D1055320

SHOWING UP FOR WORK

AND OTHER KEYS TO BUSINESS SUCCESS

MICHAEL H. MESCON &
TIMOTHY S. MESCON

PEACHTREE PUBLISHERS, LTD.

Published by
PEACHTREE PUBLISHERS, LTD.
494 Armour Circle, N.E.
Atlanta, Georgia 30324

Manufactured in the United States of America

10 9 8 7 6 5 4 3 2 1

Library of Congress Catalog Card Number 88-60002

ISBN 0-934601-45-3

Acknowledgment

Emphasizing the importance of leading by example, we have attempted to express the belief that the secret to success is that there is no secret. The effective manager-leader-entrepreneur works wonders by working and creates miracles by showing up, showing up on time and showing up on time dressed to play. Simply stated, this is what our collection is all about.

We are deeply grateful to Lidia de Leon of *Sky* magazine and to the outstanding practitioners whose contributions have provided an additional dimension of real-life credibility to this manuscript.

Michael H. Mescon

Timothy S. Mescon

Contents

3
THE POWER OF PEOPLE:
The Competitive Edge

4
THE SIMPLE THINGS

5
INNOVATION GENERATION

1

REEKING OF GREATNESS: Top-to-Bottom, Inside Out

Michael H. Mescon

Michael H. Mescon, Ph.D., is Dean, College of Business Administration, and Regents' Professor of Human Relations at Georgia State University, where he has held the Chair of Private Enterprise since its inception in 1963. Mescon is author of more than one hundred articles and books, including the best-selling textbook Business Today. *He is also chairman of* The Mescon Group.

Don't Blame the Clerk

Some years ago a tire dealer told me that the forty-thousand-mile warranty on my seven-thousand-mile tires was not applicable on a station wagon. This was especially depressing since I owned a station wagon. He cautioned me to read the small print. I was still depressed.

In my attempt to return a call, I was asked my name, business and reason for calling. Armed with these data, the inquisitor told me to hold. I'd still be holding if I hadn't grown weary. I made up my mind not to get mugged again on the phone.

On a Sunday afternoon, I was informed by a physician's answering service that the doctor only handled emergencies on Monday. I apologized for my bad planning and indicated that I'd be more careful in scheduling my own personal crises, but this was for my daughter and everyone knows how thoughtless teenagers are. I guess the only comforting feature is the realization that nobody is intentionally picking on me. On the other hand, I'd be just as happy and much more grateful if the situation turned from bad to good, and things are bad. If you agree with this observation, let me suggest that a return to basics just might be an effective remedy. I say this even though the real basics might be more a myth than a historical reality.

For example, during these especially trying times, and when weren't times trying, a possible solution to many of society's problems might be tied to our ability to identify the kind of society we actually want.

In working with organizations, I always use this as a proper starting point. Unless you can define what kind of business you're in and identify your goals, everything that follows tends to be fruitless, and if by chance it works, it is purely by chance. Quite frankly, I'd suggest that we not press our luck.

For a starting point, I'd like to opt for an open society structured about what is often loosely referred to as the American Dream. Perhaps it's called a dream because we've never really implemented it as it should be implemented. As a matter of fact, if you consider the American Dream as a kind of ideological blueprint, it is fairly apparent that we've never built according to plans. Instead, we've been a nation of ad libbers. What I am suggesting is that we take a good, long, intensive look at the plan, and if we like it, let's stick to specifications.

In examining this Dream, one factor stands out and that is the firm belief that an individual's position in life should be tied to behavior, not birth. Further, we often say that there should be a linear or direct relationship between what you do and what you receive, between investment and reward, and between pay and productivity. Mind you, this is how we talk. Our behavior in many instances is another matter that is compounded by apparent discrepancies between what we say and what we do, between mouth and movement. Perhaps this gulf between the axiom and the action led Flip Wilson's Geraldine, one of my all-time favorite practical philosophers, to caution, "Don't let your mouth write a check that your body can't cash." I fear that continued reliance on maxim instead of movement has resulted in our overdrawing our credibility account. Either we must make some deposits right now or suffer the consequences. In short, it might be well to practice what we preach. Alas, with each successive year, hackneyed utterances assume special meaning, and today, especially today, minimizing the gap between articulated philosophy and overt behavior just might alter a lot of things for the better.

Specifically, why not consider placing a premium on the ability of the individual to produce rather than to be digested and fully assimilated by the system. Further, placing real emphasis on productivity and gearing compensation to contribution might do more to correct inflation than any other suggested remedy. In addition, rewarding individual performance and moving away from the mass across-the-board approach to human behavior might have a very positive effect upon the kind of treatment we receive as consumers.

Actually, when is the last time you did business with anyone, and I use business in the broadest sense including any kind of organization, and left feeling truly pleased? For the most part, you don't expect to be pleased. As a matter of fact, you don't even expect to be satisfied. What you hope is that you won't get hurt too much. This is what I refer to as the minimum shaft expectation, and it has done more to contribute to and reinforce anti-business sentiment than any other single factor.

For the most part, products are better today than ever before. What you can't get in most instances is service provided by a well-motivated, concerned human being who gives you the impression that he truly cares about you and your problems. For example, have you ever walked into a store and gotten the distinct impression from the salesperson that if it just weren't for the customers, this would be an ideal place to work? Just the other day, I was waited on by a salesperson who took my money while talking to a friend on the telephone. Undoubtedly, by accepting this rotten service, I reinforced a pattern of customer relations that wavers between apathetic and downright antagonistic. To a great extent, we consumers, and we're all consumers, must recognize our responsibility and should register our pleasure or displeasure with the kind of service we receive. I can assure you that many organizations are especially sensitive to how you feel. Let them know.

In all fairness, don't blame the clerk. Chances are what you're getting from him, he's getting from his boss, and that is across-the-board nonrecognition. Even worse than the clerk situation is the computer confrontation.

Several months ago, I received a bill from a department store indicating that I owed $2,612,018.37. I was relatively certain that an error had been made. Subsequent correspondence with the computer and the store have led me to conclude that the easy way out is to pay the bill. Somehow, when people talk about alienation, this computer confrontation comes to mind. However, just as we don't want to blame the clerk, neither should we abuse the computer.

A basic fact of organizational behavior is that good customer relations begin with good employee relations. It is an inside-out, top-to-bottom situation that originates with the big boss and reflects itself down the organization and directly affects the organization's various publics, and as publics, I am including stockholders, employees and customers.

Quite frankly, the relationship between the inside and the outside is so very basic and essential that I've never completely understood why more smart business people don't get in on a good thing. For example, of what value is a great advertising campaign when nobody is trained to deliver the service you've been led to expect? Actually, a business is better off not promising anything and delivering accordingly than raising customer expectations and furnishing zero.

If this makes sense, consider doing away with all corporate titles and designations but salesperson. I don't think that any business can afford the luxury of a single behind-the-scenes person. Further, why not entertain the possibility of putting to rest the idea of satisfying the customer and replace it with a commitment to please the customer? The difference is more than a matter of semantics. When a customer is truly pleased, you've just added another person to your sales force at no additional charge to you or your company. Customer satisfaction as a goal is a bare break-even approach that fewer and fewer people are willing to tolerate.

The notion of having every employee function as a salesperson makes eminently good sense if you agree that the only meaningful, long-run competitive edge a company can have is its people, and here I am referring to all of its staff regardless of level, position or activities. Too many organizations tend to emphasize nonpeople-related factors. For example, when commercial banks advertise and talk about convenient locations, I suggest that what they really mean is that their locations are convenient to their competition's locations. People like doing business with other people. Advertising, physical facilities and convenience might provide the initial attraction, but it won't keep the customer coming back. Treating each staff member as a separate and distinct entity whose contributions or lack of contributions won't get lost in the corporate shuffle could not only increase productivity, but might replace customer contempt with customer commitment. It's worth a try, and the process of trying might contribute to a nicer existence for all. The logical starting point is at the top. That's where the buck stops and where the action should begin. Don't blame the clerk!

Timothy S. Mescon

Timothy S. Mescon, Ph.D., is Dean of the Franklin P. Perdue School of Business Administration at Salisbury State University in Salisbury, Maryland. Mescon, who has held both line and staff positions in industry, is widely published and, along with his father, is a contributing editor to Delta Air Lines' Sky magazine. He is the 1984 recipient of the National Award for Excellence from the U.S. Small Business Administration.

Winning Ways

The restaurant was crowded . . . . and why not? Its food was consistently excellent, the service effective, and the price right — an almost unbeatable triumvirate. The key word here is *almost*, however, as it is in most instances. For example, the automobile repair that's almost right. (You only have to bring the car back once.) It usually is the "almost phenomenon" that sets apart the outstanding from the OK and which is, in most all instances, a function of selection, training, attitude and reward.

Having said the above, let's get back to the restaurant, where the customer said to the hostess, "I have seven in my party," and the hostess grunted, "It will be at least two hours until you can be seated." The nonverbal backup to what she said literally screamed, "Only lunatics would wait two hours. You just might be one."

The customer, hungry but not stupid, quickly concluded that two hours from now it would be three in the afternoon. Hence, a two-hour wait simply wasn't a rational estimate. The customer (and aren't we all customers?) also remembered customer service originates at the top. Simply stated, don't blame the clerk, or, in this case, the hostess.

The restaurant manager was easy to locate. He was making sure what came out of the kitchen was just right. This is commendable and correct. However, if the hostess continued to welcome the hungry with two-hour admonitions, the only thing coming out of the kitchen might be cobwebs.

To the manager's credit, when the situation was brought to his attention he took immediate action, and the seven were seated in less than 20 minutes. When the group left after eating, the total time from "two hours" to the payment of the check was 65 minutes, and the restaurant was virtually empty. One more hostess like this, and the restaurant could be empty all of the time.

In discussing the matter, the restaurant manager indicated he had simply assumed too much about the common-sense quotient of the hostess. Assuming common sense can definitely be hazardous to the health of a business.

Nowhere is this more apparent than when competitive edge and advantage come from service. As a rule, excellence must be cultivated, and organizations train for excellence the way winning athletes train for competition; i.e., consciously and continuously. Never assume excellence will occur through a type of spontaneous combustion. It requires effort of an extraordinary nature and this is often alien in a society where the taste for mediocrity appears to be virtually insatiable.

Quality, productivity, excellence, first-class performance: these and many other issues inundate management today in a never-ending variety of ways. Lectures, speeches, books, articles and seminars spread the gospel of competing to win in manners that would seem to convince even the occasional observer that the message surely must have been effectively communicated, if not over-communicated. Unfortunately, for all too many organizations, the message that has been communicated has fallen on disinterested and often oblivious parade-watchers. Surely, each of us understands the difference between being laid-back and unconscious!

Sadly, the message of winning has been replaced with the

melody of mediocrity, proclaiming that in the long run everything will simply "work out." This thinking is wrong.

It was November, the middle of the holiday season, when over-anxious shoppers were rushing about making their last-minute purchases to help properly usher in a range of festivities with both spirit and joy. Despite the ominous predictions of economic doomsayers, the 1987 holiday season was a good one for business. People were buying, and overall spending was up. In particular, spending was up in "Car City" (the city's name has been changed to protect the innocent), where the delights of the holiday season are often coupled with the opening of the deer-hunting season.

November 16 and 17 were special days in 1987 in Car City and will probably remain painfully etched on the minds of managers who are left to ponder whether or not the thirst for winning was lost. On those two days, right smack in the midst of heightened business activity, in a year when our national debt saw record highs and at a time when Americans were increasingly turning to foreign-made goods, an automobile assembly plant in Car City had to close because too many employees were pursuing their penchant for deer hunting. At a time when our automobile industry has been backed up against the wall by tough competitors who produce some splendid products, management at this particular plant could not muster a production quorum to staff this facility and simply had to *shut down operations* until the enthusiastic band of hunters returned to work.

Instead of preaching the bagging of Nissan, Toyota, Hyundai and Yugo, management at this plant was placed in the untenable position of having to explain why the hunt for deer superseded the hunt for profit.

After a thorough analysis by the Chicago School Board, it was determined that in order to alleviate the "computational drudgery" of long division, the School Board would purchase 160,000 calculators at $6 apiece and distribute these to students throughout the city.

Lo, the drudgery of long division; Pythagoras would spin in his grave!

The failure to recognize the need for the enhancement of analytical skills through mathematics and science sends out a message to the world at large that "simple is always better" and "understanding the how and why" is of no great consequence. A productive and competitive nation demands a populace that cannot only do, but comprehends the how and why.

According to a recent survey conducted by Robert Half International, top executives spend 26 percent of their time, equal to 11 work weeks per year, writing or reading memos. The executives polled observed that 39 percent of those memos are a waste of time. Now, what would happen if we had a *memo-buster* holiday? That's right, let's devote a single day to not writing memos. Indeed, if this were merged with national smoke-out day, we could ignite every memo with a cigarette and make a great contribution to mankind. Eleven weeks a year of reading and writing memos would be freed.

Although many Congressmen proclaimed disbelief at the approval of a 2,000-page budget summarized in a two-page executive brief, the budget was passed. We have so sensitized ourselves to the notion that simpler is better and to act, not think, that our competitive edge has become dulled and is in a state of disrepair.

In 1987, H&R Block prepared a worldwide-record-high 11,627,700 tax returns. In defiance of all predictions, this represented the fourth consecutive-year increase in returns prepared. In the U.S. and Canada, one out of every ten income tax returns is prepared by H&R Block. The spirit and enthusiasm fostered by president Henry Block and company is infectious. The rapid and impressive growth demonstrated by H&R Block and subsidiaries like CompuServe, Personnel Pool, and Path Management is a textbook example of how to compete in turbulent marketplaces. Tax preparation, temporary help and management seminars are all people-dependent businesses. Personnel at H&R Block are the reason that earnings hit a record $127 million and continue to grow at an exponential rate while competitors try to catch up. Again, it is a matter of basics. You compete and win through constructive, no-

nonsense commitment to excellence in everything you do — from answering phones to data entry. There is no room for error.

Management theorists contend that long-term success is predicated on some relatively simple ideals that are often ignored. There are four "D's" that make a difference in win, place or show:

Direction. Everyone in an organization, top to bottom, inside-out, must have a clear sense of direction. Where is the organization now and where is it going? This building of consensus in mission and direction is essential if each person is to commit him or herself. Direction means a clear sense of goals and objectives and specifies the role of the individual in making things happen.

Dedication. There is no room for "closed for deer hunting" in the successful organization. Sure, you can deer hunt on your own time. But dedication to success and making good things happen must consume everyone in the organization. Dedication means committing yourself and your department to improvement in quality and performance. Dedication is a two-way street. Dedication to the organization mandates a dedication to the individual. Superior performance demands superior recognition. This reciprocity builds commitment and more importantly, loyalty. Everyone wins together.

Detail. You must build an organization with a love for detail. In order to make things happen all of the time, the little things must work. Defect-free performance must be the standard for all members of the organization. Anything other than perfection upsets the paying customer, and that's bad.

Demolition. Can you ever win by too much? Much of the hue and cry raised in the athletic arena today focus on running the score up. Who truly cares? Would you ever tell your salespeople, "Sell, but not too much"? Would you ever want an average profit or a mediocre market share? The answer is a reaffirmation of private enterprise and a resounding "No!" Winning and winning big make all of us better off, and that is not all bad.

Talk to winners and losers. Winners will indicate winning is much more fun than second place. Winning can become infectious and fun if you commit yourself and your organization to doing what must and should be done.

What Makes a Leader?

In a piece published several years ago, we wrote about the notion that, if one doesn't like what one sees at the bottom of an organization, it's important to take a careful look at what's going on at the top. Essentially, the article recognized the reflective nature of organizational leadership — that is, that subordinates tend to behave the way they think their supervisors expect them to behave.

Many readers not only agreed with the top-to-bottom, reflective phenomenon approach, but were often frustrated (particularly if they were middle managers) in providing a leadership style demanded by the organization but not necessarily sanctioned by top management.

Actually, meaningful, proactive change should originate at the top. If it doesn't, a vacuum is created that is eventually filled in a fashion that is often dysfunctional. Be assured, however, that the vacuum will be filled. Smart leaders understand this, and minimize vacuum-creating behaviors by building an organizational climate, or ethos, where all constituents get well together.

Leadership is not just a product of the profit-making endeavor, but it abounds in organizations that are really going places. In 1980, Dr. Alonzo Crim, then Atlanta's school superintendent, went way out on a limb and emphatically stated that Atlanta's public school students would score at or above the national norm on achievement tests by 1985. This goal was reached in 1983, and improvements are still being made by students who believe in themselves because their teachers and administrators believe in them.

Winning, like losing, is contagious — but winning is a lot more fun. It all started with one person, a leader, who said "We can do it" and personally committed himself to this challenge. The total system therefore benefited, again reinforcing the belief that one person actually can make a difference.

The late Robert Woodruff of Coca-Cola apparently felt that great things could be accomplished if people were not preoccupied with who gets the credit. There is ample evidence that this rationale is sound, sensible, and profitable for everyone involved. The leader who recognizes this, and whose behavior reflects this belief, can create an environment where the glory of success is shared and savored by the total organization — without in any way diminishing the recognition coming to certain key players. Again, everyone prospers.

Conversely, when things go awry, and one may be certain they will on occasion, failure is not viewed as a time for blame-allocation or scapegoating, but rather as an opportunity to learn, regroup, and move on. Actually, in many organizations, the climate or culture is such that others may wish you well, but not *too* well. With the Woodruff philosophy, everyone wishes everyone well. The net result is an entity where excellence becomes a way of life, not merely a motto or fad.

Most will agree there is a certain romantic quality to leadership that is difficult to describe, elusive to the touch and exciting to the organization. There is an intriguing quality about leaders that is both alluring and exhilarating. Leadership is a mysterious, exotic attribute that mesmerizes and awes.

Great leaders can do great things. Great leaders can incite people to build great organizations. Great leaders are visionaries of mountains, not molehills. These visions drive strategies, policies, procedures and people. These visions are not ordinary or mundane. They are romantic ones that allow great leaders to slay windmills or leap tall buildings. Visions drive people and people drive organizations. There is an irreverence about leaders that makes all too many all too uncomfortable.

It is the smothering of this drive that makes some companies all too lethargic. Leaders energize and electrify people, and these very same individuals energize and electrify organizations. And guess what? These very same people and companies love it! There is something about extraordinary leaders that is infectious. Good leaders are made, not born, and these good leaders make good people in good organizations, great. Great leaders are both hero-worshippers and hero-makers. Indeed, in great organizations, everyone has the opportunity to become a hero — and *that's* great.

"I want to assure you that we intend to become America's national department store." With this rather simple statement, William R. Howell, as chairman and CEO of J.C. Penney, pronounced in 1982 a vision for an organization that has slowly make believers out of skeptics and heroes out of employees. In recent years, as Howell directed an expansive and expensive redesign of more than 500 stores in the J.C. Penney network, never in its existence had this company experienced such excitement — and such fun. By the end of the decade, J.C. Penney will have radically revamped its 100 million square feet of department store space and, in doing so, will have brought up a new generation of shoppers in an upscale shopping environment.

There have been many detractors. After all, what historically came to mind when J.C. Penney was mentioned? Good, quality clothes, staple commodities, value and price are the most frequent responses. "Beautiful," "exciting," "fun," and "glamorous" were generally reserved for the other stores. However, Howell said yes, we can — and yes, they are. Howell knows it, his employees know it, and now, slowly but surely, the public knows it. This is the beauty of a leader at work.

According to *The Wall Street Journal,* one company has more women earning over $50,000 in annual commissions than any other firm in the United States. This company awards its employees with gold and diamond pins, fur coats, cruises, Oldsmobiles and Cadillacs. According to the CEO of this firm, managers motivate by praising people to success. The company is Mary Kay Cosmetics, Inc.; the leader is Mary Kay Ash.

Pageant night at Mary Kay makes you cry and laugh and cheer and applaud a leader and an organization that believes that people make profits. And people who make profits don't just happen, don't just occur. People who make profits are carefully trained and rewarded by managers and leaders who themselves are committed to making a difference. The myth of May Kay is, in fact, no myth at all. This is a great leader who built a great organization that makes great products and praises great people. Simple, isn't it?

In another context, they said never. They said you cannot introduce a new soft drink in eighteen months. (He introduced four.) They said you cannot mix soft drinks and entertainment. (He said you can and did.) They said you absolutely, positively cannot alter a time-tested formula that has been in the family for almost a century. (He said we can and we must.) Robert Woodruff brought one kind of romance to Coca-Cola; Roberto Goizueta brings another. And both seem to work. Great leaders can take great corporations on great journeys. In the years under Goizueta's guidance, direction and leadership, stockholders have seen return on equity reach unparalleled highs and sales cross the one-billion-dollar plateau. You can never say never to a great leader and succeed. Never.

The great organization encourages, cajoles and incites individuals to greatness. These individuals become the leaders who encourage, cajole and incite others who spur the organization to greatness. Romancing these leaders can be a difficult and trying experience. Not romancing these leaders can be fatal. You choose.

John L. Clendenin

A native of El Paso, Texas, John L. Clendenin graduated from Northwestern University and served as a pilot in the U.S. Air Force Strategic Air Command. Since 1984 he has served as chairman of the board and chief executive officer of BellSouth, the largest of the regional telecommunications holding companies.

Great Expectations

Leadership is a subject that has confounded even great leaders' attempts to describe it, though they've tried many times. Henry Ford said, "The question of who ought to be boss is like asking who ought to be tenor in the quartet — obviously, the man who can sing tenor."

Mid-nineteenth-century French politician Alexandre Ledru-Rollin said, "There go my people. I must find out where they are going so I can lead them."

Across the English Channel, British statesman Benjamin Disraeli put it more poetically: "I must follow the people. Am I not their leader?"

The problem is that these thoughts are much like the independent descriptions of three blind men describing the proverbial elephant. They're piecemeal, descriptive of one facet of leadership — but not the whole.

Perhaps that's the best we can expect — piecemeal impressions of various leadership qualities. After all, who really knows what leadership is, exactly? Who's got the ability, and how can we identify it? Are leaders born? Or can they be groomed and trained? Well, even though none of us can fully answer these questions, in the next few pages I'd like to offer some thoughts about what this elephant of leadership looks like from one observer's perspective.

My first premise of leadership is that leadership and personality are not the same. There's often a tendency to think otherwise, to think that a certain personality type predisposes one to leadership. But the pages of history demonstrate that many different personality types are candidates for leadership. Leaders have been outgoing or introverted, relaxed or intense, quiet or vocal, flexible or unyielding, witty or strait-laced; no pattern has clearly emerged.

Well, then, what makes someone a leader?

I confess there's nothing I'd like better than to reveal a blinding insight to answer that question. But the truth is embarrassingly simple: a leader is a person whom others follow of their own free will. A key phrase there is "of their own free will." To be a leader, a man or woman must elicit voluntary followership.

You'll recognize, of course, this definition of leadership is morally neutral. It makes no value judgments about the worthiness of goals being pursued or the means used to pursue them. Some of the attributes that enabled Winston Churchill to rally Great Britain in the darkest hours of World War II also allowed Adolf Hitler, a decade earlier, to rise to power in Germany by instilling a new sense of purpose amidst despair.

The moral quality of a given leader in a given age may be attributed to the social crucible of the time. It may be attributed, by some, to divine intervention. It may be attributed by others to good or bad fortune or, less elaborately, to luck; I'll leave it to others to explain why. But the truth is some followers have the fortune of having a Churchill to rise in their midst, and others the misfortune of a Hitler.

If luck's all it is or was, I'll take it. How lucky we were, for example, that Dr. Martin Luther King, Jr., emerged as a preeminent leader of his time. How tremendously fortunate we were to have him as our guide through the perilous passage of the civil rights movement. It was his unique gift to be a guide not only to those who marched with him but also to those frightened, confused onlookers who didn't know where all the civil rights activity would ultimately lead.

Although many didn't realize it at the time, and perhaps wouldn't have acknowledged it if they had, King's unswerving dedication to nonviolence, his commitment to the cause of universal justice and his absolute refusal to hate were torches that lit the way for our entire nation. Those torches still burn brightly here in Atlanta; I pray they always will.

And the fact is I can think of no better example than Dr. King to illustrate one central quality that I believe all great leaders share, no matter what their personality. I call this central quality "Fixation on a goal." In all spheres of human endeavor, the leader is one who clearly sees a goal and believes in it wholeheartedly, one who keeps seeing and believing that goal despite seemingly endless difficulty.

In its purest form, leadership is the quality that holds us steady on course when voices all around say the journey's pointless. Clearly, one must assume the course of action has been planned well and has at least what appears a reasonably worthwhile purpose. Leadership, obviously, is not blind adherence to an agenda lacking sense, nor is it sheer stubbornness and lack of imagination. But the moral courage to keep going when you believe you're right, no matter how discouraging conditions and people become . . . *that* is the essence of leadership.

My second premise of leadership is that it demands competence, a personal mastery of responsibilities . . . . and it's harder now, frankly, than ever before. Throughout a professional career, regardless of vocation, maintaining competency becomes more of a challenge with each passing year. That's just how fast the current of information and technology is running.

It can't be faked, this matter of knowing your stuff, and it can't be avoided by anyone who aspires to be a leader. Followers will unmask a charlatan in a second. And, once exposed, a charlatan leader loses what Barbara Tuchman, the Pulitzer Prize-winning historian, calls the "Do This" factor . . . when the leader says, "Do this" — this gets done.

The "Do This" factor means followers have ample trust their leader knows whereof he or she speaks and is giving good direction. Even when a leader's style is low-key and collegial rather than authoritarian, the leader needs the "Do This" factor, which boils down to having the respect and confidence of those being led, in order to accomplish anything.

My third premise of leadership is that it depends upon understanding people and knowing what motivates them. There are, I know, many exceptions to this rule; indeed, they spring to mind precisely because they are exceptions. But generally I believe that human nature inclines us toward leaders who demonstrate sensitivity for the aspirations, hopes, fears and other emotions we all share.

To illustrate, let me draw briefly from the research of author-psychologist Frederick Herzberg about what motivates people in the workplace. He maintains that one of the most important motivators is for a worker to feel challenged — to know someone expects him or her to succeed at an important task. Living up to high expectations is a powerful goal, Herzberg says, and I agree. My own experience both in business and in civic affairs gives me no hesitancy in endorsing at least this aspect of Dr. Herzberg's work. Expecting good things of people is a tremendous motivating force, and leaders use this effectively.

My final premise of leadership is that it requires self-confidence. And probably this characteristic grows out of all the others; out of being personally committed to a goal you clearly understand; out of knowing you're fully prepared and professionally competent; out of being aware of and sensitive to what moves other people. Self-confidence is the final line of demarcation between those who genuinely want to take on the risks of leadership and those who don't. It is the hallmark of those who want to experience the "thrill" enough to hazard the "dangers" of leadership. For when all the other qualities are in place, the final test of leadership is to have the self-confidence that you are the right person to shoulder the load and to be excited by the chance.

Only then can a leader boast the stuff Theodore Roosevelt invoked when he said, "Far better it is to dare mighty things, to win glorious triumphs, even though checkered by failure, than to take rank with those poor spirits who neither enjoy much nor suffer much because they live in the gray twilight that knows not victory nor defeat."

Roll Out Your Role Models

While the title of what follows is "Roll Out Your Role Models," it could very well have been "Hold Out Your Heroes." There is little doubt that we are a people in search of heroes and heroics in all fields of endeavor, and this is not bad.

Over thirty years ago, O. A. Ohman of Standard Oil suggested the need for "Skyhooks," or cultural reference points. Simply stated, we want something to hang on to, to identify with. What an opportunity for those who are well motivated and committed to the best. As a matter of interest, how about you? Chances are you may already be someone else's role model, and, as management professor Dr. G. Hugh Russell of Georgia State University states, "You may be the only book someone else will read." Let it be a good one.

A story. The following "essentials" were ordered, two weeks prior to taking office, by the new chief executive officer of a public-sector organization:

- A marble desk, conference table, and cocktail table: $9,400.
- A custom-made (is there any other kind?) credenza in oak that runs along two walls: $9,950.
- Ten steel conference chairs: $1,675.
- A high-back leather armchair: $1,588.
- A custom-built, curving (straight is simply too mundane) leather sofa: $8,900.

Total Expenditures — $31,513.

Seems a bit extravagant. But that's not the end of the story. Five months earlier, the previous CEO had purchased new office furniture, including a mahogany desk and leather chairs, that cost taxpayers $32,161. This furniture was moved to the office of another manager. The fact is, $63,674 can buy an awful lot of furniture. The fact is, that in a time of public-sector economic austerity, these kinds of purchases would make one's eyebrows reside in a permanently raised position. The fact is, these symbolic gestures set a distorted example for the thousands of subordinates seeking direction, guidance and leadership. Where have all the role models gone?

The publisher of a leading regional newspaper resigned after word leaked that his war record was completely falsified. The myth had grown to epidemic proportions and, indeed, had become bigger than reality. Where have all the role models gone?

The reflective phenomenon of management suggests that behavior at the top is mirrored, or reflected, throughout the organizational hierarchy. The reflective phenomenon of management argues that if we see, we do. In most instances, subordinates learn by example. In all too many instances, the example espouses more form than function. Regardless of the organization, whether it is a municipality, a publisher, a manufacturer, or a deliverer of services, emphasis must be placed on what you do — not where you sit.

Cecil Day, the late founder of the Days Inn lodging chain, insisted that the organization maintain its commitment to creating and providing an ambiance that he considered conducive to family travel. This CEO built one of the fastest-growing and most profitable lodging chains in North America. This dedication to function permeated his everyday life as well as his working life. Successful examples are maintained by doing, not thinking. Successful role models are maintained by action, not thought.

Truett Cathy of Chick-Fil-A fame has truly closed the gap between mouth and movement in building an organization that is a reflection of his belief in private-enterprise basics. Combining infectious enthusiasm with hard work, he has become every person's role model of what can be done if you are willing to pay the price. Truett Cathy has built an organization where everyone has an opportunity to get well.

Standards of excellence, of performance, of doing, don't simply happen. Standards of absolutely first-class, pristine performance don't spontaneously emerge. These very same standards are carefully cultivated and harvested by first-class organizations committed to the notion that second-best simply won't do. New entrants to the world of work desperately seek guidance, direction and support. Neophytes in the world of work, be it in the public or private sector, are better educated, more worldly, more demanding than any work force ever managed.

These newcomers are increasingly seeking leaders, heroes and role models to show them the way. This nation was founded on the principle that rewards on the basis of performance, not birth. This principle did not evolve frivolously. It was carefully cultivated by leaders and role models dedicated to setting a better example. The onus upon management is a heavy one. But can you imagine the challenge and pure excitement of managing an organization full of winning role models?

To Foster the Best,
Begin at the Bottom

In a lively executive MBA class discussion at the University of Miami, a CEO of a large, multinational manufacturing organization was leading a case analysis and discussion of his company. The firm had experienced some spectacular growth in the past five years and he, understandably, was thoroughly enjoying the comments and compliments of the students.

A financial evaluation of the firm's cost of goods sold revealed high selling expenses for high-ticket items. The CEO lamented that he probably had the highest-paid sales force in this particular industry in the world. Furthermore, he continued, it truly disturbed him that many of these salespeople earned greater salaries than he during the previous year. This comment was the source of great consternation. Amidst all the successes and achievements attained by this organization during the previous half decade, the income level obtained by those selling that company's products day-in and day-out was a source of irritation to the leader, the organizational role model of the firm. Something was not right.

At a restaurant recently, a patron waited twenty-five minutes for service. The waiter took the order and returned fifteen minutes later to explain that that particular item was not available. A new choice was finally delivered twenty minutes later, and it was cold. At the cash register, when asked the inevitable question, "How was it?" the customer uncustomarily responded, "The service was terrible and the food was cold." The manager responded, "What do you expect for minimum wage?"

At a large, newly opened department store, a customer sought to charge a fifteen-dollar purchase. It was one of those cashless days, and the convenience of credit was about to be utilized. At the cash register the clerk asked, "Why are you using your credit card? I never use mine."

Finally, at a pre-holiday sale, a frustrated customer, unable to locate a heavily advertised sale item, collared a salesperson and asked for the whereabouts of the product. The salesperson, dashing madly away, said, "Don't ask me. I only work here."

Something is not right.

The basic dictum upon which our economic system was constructed is one that argues that individuals in this (unlike any other) society shall be rewarded on the basis of what they do, not who they are. We have built a pay-for-performance system that has historically argued that we reward on the basis of compensation for commitment. Simply put, if you don't do, you don't get.

Unfortunately, while we have held steadfastly to this belief where middle- and upper-level executives are concerned, we have all too often systematically ignored the one level in the organization where sellers meet buyers. We have forgotten the one level of the organization where the overwhelming majority of transactions occurs. We have neglected the one level of the organization where mouth and movement result in sales or losses. We have snubbed the one level of the organization to which, when customers think products or services, they automatically refer.

We are referring to the first level of your organization, the bottom of that organizational hierarchy where money is made or lost. That level, inhabited by millions and millions of "salespeople," is where impressions are made, sales consummated and loyalties fortified. It is precisely at this level that the care and feeding of excellence must be constantly reinforced.

Our preoccupation with short-term performance ignores the importance of developing and encouraging the very heart and soul of the organization. When we place ourselves in the role of quality-conscious customers, we are often hard-pressed to recall a truly satisfactory buying experience. When organizations proudly proclaim a renewed commitment to excellence or a reinvigorated pursuit for perfection, careful attention and concern must be focused on those people representing the firm in the turbulent trenches.

Money is still a socially acceptable way of saying "I love you." The fact remains, however, that in too many instances, we consider the allocation of scarce resources to the first level of the organization as an uneventful act. Training, development — and, yes — compensation at all levels of the organization send a clear and important message of commitment to all employees. The role of providing customer service, customer attentiveness, customer responsiveness and customer love is becoming an increasingly important one in hypercompetitive marketplaces where product quality and performance are more difficult to differentiate.

Employees within organizations wear the mantles of salesperson and representative of the firm to the world at large. It is no longer socially acceptable or proper simply to accept poor or unresponsive service. Customers are sending a clear message to the sellers of the world; namely, *caveat venditor,* let the seller beware. First-line representatives of organizations generally reflect the service and treatment that they receive from their bosses. This reflective phenomenon of management reveals to consumers at large that too many organizations just don't care. In increasingly competitive global markets this is, quite simply, unacceptable.

Lack of service, productivity and quality are symptoms, not causes, of an organization's well-being. Therefore, attaining service, productivity and quality requires that we address causal concerns — not overt manifestations of factors that are more deeply rooted. If we want a top-notch organization, it would be well to focus on the environment or climate within which work takes place. Ideally, we need to develop a culture or ethos where everyone, i.e., owner, employer, employee and consumer, can get well together.

It's a bit like our taking a cruise down the Chattahoochee River. You're in the bow, and I'm in the stern. We're both paddling as effectively as possible. Unexpectedly, we hit a submerged rock. It's at the front, your end, and a large gaping hole develops. I've got to be less than rational to say, "Thank goodness, it's up front." You're going down, but I won't be far behind.

In an organization, we are all in the same boat. We'll sink or swim together, and we'll most certainly get sick or thrive as a unit.

In our exploration for the best, it would be logical to make everyone a salesperson — and an entrepreneur — by developing a fair and equitable system of rewards and punishments. Create a sense of true ownership and build an organization where the best is a consensus reality, not a mission statement aspiration.

In the final analysis, people actually do make the difference. Location, product, price and timing are formidable components, but people provide the organization with its most potent differential. Recognizing this is the first step. Developing a philosophy that subscribes to this is the second. Implementing this philosophy is the third. Once you've built a winning organization through steps one, two, and three, you can enhance the possibility of staying a winner by not forgetting how you got as good as you are. If this is forgotten, you become just like everyone else.

Actually, there's nothing complicated about this prescription for winning. Dr. David J. Schwartz, of Georgia State University's College of Business Administration, concludes that the dedicated and effective application of common sense, or basics, can yield some truly uncommon results that spell profit — economically and psychologically — for all involved publics.

The Evolution of Excellence

He was a nice-looking kid. It was apparent that he was ill-at-ease, but this was not an unusual student-teacher relationship; he just wanted a few minutes of the professor's time, because "he really needed some help." The problem: he was a high school All-American basketball player who received a "free pass" during his preparatory years and then found himself in college, recognizing he was not good enough for the pros and suffering from an acute attack of the academic shorts. Slightly better than functionally illiterate, the young man was both victim and victimizer.

One thing was certain: he would have to get his high-school and college educations at the same time, and he wanted to know how. Even then, there was little doubt he possessed the desire and potential. With these ingredients, there's little that escapes accomplishment. Eight years later, the "kid," now a happily married man with an excellent job, a successful wife and two children of his own, is a real-life role model for those who for one reason or another possess the desire but not necessarily the latest equipment.

This success story is inspiring but certainly not original, which makes it even more inspiring. Somehow, there is something marvelous in the mundane. Perhaps this is because there are more "mundanes" than "great danes." In any event, what he did is worth telling. After all, you never know when a young person may want a few minutes of your valuable time.

Question: What do Tom Selleck, Cheryl Tiegs and Christie Brinkley have in common with Lee Iacocca, William Norris and Malcolm Forbes?

Answer: Not much.

The fact of the matter is that the first three have been, are, and will be supermodels in the world of fashion. Each is known by millions of fashion aficionados, television watchers and moviegoers from Kansas to Kenya. Each is easily recognized and admired by throngs eager to emulate the "look" that these supermodels have created. Each represents excellence in his or her field of work.

On the other hand, the latter three are neither dashing, smashing nor particularly debonaire. They, too, are known by millions. Each is easily recognized. Each represents excellence in his field of work. These men are role models.

A supermodel is someone we aren't and will never be. A role model is someone we aren't but can be. Today, unfortunately, our society seems to be brimming with an affinity and affection for supermodels rather than role models. We are actively striving for something we will never be when we should in fact be pursuing something that we ought to be. In short, we have systematically replaced our true American heroes of yore with such transient imposters from popular culture as the Hulk, Rambo and Papa Smurf!

The simplest and most direct route to excellence is to emulate, shadow and replicate what works. Unfortunately, the media has a somewhat morbid preoccupation with failure or success. So we must be content to peruse advertising pages of periodicals inhabited by supermodels rather than role models. We are inundated with form, not function, with quantity, not quality, with illusion, not substance.

What characterizes a role model? What rings a tone of excellence that is loud and clear? What separates the role model from the rest? Let's see.

Nicola Iacocca immigrated to the United States from Southern Italy in 1902 and eventually settled in Allentown, Pennsylvania, where he built a small auto-rental business. His son, Lee, surrounded by cars all his life, aspired to work for Ford. With a bachelor's degree from Lehigh and a master's from Princeton, Lee joined Ford Motor Company in 1946. By 1970, only the grandson of Henry Ford held a higher position in the company than Iacocca. On July 13, 1978, thwarted by Ford's obsession with nepotism, Iacocca was fired. On October 30, 1978, Lee Iacocca was named president of the Chrysler Corporation; on that same day, Chrysler announced its largest-ever quarterly loss.

On Thursday, April 21, 1983, The New Chrysler Corporation triumphantly announced it earned $172.1 million in the first quarter, the highest quarterly profit in the automaker's history. Initially, many dismissed Iacocca as a hypersalesman. After all, the demise of Chrysler was imminent. Wall Street laughed, the public taunted, Congress scrutinized, and Iacocca persevered. After effectively cutting the size of the company in half, Iacocca went to work on the people at Chrysler.

His managerial style has been described as charming, demanding, arrogant, ruthless and confident. The truth is that Lee Iacocca demands no more than he gives. He is the ideal role model. He sets quarterly goals for Chrysler, for himself and for his management team. Iacocca exudes confidence. He is impeccably tailored and groomed, smokes big cigars and literally oozes assuredness. He is a winner.

On June 25, 1979, *Business Week* included an article that cited quotation after quotation from managers at Control Data Corporation critical of the recent decisions made by CDC founder and chairman, William Norris. At that time, Norris had committed more than $300 million in an attempt to position Control Data in a leadership position in education and training markets.

The company's vehicle for achieving this objective, and a pet project of Norris's, was PLATO. PLATO is a sophisticated, expensive computer-based education system offering basic English and mathematics training. Quite simply, according to *Business Week*, the majority of managers at Control Data perceived PLATO as the corporate dog. Norris envisioned thousands of small companies and school districts using PLATO as a training tool. His management and, ostensibly, *Business Week* disagreed. In ringing the death knoll, the magazine said, "It is just too far ahead of its time," and "It's the Cadillac in a market where a Chevy will do."

In another *Business Week* article in the November 30, 1981, edition, the magazine claimed, "Control Data beats the industry." At the time the article was written, the company had had its best year in history while the industry lagged behind. The two morals of the story: the editorial community has a very short memory, and Norris is a role model. Over the past decade Control Data has invested $750 million in PLATO. To date, the company says that PLATO is still not profitable, but Control Data is and PLATO will be. Norris believed, like Iacocca believed, while others openly jeered and, at times, wished for failure. Excellence is a top-to-bottom proposition, and Norris is a tiptop example.

Malcolm Stevenson Forbes is prompous, arrogant and incredibly successful. Better yet, Forbes revels in his success: "Anybody that knocks money either has no sense, or no dollars and cents, or too many dollars and no sense. Money is independence, and to knock it is silly, to deplore its necessity is foolish."

Forbes has catapulted the magazine that his father founded into a much respected and referenced monitor of the business community. Forbes argues his magazine's philosophy by stating: "We think that the greatest service to capitalism and the free enterprise system is blowing the whistle on those who can't cut the ice." And what better whistle-blower could there be than the master ice-cutter himself. Forbes also lives the life of a successful role model to the fullest. He has homes around the world, a balloon museum, paintings, sixty thousand miniature soldiers and a Fabergé Imperial Egg collection. He flaunts his success with the passion of a successful man. Forbes is without question a credible role model.

There is, indeed, a common thread of excellence that weaves its way through Iacocca, Norris and Forbes. Not surprisingly, although these three men are involved in three completely unrelated businesses, there are many common factors among them. These common factors, these ingredients for success, represent our three *A*'s for excellence: Attitude, Aggressiveness and Appearance.

Attitude. Excellence is a mind set. You must believe. Each of the role models cited in this article holds an unwavering commitment and belief in his own abilities. They adhere to a very basic tenet of business: rely on no one. Their beliefs, their mind sets, their attitudes are communicable. This is a top-to-bottom phenomenon in organizations. We all want to believe. But when the CEO believes and that belief is transmitted throughout the organization, the belief is catchy. Says Chrysler St. Louis plant manager, John Burkart: "All of us at Chrysler believe in the man. I worship the guy."

Nowhere has the top-to-bottom role model permeated and shaped an organization more than at IBM. Reflecting founder Tom Watson's philosophy of individual dignity, excellence and commitment, IBM is more an institution, a culture, than simply an organization. Today, largely due to the Watson model, many contend that the greatest threat to IBM's dominance resides within, rather than in outside factors. In essence, it will lead the best and the rest just as long as it doesn't forget how it got as good as it is.

Aggressiveness. Our society today is overcome with a national lethargy that has reached epidemic proportions. In a multinational, hypercompetitive business environment we can no longer afford this luxury. Norris's intent to build a better computer that has been labeled "too far ahead of its time" is a classic example. The global business community is populated by competitors who are both hungry and aggressive. Perhaps we, too, are hungry, but not hungry enough. The search for excellence is a top-to-bottom aggressive process. It is a preemptive strike on the business community. First you win, second you lose.

Appearance. A brilliant student could not find a job. He mailed resumes to dozens of businesses. Many responded favorably, invited the student to visit and interview for a position. The student visited a number of firms but no offers were forthcoming. The student wanted to know why.

"Are you absolutely certain you want to know why?" the professor asked. "I am," replied the student. The professor then responded, "You look like you've been on a six-month camping trip." The student indignantly responded, "Are you referring to my hair and my beard?" The professor answered, "Yes, and your clothes and your shoes — and your breath." The student said, "That's not fair." And the professor patiently replied, "You didn't ask if it was fair, you simply asked why."

Fair or not, the business community responds to appearance. Naturally, appearance must be fortified with substance but, nevertheless, appearance is important. You must reek of excellence. Many of the initial high marks received by the Reagan administration were based not on substance but simply on appearance; the White House once again appeared "Presidential." Reagan and his staff looked the part. The sartorial splendor of Iacocca, Norris and Forbes is not act. The third *A* is simply a visual manifestation of attitude and aggressiveness.

Happily, the world is full of heroes, those who have simply taken what they have been handed by nature and environment and decided not to stand pat. Having learned that success is more a matter of constantly chipping away than a function of flashes of brilliance, they understood where they were and where they wanted to be and then fully embraced self-improvement endeavors which not only got the job done but will also probably always remain an integral part of their characters and ways of life.

It is students who need such heroes as role models because it is students who become the models for future generations of students. The evolution of excellence is a simple procedure transmitted from one hero to another. The chain must not be broken.

COLD STORAGE:
Not a Winning Strategy

He certainly looked like a winner. An honor student, he had worked his way through college in a co-op program and had finished in record time. He was smart, hungry and ambitious. He also wanted out after eight months on the job. Let's try to understand why.

The American Dream is relatively simple to understand. In essence, it focuses on behavior, not birth. It says that education plus dedication (a little luck won't hurt, either) can make the dream a functioning reality. Outstanding organizations endorse the dream, pay the price and grow winners. The others endorse the dream, don't ante up and run the good ones away. Incidentally, the good one cited in the opening paragraph was, in his opinion, being run away.

Winning organizations will measure achievement, not activity.

For example, meetings are held to enhance effectiveness, and people are brought together to help themselves and the organization. Meetings are not held just to have something to do and keep folks out of mischief. In winning organizations, achievement, not hours, is the measure. Burning the midnight oil is commendable if meaningful things occur. It is dysfunctional if it becomes a hollow ritual reinforced by a corporate culture that equates achievement with kilowatt hours. This leads to form, not function — and it will cause winners to look for greener pastures, also-rans to adapt and the unproductive to think they are in heaven.

The legal community is today experiencing one of the greatest infusions of manpower and talent ever observed. Despite a leveling of the number of law-school entrants, tens of thousands of attorneys are cascading from the hallowed halls of jurisprudence into the great conundrum called the "firm." The firm, today, is employing rituals and rites of passage that make hazing look like fun. Today, there are Partners and partners. Partners (with a capital "P") are traditional shareholders in the firm. Partners (with a small "p") are partners in name only, with no equity position in the firm. The small "p" implies prestige, but not pay. Neophytes in the working world of law find that there is not enough midnight oil to burn, or to satisfy Partners and partners. Billable hours represent a negotiated game between payer and payee. Trying to extract eighteen billable hours out of a twelve-hour day is a feat that would astonish even David Copperfield. The action of inaction becomes an intricate game that rewards one's ability to sit for hours and hours because it looks right. In the firm, heaven awaits those who can wait . . . . and wait.

You'll recall the college graduate who was ready to jump ship after only eight months on the job. Be assured, it was not money. It was challenge and an opportunity to utilize his skills and energy. When he communicated these feelings and frustrations to his boss, he was promised more money and a transfer to another location where he would "cool it" for a couple of years until the company could properly use what he had to offer. Apparently, the idea of being placed in cold storage for two years was not too appealing. Now, he really wanted out.

Somewhere, there is a message. Can any organization be that blessed that it can afford to CS (cold storage) talented staff members? Expressed another way, can any organization maintain its effectiveness and profitability by "CS-ing" its talent? When this is done, what impact does it have on the people in CS, and what does it do to the organization? You do not have to be a management expert or a student of organization to know the correct answer. Therefore, the crucial issues are: why are these practices practiced, and what practices *should* be practiced?

One of the most salient examples of "CS-ing" occurred during the waning weeks of the collegiate football season. One team (let's call it Winner) clawed its way to a rare shot at a national championship. The opposition (let's call it Runner-up) was anxious for the season to end. The first half complete, the Winner was way out in front. Winner's coach substituted freely during the second half. Student-athletes who had not played a down of collegiate football in one, perhaps two, seasons (and in danger of freezing in cold storage) were now playing regularly. Second- and third-team players were sent into the game with one assignment: play to win. Do your very best. The media erupted: "Why degrade the Runner-up? Why run the score up?"

Flash to your world, the world of work. Can you imagine expressing grave concern at overachieving? Can you imagine consternation at too much profit? Can you imagine management's being indignant at beating up on the opposition too badly? In the "real" world of work, in the hypercompetitive business environment, there are winners and there are runners-up. Do you want to CS your players?

We can manage almost anything but abundance. The management of scarce resources, because of a sense of urgency and a drive to survive, is far less challenging than the management of plenty. As a nation, we have been blessed with resources of all kinds. In too many instances, we've ignored the blessings and squandered the resources. If you will, take just one more look at what the Japanese have done with virtually no natural resources except human ones. The moral is relatively simple: hungry organizations with a will to win often outperform those with everything but an appetite to excel.

Take all of the truly beautiful, desirable areas in the United States — Palm Beach, Palm Springs, Hilton Head, the Catskills, the Rockies, Padre Island, Lake of the Ozarks and the Blue Ridge Mountains. Now take Indianapolis. William Hudnut took Indianapolis. He took a tarnished, rust-belt urban center and transformed it into a world-class city. Hudnut, mayor of Indianapolis, built upon the foundation laid by Senator Richard Lugar and created a vibrant, lively community with over $1 billion in development projects under way. And guess what? Purolator found Indianapolis. Courier found Indianapolis. Even the Baltimore Colts found Indianapolis.

Hudnut was driven by a sense of urgency, with a fervor to survive and succeed. He took an entire city out of Cold Storage. With a will to win, anything is possible.

Building on Basics

There are managers, and then there are managers who make the right things happen most of the time. The difference between the two is often a matter of recognizing that people really do make the difference. However, merely recognizing this is only one part of the story. Doing something about it is the other. That is what differentiates the winning manager from the also-ran.

The mouth without the movement is less than worthless. For example, the chief executive officer who talks about the importance of training for everyone but who is "too busy" to attend training sessions makes a mockery out of a potentially good endeavor and communicates (by his non-attendance) that maybe training isn't really that important. In a similar vein, merely talking about customer service without living it out is a definite negative for the organization, the employee and the customer. Managing in this manner makes losers of us all, except for that innovative individual who steps in, fills the vacuum and walks away with all of the business. The frustrated neophyte in your organization, committed to excellence, dedicated to rate-busting, becomes disenchanted and disenfranchised. When this organizational investment walks, everyone loses.

Productive behavior merits praise and thanks. The winning manager wins because his or her staff exhibits winning behavior, and this eventually becomes a way of life. Creating a winning climate is only one dimension. Maintaining, multiplying and strengthening this climate is another.

Doing both often consists of paying careful attention to the so-called little things. In a recent poll administered by the U.S. Chamber of Commerce and the Gallup Organization, the following question was asked: "What do you think it would be possible to change so as to bring about the largest improvement in performance and productivity in most companies?" Over 80 percent of those responding stated worker attitudes and abilities and managerial attitudes and abilities. Only a very small percentage thought that enhanced computer facilities or more modernized plants and equipment would make a significant difference.

Attitudes? Abilities? At the same time we are proclaiming loudly to the world at large that intensive capital reinvestment and the inundation of the corporate arena with super-computers is our only hope for economic salvation, the greatest perceived drag on performance and productivity, the albatross around the collective necks of corporate America, is the millions of employees who are not challenged, charged and rewarded.

In a similar nationwide survey conducted by A.B. Dick Company in Chicago, the results indicated that "lack of recognition and equipment breakdown were Americans' most frustrating on-the-job experiences." It is relatively easy to fix equipment, but the radical surgery needed to reshape and repair employee and managerial attitudes is complex, costly and critical.

On a recent flight to the West Coast, an executive from Tupperware anxiously related his whirlwind travel schedule. When asked if he was touring company manufacturing or distribution facilities, he smiled and said no. During the course of the year he would visit hundreds of gatherings of groups of independent Tupperware representatives to thank them for a job well done. "You see," he said, "it is thanks to the efforts of our individual, independent representatives that millions of Americans know that our products 'burp.' And that reflection of our product's consistency and quality, that release of air indicating that our container is indeed airtight, is done on a person-to-person, seller-to-buyer level. It is my job to simply say thank you."

Let people know you truly appreciate a job well done. Tell them privately and publicly. Don't ever take anything for granted.

IBM has developed a winning climate by making certain that productive employees are recognized and rewarded. Productive employees are identified at all levels of the organization. This means that recognition, praise and plaudits are given to executives, marketing representatives, production employees, secretaries, truck drivers and janitorial staff. Wherever you are in the IBM hierarchy, if you deserve it, you get it. Productive performance on a long run basis demands this. Further, as the organization prospers through winning performance, its staff should also profit.

Simply stated, managers who are secure enough to praise generate an entity where everyone gets well. In the soon-to-be-classic, *Iacocca: An Autobiography,* the author relates a most revealing incident. In a discussion with a group of students more than twenty years ago, Iacocca (at the time, general manager of the Ford Division) was asked who motivated his eleven thousand employees while he was away from Detroit. Iacocca thought about the question and realized that, indeed, the job of a manager requires only two seemingly basic talents: motivating and communicating. There is a lesson in this for all of us.

The manager who makes good things happen generally builds upon basics that seem to transcend time. These basics provide a solid foundation. They are requisites.

For example, F. W. Taylor, often referred to as the "father of scientific management," suggested that "the basic object of management is to secure maximum prosperity for the employer, coupled with the maximum prosperity for the employee." Certainly, this guideline is as relevant today as it was when Taylor wrote it three-quarters of a century ago. That is, if the employee prospers, the employer prospers. Loosely translated, Taylor implied that in the long run all businesses are engaged in a winner-take-all struggle.

In 1776, the great economist Adam Smith talked about the economy of high wages. He fully understood that productive behavior should be recognized and rewarded. The more productive, the greater the reward — and don't concern yourself with limits.

Essentially, much of what's considered brand-new is simply a restatement of what once was. Management's challenge, therefore, is not so much in the rediscovery as in the implementation. Bridging the gap between thinking and doing, contemplation and commitment, philosophy and practicality represents the subtle difference between win, place and show.

Out of the Hawthorne experiments which began in the 1920s came the recognition that work is a social as well as an economic activity and that showing people you care is not being soft, but being smart. By caring, you focus not only on output but also upon the human dimension that provides the output and delivers the service.

The winning manager makes certain his or her staff is part of the total operation. In short, the winning manager wins when there is the firm realization that his or her success can be measured in large part by the success of his or her subordinates. In turn, the organization and the customer profit. Everyone gets well. Everyone wins. That is what good business is all about.

Ted Pappas

Theodore J. (Ted) Pappas is chairman of the board and chief executive officer of the Keyes Company, Florida's largest independent real estate company. Born in Michigan, Pappas, a Duke University graduate, joined Keyes Company as a branch office sales manager in 1962. He was named chairman of the board in 1969. Under his leadership, the company has grown from less than one hundred sales associates to a commercial and residential sales force of over thirty-five hundred in fifty offices throughout Central and South Florida.

The Formula for a Successful Business

In the many years I have devoted to building a business, I've found that the basic principles I first learned in my Economics 101 class at the university still stand. The principles of economics haven't changed, and neither have the basic requirements for building a successful business of any size. They must include these four essential elements: management, manpower, money and methods. The most important of these is manpower, or, forgetting the alliteration, *people*. The only thing that makes one company superior to another is the caliber of its people.

Management is a team effort. The first thing a person realizes when he or she sets out to build a business is that doing it alone is impossible. He or she must have help, and the first line of help is the management team. This is the CEO's number-one priority! The ultimate success of efforts to build a business depends upon success in creating an effective management team. Drafting this team is not a task that can be delegated. It's a do-it-yourself job for the CEO. If a person is going to work directly for the CEO, as the members of the management team are, then it's up to the executive personally to select, indoctrinate, and monitor that person. There's no other way to develop a management team that can be what it must be — an extension of the CEO's thinking, ideas and goals.

The process of creating the management team requires more patience than skill. It calls for a large investment of the CEO's time at the outset in order to create some freedom later on. It entails continuous coaching, daily, and a performance review every thirty days. The training should continue until the CEO is certain that each team member is on the right track. Then a performance review every six months should be sufficient.

In most cases, the CEO selects people who are experienced and competent in the areas in which they will function as members of the management team. For a service company, these could be sales management, finance, marketing and personnel, in addition to such others as engineering and production, depending upon the firm's product. Sometimes the CEO will prefer to start from scratch and train one or more of the team members in his own specialty, such as sales management or personnel.

A management team is very much like every other kind of team. Goal setting is vital to success. Each team member must be constantly aware of individual and collective goals. Each team member must know:

1. What part he will play in attaining the corporate goal.
2. What part each of the other team members will play.
3. What part the leader, the CEO, will play in attaining the overall goal.

Only if these individual and overall goals are completely understood and agreed upon can the team be effective.

Delegation of authority and responsibility requires skill — and guts. It isn't easy to give a job to someone when you know you could do it much better yourself. But, of course, it is essential. In fact, it's essential to delegate authority and responsibility as far down the line in your organization as possible, to the point where every decision is made at the lowest possible level at which it can be made intelligently.

Committees are not decision-making bodies. They can't be because the responsibility is divided. Committees have their uses, but only as information-gathering and information-dispensing devices — to report to the person responsible for making the final decision.

Delegation without control is abdication, and abdication is not for CEOs. What controls can you rely on?

First and most important are the subordinate managers. Properly selected, trained, organized and informed, they are the first line of control. The second set of controls is the company's policies that apply to many or all aspects of the business. These include hiring and marketing policies and budgets. The third set of controls is the statistical indicators that have been established to measure progress and spot potential problem areas while there is still time to make corrections. These are routine, day-to-day controls; they work well if properly established. They are designed to prevent crises, but don't depend on them if a crisis occurs.

Open communication is imperative for productivity and progress. It's obvious that no matter how brilliant the plans and ideas of top management may be, they are ineffective until they are transmitted in an understandable fashion through management channels to the employees who produce the service or product and sell it. Yet failure to establish effective communication among top management, the management team, subordinate managers and employees is a problem that seems endemic to corporations. This is true even in this age of computers that provide superior facilities for gathering, organizing and disseminating information. Unfortunately, it's not likely that communications that are 100 percent effective will ever be possible, if for no other reason than there will always be some employees who either can't or don't want to get the word. But I like to believe that maintaining communications that are 80 percent effective is an achievable goal, and 80 percent is sufficient to allow the CEO's message to get through.

These, then, are the prerequisites for a good CEO:
- He is reasonably intelligent.
- He is a good manager. He knows how to get the best out of people, to their advantage as well as the company's.
- He is willing to make decisions; he has the guts to make the tough ones.
- He must be willing to sacrifice his time, often most of it, to achieve the company's goals.

The Good Life

On January 6, 1941, in his annual message to Congress, President Roosevelt enunciated the "Four Freedoms": freedom of speech, freedom to worship, freedom from want and freedom from fear.

To no small extent, these freedoms help constitute what could be considered the "good life." Actually, many view these as standard values. They're not. To over 80 percent of this small world's population, any of these four freedoms (much less all) would be considered pure fantasy and unbridled speculation — an ideological impossible dream. To us, no big deal, and why all the fuss? We would like to suggest that we are, indeed, talking about a big deal and that it might be well to start making a fuss.

The promise of freedom attracted people to the New World. Freedom to succeed and, yes, freedom to fail. More than anything else, the lure of economic mobility is what differentiates the open society from the totalitarian state. Even though our streets weren't actually paved with gold, our dreams were. And, of all our dreams, the one with the most consistent pulling power promised an existence where one's position in society would be a function of behavior, not birth. Just imagine the pure excitement inherent in an ideology that is predicated on the notion that you just might be the master of your fate and in which upward mobility is geared not to genes but to what the individual actually gives. A dream where self-control, rather than governmental control, is the accepted norm. It was this dream in past years, as it still is today, that made this nation, with all its shortcomings and imperfections, a powerful magnet to all those seeking the good life in a free society. As an aside, it is especially interesting to note that it is often the immigrant, the stranger, the outsider, who most appreciates what this country has to offer. These individuals often have not known what we accept as a birthright. For living, breathing examples, one need simply examine the economic explosions in San Antonio, Los Angeles and Miami.

The four freedoms which serve as a basis for the good life are not the permanent possession of any individual or nation. Like it or not, dues must be paid each day in order to keep these precious assets. This is contrary to the belief of some who tend to feel that the most important freedom of all is freedom from responsibility.

Today, we are constantly reminded of our unpaid dues in a globally competitive business environment. Between 1982 and 1987, the U.S. slipped from serving as the world's largest lender to become the largest borrower. This year, Fortune 500 firms employ 500,000 fewer employees than in 1986. And, while average worker productivity in the United States is still the most advanced in the world, our lead is rapidly narrowing.

In contemporary society, you attain freedom from responsibility when you decide to swap self-control for societal control. Do this, and you're like an animal in a zoo. Well cared for, perhaps, but the bars, the cages, prevent you from going anywhere. Yet, there are some naive enough to believe that individual freedom can be maintained in a situation where you are completely dependent upon one area of society — and this is dangerous, no matter what the segment. In short, there is no freedom without individual responsibility, and this thought should be paramount each time we contemplate the possibility of a nation where each person always does his or her own thing.

There is nothing quite so expensive as a free lunch and nothing as debilitating to individual or national purpose as a free-lunch mentality. Unless you're a certified hermit, life in the United States is shaped and affected by quid pro quo relationships. In simpler language, you have to pay for what you get, and here we use "pay" in its broadest and fullest sense to include effort, commitment, dedication — the idea that the goal must be worked for or it isn't really worth having.

Somehow, we've managed rather miserably to communicate the function of trade-offs in a free society. Actually, a basis of our freedom or, more specifically, one of the prime advantages of a free society is the existence of choices or options. In the totalitarian state, they are virtually nonexistent. However, it must be understood that while the best things in life may be free, the material things have to be paid for. Many young people, especially, fail to understand this. What we need to explain is that you have every opportunity to study what you wish. However, society really doesn't owe you a livelihood. As a matter of fact, you should be prepared to offer the world something of worth, something it is willing to pay for.

Robert Satter, CEO of Satter Companies of New England, has built two hypersuccessful real-estate development firms by dues paying and a commitment to quality that doesn't quit. Satter bases his approach on an ongoing commitment to customers (the most important ingredient for success), commitment to excellence and reliance on people (the most important resource). Satter's success illustrates that if we want understanding and appreciation, the system must be merchandised; after that is accomplished, steps must be taken to close the gulf between what we've sold and what we deliver. Actually, our weakness (a kind of national Achilles' heel) is primarily our failure to deliver. When this happens with any degree of frequency, our words lose credibility and our statements of philosophy are then perceived as ideological facades.

American Bankers Insurance Group has closed this gap between what is said and what is done by creating a "Boss's Bill of Rights." The "boss" is American Bankers' accounts and customers without whom, CEO Kirk Landon argues, the company would cease to exist. How right he is.

In a *Christian Science Monitor* column, John Marsh, former head of the British Institute of Management, observed that yesterday's conditions will not reappear. He argues that in contemporary democratic societies, managers and workers will have to work toward forms of partnership that are free of the damaging conflicts of strikes, go-slow tactics, or sheer lack of interest in change. And managers must, he insists, manage less and innovate more.

No one has implemented this philosophy and commitment to innovation more than Michael Eisner, CEO of the Walt Disney Company. Eisner claims that the entrepreneurship needed to keep America competitive today must come from inside existing companies, bureaucracies and industries demanding protection from foreign competition. In recent years, Eisner has managed to energize and electrify Disney's thirty-two thousand cast members and team players, ensuring a pattern of success that will continue for quite some time. Management history says Eisner is right on track.

Robert Owen, the "father" of industrial relations, was a revolutionary in his own right when he devised his now-famous silent-monitor experiment in the early 1800s. It enhanced the profitability of his enterprise, as well as the social and economic conditions of his employees — or what he referred to as his "living machinery." During the early part of this century, the often-misunderstood F. W. Taylor ran roughshod over accepted views by insisting that there was a better way to achieve what he considered to be the basic object of management: to secure maximum prosperity for the employer, as well as maximum prosperity for the employee.

Today, more and more individuals in power positions, along with many concerned "bystanders," somehow feel there must be a better way to fulfill our productivity potential, as well as enhance our lives. We carefully emphasize that productivity and quality should be complementary and supportive. In addition, the effective utilization of our human resources must be the basis of whatever we do if we value a free society characterized by productively responsible behavior and a diffusion of power.

If the good life is to become a living reality, each one of us must decide if he or she is willing to pay the price.

Peter R. Spirer

The founder, chairman and chief executive officer of Horizon Industries, Inc., in Calhoun, Georgia, Peter R. Spirer oversees operations at one of the leading manufacturers of carpets and rugs for residential and commercial markets. A native of New York City, Spirer attended Hiram College and graduated from the University of Miami in Coral Gables, Florida.

From Chenille Spreads to $300 Million in Sales — The Tufted Carpet Industry

The tufted carpet industry emerged in a serious way in the mid-1950s. This strictly home-grown Georgia technology has its roots in handmade cotton chenilles crafted by farm ladies. Not surprisingly, the industry emerged in northwest Georgia where this handicraft was centered. Seeing its commercial potential for bed-spreads and scatter rugs in the 1940s, enterprising residents of the Dalton, Georgia, area began tinkering with machines that could duplicate the nature of the stitches, or "tufts," that formed the chenille pile. The result was inexpensively made bedspreads that could be produced at a fraction of the cost of woven spreads.

The evolution of machines capable of tufting denser, wider and heavier pile products, namely carpets, took place over the ensuing years. By 1950, entrepreneurs began to market tufted carpets.

Crude and questionable in quality as these early products were compared to their woven counterparts, they would, in just a decade, transform what had been a rich man's luxury item into a standard building material. By 1960, it was clear that the technology of tufting, in concert with synthetic fibers (principally nylon), would be the dominant method of manufacturing carpet.

My career in carpets began in 1955, at the very outset of tufted broadloom. It was a special point in time and Dalton, Georgia, was the Mecca, the legendary epicenter of industry activity. The company I worked for was a wholesale floor-covering distributor in New York owned by Tom Carmichael, a visionary whose belief in the new technology earned him scoffs and jeers from competitors steeped in the traditional woven mode.

Mr. Carmichael's fascination with and confidence in the new tufted products was absolute. His firm distributed woven carpets from some of the great mills of the day, yet it was in Dalton that Mr. Carmichael's heart resided. There was no doubt in his mind that the same wonderful mechanics who had built those early tufting machines would overcome the quality problems associated with the products.

He was right. By 1957, important technical innovations were made and a respectable product emerged, marketed at less than half the price of wovens. The scoffers quit scoffing, the jeerers fell silent, the gold rush was on. Not surprisingly, I wanted in on the action, and in 1958, I left Mr. Carmichael's firm and started my own sales agency, representing three Dalton tufting companies in the northeastern United States.

It is said that luck is the point at which opportunity and experience merge. Experience told me that while the new tufting technology had advanced to a respectable state, it was still in its infancy. Everywhere one looked in the Dalton of 1958, there was a new breakthrough — a series of pattern rollers for tufting hi-lo pile, a new continuous filament yarn, a woven secondary backing material to improve stability, a better adhering latex — the improvements were rapid and remarkable.

I was thrilled at the opportunity to be right there at the outset of a great new industry. Fortunately, I was able to witness the stream of innovations at close hand. One of the manufacturers I represented as a selling agent was Painter Carpet Mills, a small operation run by Mr. Mose Painter, the industry's most celebrated innovator and inventor. Although there has long raged a debate as to who actually built the first tufting machine for carpet, Mose Painter is generally conceded to be that man. This rough-hewn, colorful mountain man came to Dalton from the backwoods of West Virginia in 1941, set up a crude machine shop and almost single-handedly forged the key equipment elements for tufted carpets.

I saw a lot of Mose Painter. While my sales territory was in the north, I came to Dalton for several days each month to visit him and to collect my commissions (no easy task in those days). I learned early on that no thrill is quite equal to that of invention, no satisfaction as complete as creating that which did not previously exist. If Mose had an idea for a new product, he'd go to any lengths to produce it. The fact that no machine existed to achieve the effect was incidental — he simply built one! Seemingly, financial reward from all his inventions and innovations meant nothing to him. To my knowledge, he never applied for a patent, nor did he ever charge a license fee. He freely shared his insights and his inventions with competitors who, more often than not, brought his ideas to market before he ever got them there.

That is not to say he never scored a triumph. On those rare occasions when he got to market first, the orders from customers flooded the company with business. Seldom did a Painter carpet look like any other carpet. Strangely, these successes meant little to him — for Mose Painter, a compliment or a hearty pat on the back was reward enough.

Ultimately, he was unable to hold onto the company which bore his name and which blazed so many trails in the early years. Mose Painter, the mechanical genius, the brilliant product innovator, had committed an unpardonable business error — he tried to be all things to all people, dissipating his time and energies in areas of the business he should have left to more qualified associates.

Perhaps I have taken too long a look back to trace the roots of those events and people who strongly influenced my business philosophy. Yet, three useful lessons emanate from this trip down Memory Lane:

1. It's true what they say about better mousetraps.
2. There is no such thing as a commodity.
3. Know your limitations.

Let me take each in order.

Lesson 1. As exciting as the industry was (and is), the tendency has always been to duplicate the competitors' best-selling styles. In this sense, Dalton, Georgia, has traditionally demonstrated a kind of "Xerox mentality." Copying one's neighbor but doing it cheaper is undeniably the dominating product-marketing strategy.

To this day, whenever a clever stylist makes a unique product, people rush to buy it. The lesson is clear — great products make great salesmen. It's easy to sell what people want to buy. The most effective marketing device known to any industry is an innovative product or service.

My company, Horizon Industries, started as smallest among four hundred carpet mills in 1972. We began with the belief that the American carpet consumer wanted variety, and we assumed some major risks by introducing uniquely styled carpets. The strategy worked. Today, Horizon is approaching $300 million in sales, and we are among the fifteen largest carpet manufacturers in the world. While we produce the "basics," we continue to bring to market the different, the creative, the more colorful products on which we established our reputation. Product innovation is the shrine at which we worship.

Lesson 2. The U.S. carpet industry has much to be proud of. It is a world-class industry which has consistently shown its extraordinary ability to control costs through efficiencies and productivity gains. Its record of price stability in the highly inflationary twenty-five year period from 1960 through 1985 is enviable. While automobiles increased in price by 127.2 percent and the consumer price index soared by 215.9 percent during this period, carpet prices rose only 52.3 percent by comparison.

However, this focus on lowering costs has dealt a damaging blow to the industry's marketing prowess. With its relentless reliance on price as the hook to attract consumers, such concepts as brand merchandising, fashion emphasis, sales training, specialized distribution and advertising and promotion have been largely neglected. The industry makes the most technically outstanding floor-covering products in the world, yet it peddles its products as so much "colored concrete." Its mind set suggests that carpet is a commodity, and the best a manufacturer can do is to conceive ways to sell it cheaper.

Horizon has resisted this commodity premise from day one. We put no stock in the suggestion that one mill's product is the same as the next's and that the order should go to the lowest bidder. This is not to say that we don't compete aggressively or take a lot of low-margin business. We do. If we didn't, our massive continuous production lines would come to a halt, with resulting losses much greater than the profits lost by accepting marginally priced orders.

We live in a real world of fierce competition, and we tough it out with the best of them. Still, we strive continually to make our customers and the ultimate consumer aware of the added benefits in our product. We don't believe any company makes carpet quite like Horizon. We are convinced that we market the most attractive, best-performing, highest-value products in the industry. We are committed to fashion and believe that the consumer is looking for ways to make her home more beautiful when she shops for carpet. We know that she will pay dollars more a yard for the color she wants. But she will resist the wrong color at any price. While competitors offer twenty to thirty colors in a plush style, we offer fifty. We want her satisfied.

Horizon has been awarded a trophy for "Best Style" by the Retail Floor Covering Institute every year since that organization initiated its awards program. We're very proud of this recognition from those who bestow it — our customers.

Lesson 3. I often wish that I was a complete businessman, the sort of guy who can do it all. Unfortunately, I'm not. For that matter, I'm not sure I know any corporate head who fits that description, unless he's an entrepreneur running a small business. I started my own business because I wanted a situation in which I had to answer only to myself. I felt I was capable of making the right decisions, and I sought the recognition and financial rewards that result when right decisions pay off.

My recollection of Horizon's early years is that they were among its best and most productive. As in most new and small ventures, we operated as a close-knit team. We knew one another's strengths and weaknesses, and communication was virtually instantaneous. If I wanted something changed, I had only to mention it to a colleague and it happened. Although the paucity of working capital created a constant struggle, the first phase of our business was very gratifying. We had a great time. We prided ourselves on our flexibility, vowing never to complicate our structure to the point that flexibility was seriously diminished.

I kept in mind the memory of my mentor, Mose Painter, and how he lost his business because of his unwillingness to delegate authority. Mose just had to make every call. In areas where his education or experience were lacking, he often called the wrong shot. I quickly saw that this was no way to manage a business.

I am a marketing man with special interest in product development. After thirty years of tinkering with products, I think I've become pretty good at what I do. Yet, however important they may be, a business is much more than just making products. At various stages in Horizon's growth, I have sat down to ask myself a hard question: "What are you not doing well that someone else could do better?" If I came away from this period of introspection convinced that I was hurting the company by stretching myself too thin, I took corrective steps.

The toughest of these for me turned out to be the most gratifying. By the spring of 1984, following years of rapid growth and change, I found myself in a quandary. The company had become complex, we had lost the flexibility we so treasured, and our profits were heading south. I spent my time rushing around trying to put out fires. I neglected product development, and our line suffered accordingly. I knew the time had come for a change.

That summer I asked Ralph Boe to join Horizon as our Chief Operating Officer. He had spent his entire career with DuPont and knew how large companies operated. I recognized that we needed a gifted manager of his caliber to set Horizon back on track. He has done a splendid job of streamlining, simplifying and reshaping our organization. Today, we plan, communicate and execute far more smoothly and with lower SG&A costs as a percentage of sales. Profits are making a strong comeback, and the business is becoming fun again.

Now, I devote my time to creating exciting new products and marketing programs to position them successfully. Together with Ralph Boe and Dennis Fink, our CFO, I plan the strategies of the business. Horizon has moved ahead with renewed vigor; so have I.

Training, Dues-Paying and Profits

The hotel was beautiful, the location perfect. Then the nightmare began. Perhaps nightmare is too strong a word. After all, there are worse things than the failure to deliver, but when you are on the receiving end, it is difficult to think of it as anything but a nightmare. When it happens to others, the reaction can range from "Tsk, tsk" to "Oh, really?"

Simply stated, the newly registered guests had just spent more time changing rooms, looking for one where the air-conditioning worked, than they did traveling portal to portal by air from another city five hundred miles away. They had been exposed to almost everything but an apology, and they got the distinct impression from one of the hotel's assistant managers that in a couple of months cool weather would arrive and air-conditioning would not be necessary. So much for dismissing the curse of an Indian summer.

They got the impression from another of the hotel's assistant managers that this would be a great place to work — if it weren't for the customers. To the sweating guests, still perspiring after room number three, the prospect of cooler weather in a few months had little appeal. In their present state, they were sure-fire shoe-ins for a Gatorade commercial or a Lipton plunge.

Actually, checking into another hotel seemed far more rational and appealing. What convinced them to give room number four a try was a bellman who expressed concern and care for the hapless couple and who was also visibly embarrassed by conditions over which he had absolutely no control. For the most part, the assistant managers (one and two) were either defensive or devious. At best, a rotten combination.

Happily, room number four was the jackpot. But while the two guests were now cooled off, they weren't truly pleased. Perhaps, they thought, a nice meal would nurture both the body and the spirit. Alas, the search for the air-conditioned room was more time-consuming than they had realized and resulted in a decision to eat in the hotel rather than go out. As it turned out, it would have been better to retire hungry.

The menu by the dining-room entrance made great, but expensive, reading. However, why not? They were on vacation, and weren't they supposed to splurge?

To the maître d's question about whether they desired to sit in a smoking or nonsmoking section, they opted for a smoke-free section — and were promptly seated next to a threesome who appeared to be enveloped by fog.

You guessed it. When the couple asked the maître d' about this, he matter-of-factly replied that during happy hour (9 P.M. to midnight), the hotel did not enforce its smoking policy, and if they looked at their watches, they would see that it was now 9:30 P.M.

The now not-so-happy guests were wondering why they were even asked their preference unless it was part of a research project. Worse, it was part of an ill-conceived and ineffective training program which served only to reinforce these consumers' minimum-shaft expectations.

Quality service is more than skin deep. It is a top-to-bottom, inside-out result of quality training and quality commitment. Too often, the exterior — or what you see — lacks substance that can be built on a foundation only by people who know what they are doing and why they are doing it. This is the *essence* of training.

While quality service is composed of many little things, delivering such service requires a staff, from top to bottom, that understands exactly how all these little things mesh and interact. This is a *function* of training.

Too often, we concentrate on techniques and mechanics before we provide an understanding of the why. People who deliver and who do things right the very first time usually have a sound conceptual understanding of not only what they are doing but also the reasoning behind it. This is the *mission* of training.

The fact remains: what most consumers see of an organizational structure is quite contrary to the picture painted by management. While firms go to great effort to capture effectively the pyramid structures that carry them along, most consumers only encounter the lower levels of organizations. To these customers, the rest of the structure is irrelevant; all that really counts, all that truly matters, is the quality of information, service and delivery at the level of the organization where buyer meets seller. It is at this lowest level of the firm where training is most important. However, it is at this lowest level of the firm that management generally places the least resources and the least effort.

Training at this level can make the difference between satisfying or alienating customers. By inverting the company's structure, you place emphasis and energy at the level of greatest impact: where seller meets buyer, where money is made.

While the requisites for effective training could consume entire volumes, there are four simple concerns that should be recognized if management is indeed serious about enhancing service at the level where transactions are consummated.

Employees must be motivated to learn. Turnover in the fast-food industry does not exceed 100 percent annually because of a genuine lack of talent. Rather, this industry suffers the malaise encountered in all too many industries, that affliction felt by so many line employees: a genuine lack of recognition as to why things are the way they are. What difference does it make if I forget to put a pickle on the bun? Who cares if a drive-in customer said absolutely no ketchup and I put it on anyway? The fact is that these employees, like all employees, must understand the objectives of a training program and the impact that this training will have on their individual and company performance. If you emphasize the big picture and this employee's role in it, you will augment this individual's sense of contribution and worth and convince each and every employee that his or her efforts can make the difference between winning and second place.

Training should emerge from an organizational climate that recognizes its contribution to financial performance. All employees involved in training should perceive that this is a give-and-take process. Their questions and concerns are valid and necessary. Training represents a significant financial commitment that should pay off in terms of employee and company performance. In too many organizations, training is perceived as a necessary evil which delays the new employee's entry to the job.

If a diverse and complex set of skills is taught, trainees should have the opportunity to practice given components in phases. There is nothing more frightening or damaging to an organizational neophyte than to enter a new position without confidence and support. Your training investment will be disastrous if the newcomers are programmed to fail. A little more time up front will yield a greater sense of self-assuredness and probability for success.

Finally, constant feedback is a must. Too often, we dwell on what's bad rather than what is good and works. While mistakes should be identified, these new entrants into the world of work need constant encouragement and support. These words of recognition are inexpensive, but if they are passed on in a timely manner, they can yield great benefits to your employees and your organization.

Twice they said it couldn't be done. When Bob Hazard and Gerry Pettit went to Best Western Hotels in 1974, the prognosis for this rather stable confederation of independent lodges was unexciting and uninvigorated. In six years, the chain grew from eight hundred to twenty-six hundred properties and the average member's earnings increased by more than 500 percent. Why? Hazard and Pettit knew that quality in this marketplace was a function of product and people. Product could, over time, be systematically standardized and upgraded. The people, however, had to be trained and oriented to a mind set of competing in a fiercely competitive industry. The training that evolved from corporate headquarters in Phoenix was a recognition that the people in the field — the desk clerks, housekeepers, maintenance people, pool cleaners — made the difference in customer satisfaction and, in the long run, training dollars invested in these people were transformed into profits at all levels of the organization.

In 1981, Hazard and Pettit went to Quality Inns in Silver Spring, Maryland. In recent years, these executives have cut over two-thirds of the franchises they inherited and built an organization represented by more than one thousand hotels with 122,000 rooms worldwide. The industry said they couldn't do it. Many franchisees said it could not be done. But through a systematic and aggressive commitment to retraining and redirection, as well as a rededication to customer needs, Hazard and Pettit have done it again. They recognize, however, that their success has been directly tied to the performance and effort displayed by every employee at every lodge — *and this is a function of training.*

Getting the best is simply not enough. It never has been enough. As a matter of fact, selection techniques, no matter how sophisticated, are far from perfect. Hence, what an organization does with those it recruits, selects and trains is often more critical than the people it originally attracts. For this reason, training must be viewed as an organizational essential rather than a company extra.

Productivity, quality and profitability are often characteristics of organizations where training for excellence is an integral part of a company's culture or ethos and where staff members are always recognized for achievements.

Realistically, the continuously profitable enterprise is a consciously developed endeavor whose leadership understands that the company must pay its dues each and every day, with each and every transaction and at each and every level of the organization.

James W. McLamore

A pioneer of the franchise restaurant business, James W. McLamore co-founded Burger King Corporation in 1954. He has served as president or chairman since 1967, and Burger King is now the second largest fast-food restaurant chain in the world. A native of upstate New York, McLamore is a graduate of Cornell University.

Find a Need and Fill It:
A History of the Whopper

In 1954, my partner, David R. Edgerton, Jr., and I decided that we could build a chain-restaurant business around the simple concept of a limited-menu, fast-food restaurant that employed a self-service concept. Today, it may seem strange to reflect on that, yet self-service restaurants were unknown then, as were restaurants with limited menus. "Fast food," which did not exist in 1954, now generates fifty-eight billion dollars in sales, or almost one-half of a $120-billion food-service market. Burger King Corporation is the strong number-two contender in that important market.

The road to the top was not an easy one. As always, when pioneering a new service concept, there were many hurdles to overcome. In the first place, the consumer was unaware that this novel service offered an advantage. We had created a business based on offering customers very low prices, a very limited menu of quality popular products and, perhaps most importantly, speed of service, but consumers were initially skeptical about it all.

I opened my first restaurant in 1949. It featured hamburgers and short orders. It had fourteen seats and was open twenty-four hours a day. At that time the total dollar volume of the entire food-service industry, including liquor sales, was under nine billion dollars. Today, the dollar volume of McDonald's Corporation is over fourteen billion dollars a year in food sales alone — nearly one and one-half times the total industry's sales of forty years ago.

As America emerged from the war years, eating out was pretty much a luxury. There were few suburban shopping centers. Restaurants usually were Mom-and-Pop affairs located in urban centers. There were few restaurant chains, and those that existed were local and very small in number. National and regional chains were nonexistent.

Dave and I sensed that the consumer was ready for change. Service in restaurants was slow. Restaurateurs tried to be all things to all people. Food quality was mediocre. Service was poor, and eating out was generally not a pleasant experience. I used to say in those days that customers had two things to spend — time and money — and they'd rather spend their money. Speed of service seemed important to us, and we addressed it!

We built a restaurant system that concentrated on hamburgers, milk shakes, French fries and soft drinks. We served them in disposable paper containers and designed the system to serve the food as quickly as it was ordered. We thought it was important that the customers have their food products before the cashier could make their change. That was quite unique in 1954!

Our plan was hardly a formula for instant success, and the sailing wasn't smooth. The customer didn't understand a style of service where he had to wait on himself. In addition, he had a distrust of the low-priced hamburger because the quality was automatically suspect. We had to overcome these concerns. It wasn't easy. We concluded that if we could build a number of Burger King restaurants in a given community we could communicate the style of service we were offering on television, which, like Burger King, was in its infancy in the early 1950s. Further, we felt that we could expand the business by selling franchises. Franchising was essentially in its infancy, also.

Not every kind of service business can be franchised. The business we had developed, because of its simplicity, enabled us to teach others to operate under our name and trademarks. We developed operating systems and standards for managing the business. The standards we set forth dealt with customer needs. We concentrated on the customer. We knew that people appreciated fast, courteous service. They appreciated clean, sparkling restaurants. They appreciated attentiveness. They appreciated good food — hot fresh hamburgers, crisp, golden French fries, thick, creamy shakes and cold, sparkling soft drinks. We concentrated on these few tasks. We emphasized to our employees and our franchisees the importance of delivering excellence in the products and services we had for sale. Excellence in our offering began to pay off.

As Burger King grew, it attracted competition of all descriptions. We had what appeared to be a simple food-service concept that was very easy to emulate. Many did. Many of our imitators thought the trick was in the design of our buildings, our equipment, the menu items and the service techniques. They were, after all, the basic ingredients of success, but they had to be managed with another element, *proper attention to details of every kind* — details such as employee courtesy, cleanliness, speed of service, quality of products and the insistence that this quality be available to the customer at any hour of the day or night.

Most businesses that fail do so simply because management doesn't concern itself with the customers' needs. That sounds simplistic, but most managements think in financial terms rather than in marketing terms. The remote and unenlightened "bean counters" can destroy a business if they cannot relate to the customers' interest as the guiding, most important focus of the business. I have owned and operated restaurants for forty years. The restaurant business has one of the highest mortality rates of any business in the United States. I have heard countless restaurant managers fretting over controlling food costs and labor and utility costs. This is

usually the easiest, most direct approach to profit management —
controlling costs. I subscribe to the notion that management must
know its costs and that not knowing costs can lead directly to
business failure. Controlling cost is a must. Many times, though, it
fails to take into consideration what the customers' interest in all
this might be.

My approach has always been to position the consumers' preference as the number-one priority, in terms of both food quality and
service and the insistence that standards of excellence in all catego-
ries be the primary concern of management. After determining
those very high standards, management must then be charged to
apply its expertise along lines of productivity. How can we make
our food products the most efficient in terms of value and quality?
How do we motivate our personnel to deliver our products and
services as thoughtfully and carefully and courteously as we can?
What new innovations can we introduce to build efficiencies into
the system? These were our overriding concerns in building Burger
King Corporation into an important business entity.

Some examples:

I mentioned that we pioneered a new food-service concept. We
knew that by mass-producing hamburgers we could sell them very
inexpensively. We sensed that price would be a real attraction to
consumers. But we had to overcome uncertainty about quality in
those days. We realized that if we could build and expand the
number of Burger King restaurants, initially in the Miami market,
we could advertise on television. We sensed that this was a very
efficient way to communicate and sell our idea of our service and
quality. At the same time we innovated the franchising of our
restaurants to help fuel growth. We were confident that we could
teach others to operate our business because it was quite simple.
We became one of the earliest of the restaurant industry's fran-
chisors. Perhaps the most important innovation was our franchise
agreement requiring franchisees to join us in spending a fixed
percentage of sales for advertising. We went immediately to spot
television advertising in the Miami market. The results were
impressive. Our sales began to grow as people discovered us and

tried our new restaurants. It was our mission to see that our new customers were completely satisfied with everything we offered — price, efficiency, speed, courtesy and cleanliness. We insisted that these elements be delivered in spades, and they were.

I must admit that I am a detail person, basically a hands-on manager. I realize that this can present serious drawbacks to thinking in strategic terms, long-range goal setting and the like. But it was my own style never to lose sight of the very basic elements of the business, all of which pointed toward the customer and the customer's requirements. I felt, and still do, that if we could not meet the needs of our customers on each and every one of their experiences in a Burger King restaurant we were flirting with failure. In our training programs we tried to convey this concern to our employees so that they, too, would sense the need to satisfy the customers' interests thoroughly. The record shows that Burger King, from its inception, delivered excellence in the areas of service, quality of food, cleanliness and courtesy. We built a business on those principles of excellence, and we pay attention to them today. Indeed, this is the only insurance we have that we can continue to exist in this changing market place.

Sensitivity to the market place takes very sophisticated forms in a large chain organization. Constant inquiries by management as to how the market is changing and reacting have to be made. Are the physical facilities, seating, parking sufficient? What different kinds of service are being demanded? How important is lighting? Can the design of the building be improved? Is the customer asking for new menu items? How do we communicate their availability? Market research became an important function. Our original service concept sprang from intuition, mine and Dave's, but market research into a rapidly changing consumer, in a far different market place, dictated change — changes such as drive-up windows with telephonic advanced ordering, greater ambiance in the dining rooms, attractive landscaping, a remodeling of buildings, a different look, new products, a variety of products, different packaging, the targeting of different consumer groups by focused advertising, the sophistication of mass-marketing techniques. Such innovations required the energies and discipline of professional talent.

The first commercial jet transportation in the United States occurred in December of 1958. That moment in history ushered in the age of air travel that enabled a Miami-based food-service organization to consider building a franchise network of restaurants in major cities across America. A new opportunity for growth was offered by this technological advance. We took advantage of it.

Suddenly, we could travel nonstop from Miami to distant cities such as Dallas, Houston, New York, Chicago, Cincinnati, Boston, Minneapolis, St. Louis and many, many others. Our success in Florida was receiving national attention. Franchises were sought in these distant cities, and it was easy to get there. We had developed an expertise in the area of real estate. We made few mistakes in identifying the best locations for our new restaurants. Our franchisees became successful overnight. Their success triggered new interest and fueled additional growth. Our development strategy concentrated on television markets or ADIs (areas of dominant influence). Burger King and the Whopper (more about that later!) started to become household words. We envisioned becoming a national presence. We could see the prospects of network television advertising and the efficiencies that could bring.

Restaurant franchising, particularly in far-flung markets, was quite new and innovative in the 1950s. It grew rapidly in the 1960s and 1970s. As jet travel enabled us to reach distant markets, we drew on the entrepreneurial energy of a family of franchisees who were committed, as we were, to the growth and expansion of the Burger King system. Our customer loyalty was building rapidly. We were receiving ever-increasing patronage and support.

We built on many strengths: the franchisee family, mass marketing, advertising, our building and equipment design and construction, development of a system of food-service commissaries in markets throughout America to serve our growing chain of restaurants. The foundation and underpinning of our success rested solely on our high quality standards of food products and service. This was the base. This was the fabric of our success. We felt we had to be better than anybody else in our field. We believe to this day that we were — and that we still are.

But there are other, more elusive elements which have become the warp and woof of the fabric of our success: innovation and change. Back in 1956, two years after the founding of the company, we were struggling. We just didn't have the spark. We were too small to advertise, and it was hard to get across to the public a compelling reason to try our new Burger King restaurants. Our menu needed a superstar, a standout. We had to become a specialist, offer something to set us apart from the crowd. We had to project a unique image. We found that spark, that specialty. Indeed, it was the turning point in the history of Burger King Corporation. I came up with an idea — a new sandwich which I called the Whopper. For the first two years of our existence we had just an eighteen-cent hamburger and a twenty-three cent cheeseburger. Although they were of high quality, there was nothing particularly unique about them. One day in Gainesville, Florida, I noticed a restaurant serving a very large hamburger and tried it. It was delicious. Out of that experience came the idea for building a quarter-pound hamburger patty, broiling it, placing it on a five-inch bun with lettuce, tomatoes, pickles, mayonnaise, onions and ketchup. I decided to call it a Whopper because that meant big and because we could then promote ourselves as specialists. At the same moment in time, I decided to put under the Burger King name "Home of the Whopper" to call attention to the fact that we offered a unique kind of hamburger. The Whopper made Burger King. It still sets Burger King miles apart from its competitors. In 1987, it is probably the world's best-known sandwich. I doubt that any other sandwich can take its place as the most popular sandwich in the world.

Innovation and change are critical to the longevity, growth and prosperity of American business. Time doesn't stand still. Markets change. People change. Styles and personal preferences change. Failure to respond to change is the death knell of any business organization.

The Burger King story is a study of change. It is more than a study of a single company. One could say that it is a study of the founding of the "fast-food" industry now so much a part of the daily lives of the world's people. We had the good fortune to sense that change in the air and knew that an opportunity existed to grow as the change unfolded. We addressed that opportunity well, and, for a variety of reasons, we succeeded. It was fun, exciting, and we believe we did some good along the way. Yet there is nothing unique in our story. If you look at the majority of the great modern-day corporations, it is evident that most of them are really not very old at all and those that are old have been masters at dealing with change. They've kept their markets and their prosperity because they addressed consumer needs in the most efficient way. Many have been built by entrepreneurs who have sensed a need, a void in the marketplace, and have rushed in to fill that need. The exciting part of the story is that there is more opportunity in the marketplace today than ever before in our country's history. There are thousands of success stories, and there are thousands more in the early stages of being written. That is the history of America enterprise. The marketplace is constantly confronted with needs — consumer needs. Where those needs exist, profit-minded innovators will be in the midst of them, searching for ways to provide them.

John C. Portman, Jr.

John C. Portman, Jr., is founder and chairman of John Portman and Associates, architects and engineers, and nine other Portman businesses based in Atlanta. He is internationally known for his innovative hotel designs and his success in designing and developing urban mixed-use projects. He attended the U.S. Naval Academy and served in the U.S. Navy during World War II. Portman holds the B.S. in architecture from the Georgia Institute of Technology.

Making Practical Idealism Work

The success of The Portman Companies reflects four key factors. They are not unique to our operation, but they have been essential to our development. The four factors are vision, innovation, flexibility and perseverance.

Vision. Envisioning one's objective is the first step in making it a reality. My goal as a practical idealist has been to create environments that enhance the human condition and also add to the economic health and vitality of the community by adding to the tax base and creating new jobs.

When I graduated from Georgia Tech with a degree in architecture in 1950, it was obvious that the world was undergoing major changes that would significantly alter the way we live. (Architects historically have been interested in master plans for cities.)

Immediately after World War II and while I was a student, Tech had some excellent professors of architecture and also presented many famous architects, such as Frank Lloyd Wright, Mies van der

Rohe and Walter Gropius, as visiting critics. I also became very interested in philosophy and, in the process, read Emerson's *Self-Reliance* and ever since have seriously taken it to heart. Upon graduation, I truly believed that it was possible to make a significant contribution to our changing society through a meaningful and motivated practice of architecture.

Designing major inner-city complexes did not begin immediately. I first completed my apprenticeship with a major firm and, after obtaining my registration, began my own two-man practice. Our early commissions were modest. During that period, however, I progressed philosophically through intent observation. I watched people as to how they responded to their environment. I also studied the physical evolution of the great cities of the world to understand how and why they work well or, in some cases, do not.

One of the turning points in my career was a trip to the dedication of Brasilia in 1960. The much-lauded new capital of Brazil was one of the world's first modern planned cities. I traveled there with great expectations but left sorely disappointed. Brasilia was not an environment that responded to the basic human needs for order, variety, charm, nature and spirituality of the people who lived in the city. From that point my work became increasingly involved in creating environments which truly respond to the innate physical and spiritual needs of people.

In the 1960s, American cities underwent major transitions. In some cases, racial strife caused white flight to the suburbs. Also, expanded expressway systems pulled more people into their cars and into the suburbs, away from the inner city. The traditional town concept was altered radically. It was necessary to focus more intently on what a rapidly changing city could be in order to respond to the new realities. In all strategies, it was determined that the heart of the city must remain strong and viable! Economically, functionally and visually, it should work as a unit.

In the 1980s, we have addressed the new problems of the expansive suburban sprawl that has evolved during the past decades. Without losing sight of the importance of the heart of the city, we are now addressing the importance of concentrated, planned pedestrian-oriented environments in the suburbs as well.

Knowing what you are trying to accomplish — that vision of where you want to be — is the first step in getting there.

Innovation. Usually, the way to accomplish significant work is not to do it just like everybody else always has. Some have accused me of being a maverick, because I often take a different approach. Sometimes that is not popular; sometimes it is controversial. But change calls for new thinking.

A few years after starting my architectural practice, I was eager to make things happen. I realized that by becoming more involved in the development process, I would have more control over where, when and also how projects are designed and built.

The traditional architect's role was strictly limited: he was neither owner nor developer of the project. An alternative would be to approach things in an entrepreneurial way. I had ideas about business that could or should develop downtown. I also took the opportunity to design the buildings needed for the development projects. The idea for developing the Atlanta Merchandise Mart began by recognizing that the time and need were right to develop regional wholesale facilities in Atlanta. We "tested the water" by renovating a parking garage that had been converted to office space.

We modified the garage to provide forty thousand square feet of space, which we leased to furniture manufacturers for regional wholesale showrooms. The demand was so great that it grew to 250,000 square feet in one year, and we proceeded with plans for a new one-million-square-foot facility, which opened in 1961. Today, from that beginning, we have the Atlanta Market Center, now approaching eight million square feet, serving many industries and still growing.

With the opening of the Atlanta Merchandise Mart and the experience gained by visiting Brasilia, I saw the potential of a mixed-use development growing around the Mart which would include offices, hotels, retail businesses and — in the future — housing.

The offices came next. We approached the problem of urban high-rise office building design in a slightly different manner than the traditional and more typical way. Rather than construct the buildings up to the edge of the property lines, we pulled them back, extending the sidewalk back into the site. We provided space for greater pedestrian interaction within the property and created multilevel public space, freeing the heart of the city blocks for human use. We brought all forms of nature, flowers, trees and water back into the city. We also commissioned major sculpture which became part of the urban community. This may not seem like a radical departure today, but it was not the typical approach at that time.

Next came the need for a hotel. Again, why duplicate another conventional, traditional set of guest rooms stacked on top of a lobby with its registration desk and coffee shop? I tried to think about what a hotel should offer in a congested city, what a guest would seek in entering his temporary home away from home. As city streets are crowded and congested, the guest experience should be the antithesis of this. The most precious commodity and greatest need in an increasingly congested city is an increase in public space, so that is what the architecture must encompass. I literally allowed the space to explode up through the center of the building, creating a twenty-two story sky-lit atrium which provides a sense of spacial grandeur, an atmosphere of serenity with expansiveness and, at the same time, a feeling of quiet excitement.

When investors saw the plans, they thought the idea was crazy. Space was being wasted that could produce revenue. In fact, we had major problems in gaining backing for this project. Our original partners became nervous halfway through the construction of the hotel and had us seeking a new owner. We courted every major hotel operator in the country, but little interest was generated in this radically different approach to hotel design. After our inability to make a deal with the Sheratons, Lowes, Marriotts, Hiltons and others, we invited the Pritzkers of Chicago to have a look. At that time, they owned a few small West Coast motels, but were not considered major hotel operators. Here again, "vision" impacted the project. Don Pritzker was able to envision what we were trying to achieve and shared our enthusiasm for this new concept.

The Hyatt Regency Atlanta responded to what people were seeking. They stood in line to see this different new building with its glass elevators and revolving blue-domed roof-top restaurant. The space responded to the hidden needs of the people, and the people, in turn, responded back. Occupancy was incredible, and expansion plans were started almost immediately.

That radical, never-will-work idea has since become almost a prototype for contemporary hotel design the world over. It serves as but one example of the importance of looking at each set of circumstances in a fresh and innovative way. Our firm always tries to look for solutions that will best serve the circumstances at the time, not just those that are the traditional, safe way of doing things. We seek the essence of the problem and solve it by opening the windows of our minds to new realities and possibilities, always seeking to make a greater contribution.

By example, our approach to surburban development is now being reflected at the Northpark and Riverwood developments in Atlanta; the problems of Times Square were addressed with the New York Marriott Marquis; Marina Square in Singapore took a fresh new look at lodging and shopping in the Far East, and so the story goes. Each problem or set of circumstances is unique and residing within lies its own unique solution!

Flexibility. Translating ideas and objectives into reality takes old-fashioned hard work with a clear focus on fact, content and priorities as well as good organization. Reams have been written on management style. Since each set of circumstances is different, so must be each organization.

If someone were to diagram the organizational structure for our companies, he could create a traditional vertical pyramid chart of little boxes showing logical relationships of people and jobs. However, if that same person were to study how we function, his diagram would more likely consist of a series of overlapping horizontal levels. We have pioneered unique roles for individuals to grow and contribute through a broader base of interchange. By creating a more global understanding, it is possible to make a more significant contribution at the individual level. New and greater understanding and insights improve the quality of our work.

We hold some traditional staff meetings and implement certain procedures in a formal manner; however, the majority of our decision-making is done in a more spontaneous, less structured environment. I try to be readily accessible to all of our key people, and they, in turn, try to stay flexible as well. It is not unusual for key decisions to be made during unscheduled meetings in office corridors or on stairway landings. This is made possible by the practice of seeking the essence of the problem and going straight to the heart of the matter. Good ideas and critical decisions need not wait for scheduled meetings if broad-based horizontal interchange is allowed to prosper.

This style may have evolved because the basis of our company was architecture and design, which are creative by nature.

Today, as our organization has grown to over twelve hundred people, we are challenged not to lose the enthusiastic "can do" environment that fostered creative new thinking.

Perseverance. Once one has an idea or conception, never giving up is critical. Perseverance is essential. When ideas are innovative, they often are not readily accepted. Then, more than ever, it is important to know and understand one's objectives and to be a practical idealist. One must creatively pursue all means within one's power to make the ideas a reality.

If I had given up on the idea for the Hyatt Regency Atlanta when the first person told me it would not work, or even when I was told by the second, third, fourth or fifth person, the evolution of hotel design might have taken a different course. So, in fact, might the development of the Hyatt Corporation have been different.

The New York Marriott Marquis is another example of a project that tested the perseverance of all involved. Beginning in 1972 at the request of Mayor John Lindsay, that project weathered the administration of three mayors, with Mayor Ed Koch making a tremendous contribution in the later years. We had to deal with a major economic recession, the concerns and protests of preservationists and the rules and regulations of an infinite number of city and state agencies.

At times, the large convention hotel in the heart of the theater district appeared to be a lost cause. I hesitate to tally the hours spent in negotiation for that project. Yet, if we had not persisted in our commitment to revitalize New York's decaying theater district, Times Square would not be experiencing the dynamic renewal we see today.

With vision, innovation, flexibility and perseverance there is no limit to what can be accomplished.

2

DEAL
SEALING

It's Not Over 'Til It's Over

"Why me?"

How often do consumers raise this cry? How often do buyers of the world proclaim to sellers of the world that they have been abused, humiliated and humbled one more time?

Mind you, it isn't the major catastrophes that disenchant and dishearten. It's the aggregate of the little things that makes the difference between satisfaction and sadness. It is the simple things during the entire buying and selling process that consumers at large remember. It is the seemingly insignificant actions that take place from the moment buyers enter the store to the instant they leave that, in fact, determine whether they will ever return to that same commercial establishment. It is these little things that all too many sellers simply forget. The little things are killers. They kill customer satisfaction. This kills customer loyalty. And this kills sellers. Simple, isn't it?

Twelve dollars for a movie. As long as you're not interested in catching the mid-morning showing on a Sunday, this is what an average couple can expect to pay for the opportunity to view one cinematic venture. Not so bad, you say? Perhaps not. But when the typical moviegoer throws in popcorn, soda, nachos, hot dogs and maybe a candy bar or two, moviegoing becomes a major discretionary purchase.

No problem. We decide we want to go, and we pay for that privilege. Last Saturday night, a great new Whoopi Goldberg movie came to town. Good reviews, great actress — this is what weekend fun is all about. Twelve dollars at the box office, eight dollars at the snack bar, and two dollars (we knew we shouldn't have) for the video games in the lobby.

We move into the theater and are quickly confronted with a blast of hot air that would lift a dirigible. (This is Florida, and the outside temperature is eighty-two degrees.) A naive question is posed to the manager: "Is the air conditioning broken?" To which the manager calmly replies: "What do you think?" We're thinking he would look terrific dipped in nacho cheese.

Over three hundred people have now gathered to see the film, and, having spent thousands of dollars on various edibles, are now perspiring profusely. Not a pretty picture, and no remedy in sight. Sure, the theater will refund the money — but you've already invested next week's paycheck on popcorn. You see, the transaction isn't finished until that customer leaves the establishment truly satisfied and truly pleased. We will never go back.

There must be a collective vendetta being waged by the car dealers of the world against consumers. You know it, we know it, and worse yet, they know it. While buying a new car can be humbling, repairing that car can be downright humiliating.

Example: customer had recently deposited $1,236.78 into a dealer's coffers for brake work and dealer add-ons. The problem: where is the car? Repair was promptly paid for in full by a customer taking valuable time away from work to pick up car. Where was it?

The bill was explained in detail, including a colorful narrative on how difficult it is for the dealer to obtain parts (for cars that the dealer sells). The bill was paid, and customer, on her time, waits and waits. Cashier explains that there is only one person available to bring cars up front. Customer explains there is only one person available to retrieve her child from the day-care center. Still no car. Forty-eight minutes later, the car is driven into the delivery area at the speed of sound.

Floor mats are dirty, air conditioning is blasting, radio is tuned to a station used only by car jockeys, and there are cigarette butts in the ashtray. The brakes are fine, but what the dealer fails to realize, as so many sellers do, is that the transaction isn't over until it's over. Until the merchandise is delivered in a timely and professional manner to that customer who must perceive herself as someone important to the livelihood of that firm, the deal is not done. Customer will not take car back for repairs — ever.

One more time. It was a nice dinner. Reservations had been made well in advance, the ambiance was delightful, service was fine, food was good . . . it was now time to pay the check.

Problem: no waiter in sight. Each course had been impeccably presented, and following a delightful flambé and a nice cup of decaf, it was time to leave. Unfortunately, it appeared that the waiter had already left. The maître d' who had graciously escorted us in was not at all inclined to escort us graciously out. Even the orchestra had packed it in. Our last course (the check) had taken as long to consummate as the first three. Consequently, we forgot the delightful appetizer, entrée, and music. We ignored the lovely place settings and flowers. By the time the check had arrived, indigestion was well entrenched.

Good or bad, right or wrong, customers are most likely to recall the last — not the first — experience. Consumers will remember the end of the story, not the beginning. Unfortunately, sales and management energies are expended as if companies were running sprints rather than marathons. What the consuming public wants (and demands) is consistent service, start to finish. Yet, most deals end with a whimper, not a bang.

Whether they are called customers, clients or patients, business is rotten without them. Too often, this basic fact is forgotten. It must be remembered and subsequently become an absolute way of life for the individual who interacts with the consumer. Yet, as elementary as this might appear, putting it into practice is too often a rarity.

A woman had just spent more than four hundred dollars in a national discount department store. When she got home, she discovered one eighteen-dollar sport shirt was the wrong size. Certainly a common mistake and one easily rectified — or so she thought.

When she presented the problem to the clerk in the customer-return booth, the clerk insisted that it was not the store's merchandise, even though the customer had yesterday's receipt and the shirt had one of those tags that defy removal stapled to it — along with the name of the store. The clerk, like many true believers, wasn't fazed one bit by the evidence. By now, the customer was beginning to feel like the main character in a mediocre psychological drama, where you vaguely sense you may be losing your mind.

Finally, after enlisting the "support" of a dubious department manager and, ultimately, the store manager with a "Don't-think-I-don't-know-what-you're-trying-to-pull" mentality, the eighteen dollars was returned. But the customer won't. Neither will her circle of friends and acquaintances who don't object to paying for merchandise but feel that abuse, like butterflies, should be free. Too bad. It was almost a good deal for the seller and buyer. It turned out to be a loser for both.

Let the motto be "Remember the small room," and doing business will be a pleasurable experience.

Sellers should handle each and every transaction as if the seller had to live with the buyer in a very small room for the rest of the seller's life. Do this, and the customer will be pleased and the seller will make a profit. Each party wins. It is truly a good deal. From an even more practical perspective, the customer becomes a salesperson for the selling institution, and that is an even *better* deal.

The Externalization of Excellence

It was Mother's Day. Therefore, the florist's arrival was not totally unexpected. The arrangement was lovely, and the card read, "Love, Aggie and Uncle Joe." But there was a problem — no one knew Aggie and Uncle Joe. Having the name of the florist, the recipient called to discover who was wishing her a Happy Mother's Day. If everything had been perfect, there would have been no phone call, and the introduction to this article would have taken another turn. Evidently, someone put the wrong card in the right envelope without bothering to make absolutely certain that this was not the case. As a result, several people were going to be unhappy, i.e., the senders and the receivers.

When the call to the florist was made, the person representing the florist suggested that she didn't know an Aunt Edie and Uncle Harold. Further, she was too busy filling Mother's Day orders to "waste time" on the phone, but if the customer would call back later that afternoon, she'd try to straighten things out. Later that afternoon, the customer did just that, and was told, "Listen, and listen very carefully. I'm only going to say this once, so you'd better get a pencil. The flowers were sent by Tom and Diane." Before a tentative thank-you could be uttered, the bearer of glad tidings hung up, leaving the customer hoping that next year she'd receive an IRS audit notice rather than a floral offering.

Unbelievable? Not quite. The following day, a successful attempt was made to find the store's owner. This was not as easy as it sounds, since yesterday's "Listen very carefully," employee was answering the phone and screening all calls. When the owner-manager was located and the situation explained, he was apologetic but not surprised. You see, his aunt was handling the phone, and because she was a family member, he "really didn't know what to do with her." The customer made a few excellent suggestions, the most humane of which was to keep the aunt dealing with dead flowers and away from live customers.

Now, while one is prone to fault the aunt, the fact is the blame rests with the boss. If you don't like what you see at the bottom of an organization, you'd better take a careful look at what's going on at the top. In a society that is becoming more and more service-oriented and quality-conscious, top managers must put into practice the excellence they espouse.

Not since 1957, the year Russia launched Sputnik, has the nation been so captivated by the promise and potential of high tech as a panacea for virtually all of society's ills. How well we manage change and, specifically, the manner in which we mesh social and mechanical dimensions are certain to be tested. Unless service and quality are basic system components, high tech — rather than being a panacea — will operate like the mermaid's siren song, luring unsuspecting mariners to their destruction.

In a similar fashion, management must maintain, in a creative fashion, control and direction of what high tech promises. A not-so-remote danger is that high tech might result in overall increases in productivity — coupled with a diminution of quality and service. This does not have to occur, but unless we learn from past errors, it will.

According to market researcher William C. Brekke, even first-level supervisors are more concerned today with human problems than purely technical ones. Again, high tech alone can't do the job and should be viewed as a means rather than an end.

Some time ago, Georgia State University brought together a large group of businesspersons, academicians and students for the first annual Sun Belt Strategic Management Conference. At one of the discussion sessions, a chief executive officer was asked by a professor what educators could do to better prepare students for the world of work. The CEO, an aeronautical engineer by background and training, suggested we need to expect and demand more from our students, and here "I am referring not to technical knowledge, but to work habits and commitment." He felt his company was spending far too much time explaining to new employees such basics as the importance of punctuality and reliability.

A minor matter? Hardly, particularly if this lack of commitment spills over into the areas of quality and service, and as producers and consumers we know it does. Realistically, this spillover pollutes our quality of life as much as the more celebrated chemical and physical wastes.

"He said 'hello.' Absolutely unbelievable. He said 'hello' just like a real person." Happily, Ben Gilmer was and is a real person. When he said "Hello," he was also chief of AT&T. The call had been placed to Mr. Gilmer to secure a bit of advice. The caller was certain that reaching Gilmer would be a virtual impossibility, involving dozens of "holds" and "what kind of business are you in?"-type questions. Not so. The number was dialed, and Ben Gilmer answered by simply saying "Hello." The old cliché about being stuck for a response became an embarrassing reality; here, the caller was talking to a courteous, attentive and interested human being who also happened to be the CEO of one of the world's largest corporations.

Although this incident occurred many years ago and the exact purpose of the call has long been forgotten, the lesson remains. Specifically, the class-act manager, whenever possible, makes certain that he or she stays approachable and accessible to the many constituencies that interact directly or indirectly with an organization.

All too often lacking at the top, it is precisely this form of sensitivity that cascades level-by-level downward and outward until it reaches you. The good news is that when the sensitivity, approachability and accessibility are present, they *also* cascade downward and outward until they almost literally engulf all involved in a manner that generates loyalty, commitment, productivity, quality and an overall sense of everyone's believing he or she is "someone special."

Joel R. Wells, Jr., chairman of the board and CEO of SunTrust Banks, can best be described as a "functioning private enterpriser," one who is able to close the gap between the fundamental tenets of private enterprise and the way he runs a growing, exciting and effective enterprise. It is Wells's contention that "People like banks and want a relationship. However, they want the bank to know them and to care about them."

Of running one of Florida's largest financial institutions, Wells says, "The key thing I want to avoid is becoming no different than everyone else who is in the financial-service business. This is why I want our people to see themselves as serving a market, rather than marketing a service.

"I don't believe we can create products that are better than others, or even market them better. However, we can know more about Tampa or Orlando or Ocala. We can know better the needs of our customers . . . . banking is a noble calling . . . . and can have a powerful effect on community growth," he says, adding, "Today, our people ask, 'Will we survive?' I tell them we will if we make ourselves necessary."

The evolution of excellence is not a random process. The achievement of excellence does not simply happen; we are the masters of our own destinies — the makers of our fates. The road that stretches from mediocrity to excellence is long and sometimes arduous. But it is also paved with numerous simple steps that many of us simply refuse to follow. In a society insistent on instant gratification, all to often we leap when we should step lightly, we run when we should walk and we cut corners where there are no corners to cut.

When a publisher of a leading west coast financial newspaper called, he was, to say the least, angry; he was, to say the most, livid. Over the years, he had contributed hundreds of thousands of dollars to a leading university, and one of the school's deans had called him wishing to discuss the possibility of his endowing a business journalism professorship. The publisher, always eager to help, checked his calendar and found a ninety-minute block of time during lunch the following week. The appointment was set.

On the prescribed date, the publisher arrived at the restaurant three minutes early. He sat in the lobby and waited until the dean showed up thirty minutes later. No apologies, no excuses (in fact, according to the publisher, the dean's attitude was that the publisher was fortunate that the dean was only thirty minutes late!). The publisher stayed long enough to tell the dean not only that the endowed professorship was out of the question but also that the institution would never again receive any funds from him. Why? The publisher, like so many who have achieved excellence, insists on promptness and courtesy. Showing up, showing up on time — and showing up fully prepared — is but one simple step on the road to excellence. We can demand no more than we give, but if we give, we can also expect the same in return. This simple lesson was simply painful for the university.

If there is one important lesson to be learned by corporate America from the small-business sector, it is an obsession with service. After all, in many instances the small-business owner cannot compete in quantity of selection, location or price. So what's left? Service, simply service.

At a shoe department in a large retail store, a frustrated mother asked a frustrated salesperson to measure her child's feet — the salesperson didn't know how.

At a national movie chain, an acquaintance complained to the manager that it was difficult wading through the many boxes, cups and wrappers in the aisle. In fact, she expressed that there was more excitement in getting to her seat than there was in the film.

The manager responded with a smile, "It's too bad we're the only theater in town showing this movie."

A local grocery store, although part of a regional chain, is not a paragon of cleanliness or hygiene. In fact, it is rumored that the store grows its own vegetables — inside. Recently, a patron stopped the manager one evening and suggested that she might want to consider investing in a few basic janitorial supplies. The manager replied, "Why should we? The closest competitor is three miles away."

Small-business owners *stay* in business because of an exceptional degree of service delivery. The customer is constantly pampered, wooed and ultimately sold. The lesson for all of us is clear: getting to the top is long and painful; falling from grace can be swift and complete.

The reflective phenomenon of management examines the nexus between the behavior of top managers and that of employees. Excellence at the top begets excellence throughout; mediocrity at the top begets mediocrity throughout. More importantly, the internalization of excellence creates an organizational climate that exudes excellence externally. Quite simply, if you've achieved excellence within, you will reek of excellence to the consumer. (Pssst! Consumers love it.)

Perhaps what really differentiates the Wells philosophy and gives it a refreshing uniqueness is its emphasis on *pleasing* employees, customers and shareholders. During a period when many emphasize just getting by or aiming their sights to *satisfying* employees, customers and shareholders, Wells advocates that the satisfaction objective is simply not good enough, and, he argues, with extra effort, expertise and especially commitment, you can be a winner rather than "an also-ran."

Somehow, there's a simple lesson there for all of us.

Betty R. Smulian

In 1982 Betty R. Smulian founded TrimbleHouse Corporation, a company that designs and manufactures architectural indoor and outdoor lighting. Born in Philadelphia and a graduate of the University of Pennsylvania, Smulian moved to Atlanta in 1958. At TrimbleHouse, as chairman of the board, she is responsible for product design and development, financial and administrative management and dealing with international supplies.

All for the Want of A Dining Room Light

TrimbleHouse, manufacturer of commercial lighting fixtures, was started in 1962 because I couldn't find a lighting fixture I liked for my dining room. Since I was trained as an industrial designer, I designed one and had it made by a blacksmith. The wrought-iron chandelier received compliments from those who saw it, and people recommended that I design a line of fixtures and hire a manufacturers' representative to sell them. So TrimbleHouse was born. The building boom of the 1960s enabled the company to grow rapidly and change from residential to commercial specialization. I was aware that there was only one lighting manufacturer in the South at that time and that they made only fluorescent fixtures, so there was a big niche to fill locally. Since my training was in architecture and design and I had also worked in an engineering office before moving to Atlanta, I found that I could work closely with architects and engineers in the development of special designs for their projects. My husband was trained in sales and manufacturing, so his expertise became important in forming a partnership of talents.

Specialized custom work was the first stage of TrimbleHouse, and satisfied customes enabled us to grow and expand from the beginnings in the basement of my home to the second stage, which was contained in a warehouse space of about three thousand square feet. As welders and electricians were hired, we were able to produce a more varied line of products; however, no growth is without some problems along the way.

The first major one was a fire on April Fools' Day in 1968 when a welder arrived at work in a very drunken state and welded packing materials instead of metal parts. The building burned to the ground. The decision then was to either close the business or build from scratch. After viewing the ruins, I noticed that there were many wrought-iron materials left in a charred state, so using the theory that if you can't sell the steak, sell the sizzle, I decided to design a line of weathered chandeliers using the remains of the raw materials which came through the fire. Manufacturing them in a new space was accomplished, and they sold like hotcakes. Innovation and flexibility became important words to live by for Trimble-House. I set out to acquire the skills I didn't have by taking courses in finance, attending business seminars and reading about business.

Using the talents that we were educated and trained in and developed through experience enabled us to concentrate on designing and producing products that sold well. As entrepreneurs we went through many stages and processes. We found that we had to have a great deal of fortitude and stick-to-itiveness through all the ups and downs of building a business. We found that we had to surround ourselves with people who had skills we didn't have. In the early stages that especially meant proper budgeting and planning. Running a business by the seat of your pants is very short-lived, and we soon found that we had to put organized systems into the administrative, financial, manufacturing and sales areas.

I was not afraid to bring in management consultants even though it hurt our egos and our pocketbooks. Each time we brought in consultants, we found that the business advanced and grew, and we followed most of their advice. We also found out early in the game of building a company that any fool can spend money. Most employers seem to think that by adding more people, machinery and space their problems will automatically be solved. The truth is that most people are underused for their greatest productivity. Machinery is usually underused in our type of business (non-mass production), and most people cannot see the most efficient use of space. Our challenge is to make each dollar that we spend be the most productive. For example, instead of adding machinery and space, we add shifts. Another example is that in designing products we take into consideration the capabilities of our present machinery, the multiuse of our present space and the inter-changeability of existing parts. Space has been added only when all these other conditions have been met. We have been told we produce more lighting fixtures per square foot than anyone else in our industry. I believe we accomplish that because we think through a problem afer weighing input from the people involved.

An important aspect of the company has been the association of the people we work with. It is important for us to know something about their families. We plan many family activities, including outings at such local amusement parks as Six Flags Over Georgia and Christmas and Fourth of July parties. Checks in celebration of birthdays, marriages and births are given to employees as an expression of extra appreciation. We send employees to seminars and courses to increase their skills.

Suggestions by and innovations from employees are generously rewarded, and our workers are encouraged to communicate with top management. Every employee can walk into any top management office. We encourage relatives of employees to work in the business and that establishes loyalty and trust. As a matter of policy, top management visits all departments each day to greet and listen to employees. Each month the President meets with all employees to distribute birthday checks, to recognize the employee of the month and to discuss current economic conditions inside and outside of the company. The meetings are open for discussion, complaints and suggestions by employees and management. We try to pass on information that will be useful in their day-to-day operations.

Our business has been based for twenty-five years on giving better service than our competition. We stock raw material but not finished goods so we have more flexibility in manufacturing when we receive the order. The Japanese call this just-in-time inventory, and we did it for years without knowing what it was called. We can still give approximately four-week delivery to orders while our competition runs anywhere from six to sixteen weeks for delivery.

We have twenty-four-hour answering service, so there is always a voice who can take a message. Our switchboard is trained to answer the phone by the second ring, and if the person on the other end of the line has to wait, there is a message to listen to that explains the company and its products. It is amazing how many positive comments we get based on these messages, which are changed periodically. We are always trying to educate our callers.

If there is a problem in the field, we try to respond within twenty-four hours so the customer at least knows what we will be doing to remedy the situation. There must be a response. The customer needs to know that something is being done. Even if the issue can't be resolved right away, the customer has to know that someone from the company is in contact and that we are going to be taking care of them.

We have tried to take a new approach to marketing, for example, hiring recent architectural and marketing graduates whom we train to know our company's capabilities in design and manufacturing of custom lighting products. These individuals do not actually sell TrimbleHouse lighting products (they are not salesmen), but they sell the company's image as an innovator and producer of quality products. They make potential customer, architects and engineers, see the advantage of working with TrimbleHouse in answering their lighting needs. Involved in this approach is the special invitation to these leading architectural and engineering firms to a white-glove luncheon served in our board room, a tour of our facilities and a demonstration of our best products by the top management of this company. These individuals are picked up and delivered back to their offices by limousine, a round-trip program taking two hours or less. These special luncheons have developed into producing a TrimbleHouse awareness among the attendees, which, in turn, has created a demand for our services and products. We are now in the process of developing this program nationally.

We realize that we can't compete with those companies who offer less quality at lower prices, so we offer more customized service and products that our customers are willing to pay for. The theme woven throughout our advertising, marketing promotions and employee programs is "Why Not the Best?" The theme is constantly repeated and reinforced in our national ads and sales programs and in our home office and factory.

We offer a wide variety of products so that we don't depend on a single area of lighting. We constantly review competitors' products, seek ideas from customers and overseas markets and keep up with changing architectural style so that we can produce fixtures to complement what is being built today. My architectural background gave me the awareness to recognize the change that developed when the stark modernism of the glass-box building gave way to the more decorative and colorful post-modernist curves and angles being built today. Our foresight and flexibility enabled us to design lighting to match the change in building styles earlier than our competitors. Being able to offer new designs, top quality and customized service has made us find our niche in our industry. Things change quickly, and I have found that we can't be afraid of change but must always think ahead, anticipate change and use it to create new opportunities.

The second generation has now entered the business. Our son Rob became a member of our team in November, 1987. The entrepreneurial skills which led to the founding of the business will now be complemented by the analytical and organizational skills he will bring to TrimbleHouse. I look forward to the future with confidence.

More Rigor or Rigor Mortis?

In *Megatrends*, John Naisbitt's best seller, the point is effectively made that, with the advent of high tech, comes the need for high touch. Loosely translated, what this means is that for every vacuum filled by technological innovation, another is created; and it is this other vacuum that must be filled by the so-called human element.

To organizations of all kinds, the implication should be crystal clear: no number of computers or robots will affect the plain simple fact that people will make the difference. However — and here's the rub — people who *can* make the difference don't just happen. They are carefully selected, trained and rewarded by organizations who are committed to excellence and recognize that the attainment of excellence is a never-ending process.

A number of consulting firms have failed to attract or lost clients because, despite their textbook approach to strategy development, one integral element — the human factor — was consistently ignored. Even the best-laid plans emanating from the most sophisticated data bases are inoperable if the right people are missing. Pages of diagrams, flow charts and matrices are difficult to render operational without a thorough assessment of the human skills necessary to transform the abstract to the applied.

Few would question the social and economic benefits of specialization; advancements in virtually every dimension of society have been brought about through its advent. Certainly, when one considers the great inventions of all time, the division of labor would be ranked near the top.

Actually, the division of labor, like the pursuit of excellence, is a continuous process. Once you quit the quest, you quit the race. In our search for productivity and quality, specialization and the resultant atomization of labor have played key roles. In all too many instances, we have complex people performing routine tasks resulting in situations where work is viewed as an unpleasant interval between weekends. This condition might very well be the subject of another essay. But in this instance, our primary concern is what happens to those who view life through a keyhole without even the interest and excitement of a societal voyeur.

William Norris, founder and chairman of Control Data Corporation, is far more blunt in his assessment of the human condition. He chastises corporate America as a "risk-free, selfish society," intent on self-destruction by virtue of inactivity. The collective mental and physical abilities of our nation seem to be atrophied from a continual lack of stimulation.

It was December 15, the middle of the holiday season. Overanxious shoppers were anxiously making last-minute purchases preparing to usher in the festivities. At the time, the man was stuck in line at the bank. His checkbook was at home, and in order to withdraw funds from the bank without it, it's necessary to have a withdrawal slip punched up. The line of customers needing withdrawal slips was long — very long. The lone bank clerk steadily responded to each of us requesting his services.

To his right sat another bank clerk, this one responsible for punching up deposit slips (not much depositing going on during the holiday season). In fact, there was no one in the deposit-slip line, not a single person. The deposit clerk sat there, completing a crossword puzzle, clipping his nails and eating a pastrami sandwich. In short, the deposit clerk wasn't very busy.

By the time the customer finally reached the withdrawal clerk, the slip was quickly processed. As he walked away, on a whim, the customer remarked to the deposit clerk, "Excuse me, you might want to consider helping out here with some of these withdrawal slips. After all, it's not very complicated, and your co-worker is swamped." In response to this comment, the clerk looked up and responded, "I know, but it's not my job."

That same evening, a newspaper offered an encounter with another baffling situation. A local elementary school teacher with a master's degree and fifteen years of experience publicly announced her inability to teach social studies. Her 150 sixth-grade students were failing at a rapid rate with no end in sight. She stated, "I know I'm not competent. . . . It's most unfortunate that our future leaders of tomorrow must suffer along with me."

In the same breath, her boss adamantly claimed that, "She has the ability to teach her classes." The teacher, having been given time off to prepare for the course, freely and openly admits she is simply not qualified but, more importantly, not interested in learning the material. But she says it much more eloquently: "I'm not going to go to work early; I'm not going to stay late; I'm not going to take work home. I'm not interested in knowing it [the course material]."

The unfortunate fact of the matter is that behaviors such as these are becoming more the rule than the exception in organizational life today. Our contentment or complacency, our commitment to sameness, permeates our everyday lines. As historian Will Durant once put it, "A nation is born stoic and dies epicurean." In our eyes, rigor mortis is slowly setting in.

As professors of business we continuously preach the gospel of the reflective phenomenon of management. That is, that subordinates consistently and invariably reflect the behavior exhibited by their bosses. Indeed, if you don't like what you see at the bottom of the organization, chances are that this behavior is simply reflective of similar behavior at the top.

Today, we as consumers can view the distorted behavior of personnel reflecting that of their superiors. Collectively, the behaviors exhibited in many organizations reflect a genuine lack of concern for the one group that most deserves red-carpet treatment: the customers.

One important key to the success of companies like IBM is the fact that the customer is placed on a pedestal and never loses his or her identity. Over the years, it has been the implementation of the Tom Watson philosophy that has helped transform IBM from just another organization into a very special institution. For example, with over 360,000 employees, IBM's basic philosophy is built upon the dignity and worth of the individual. Reinforcing this philosophy are myriad programs that tangibly say to the producer, regardless of title, job or level, that he won't get lost in the shuffle.

For many involved in the business of teaching, real happiness is coming into class and finding a clean blackboard. For almost an entire quarter, each morning one of us entered a classroom where all blackboards were covered. Thus, valuable class time was routinely spent erasing the markings, apparently written in tongues, of the colleague whose class met the previous hour.

Towards the end of the quarter, the "eraser" gained enough courage to ask the "chalker" if he felt obligated to fill every bit of blackboard space. With no small degree of pride, he responded that he certainly did, as if this were some sort of modern miracle. It was suggested that if he were, in fact, responsible for putting it up, he might also wish to consider the merits of using an eraser. His reaction was a mix of wonder, amazement and put-upon pride; he had never considered cleaning up to be part of his job, but had believed that, somehow, academic elves magically and mysteriously handled this chore. Simply stated, he knew what to do but felt that it wasn't his job. A petty illustration of a problem of gargantuan proportions, *i.e.*, the "I-know-what-to-do,-but-it's-not-my-job" syndrome.

This kind of attitude is not solely an on-the-job phenomenon. Many sadly recall the Kitty Genovese incident where a young woman was assaulted and then killed in an area where well-intentioned citizens rationalized that while they could have gone to her aid, they "didn't want to get involved." It was, simply put, not their job.

Today, in many communities, neighborhood watch programs have been instituted that recognize that public concern, awareness and sensitivity might very well provide the foundation for personal and private safety. Essentially, here is an attempt to alter the "I know what to do, but it's not my job" perspective.

The greatest medical crisis confronting our nation today is not any of the popularly touted diseases. Rather, it is that, as a nation, we are suffering from an insensitivity, a lethargy and a form of national narcissism that has reached epidemic proportions. It's bad enough when management becomes infected, and it's worse still when employees catch it, but when the youth of this country start to exhibit the same symptoms, it's time to panic.

One of us received a call a few weeks ago from a regional vice-president of a multinational snack-food manufacturer and distributor. He described his lack of success in recruiting students interested in a managerial career with his company. The author was a bit surprised because jobs in general and career positions in particular are not in abundant supply. His experience revealed the extent of the epidemic.

While visiting a midwestern college campus on a recruiting trip, he had systematically interviewed thirty-two students interested in a management trainee position. At the end of the interviews, he casually asked each student if he or she was still interested in the position. Every one of the thirty-two said, "No." It turns out that the firm's managerial training program required each candidate to spend six to eighteen months driving a truck on various delivery routes for the company. The hours were less than desirable and the work hard, but the $22,000 annual salary would seem to compensate for any temporary discomfort. Still, each of the thirty-two applicants argued that they hadn't gone to school for four years in order to drive a truck. Rigor mortis is setting in. Protecting one's turf in an irrational fashion has become definitely unprofitable. Holding up a project for fear of stepping on someone's occupational toes is dysfunctional, counterproductive and a violation of what the division of labor should be about. For years (and many of us must share the guilt), we've sanctioned occupational practices which provide short-run protection and long-run devastation.

Operating in an almost make-believe world, where inflation and loss of competitive edge have been part of the payoff, we must now recognize that we're going to get out of this situation the way we got into it, i.e., together. Together means management, government and the educational community. Together means less conflict and more cooperation. Together means we can differ without destroying. And together means understanding what the puzzle looks like once all the pieces are in place.

In many instances, the difference between being a winner and a runner-up is virtually miniscule. Usually, the also-ran knows what to do to become a winner. What is generally lacking are the desire and the willingness to do what must be done. For example, in the successful organization, the concern is more with total mission than specific tasks. Pleasing the customer keeps us in business; therefore, this is everyone's job, regardless of title or position description.

A most vivid recollection for a then-neophyte manager was seeing the president of Rich's department stores in Atlanta, the late Dick Rich, carrying a customer's packages to her automobile. The message conveyed, by example, was clear and direct: we're all here to please the customer, and this responsibility is a basic ingredient in each person's job description, from top to bottom. Compare and contrast this with the overspecialized organization where the customer, e.g., student, patient or taxpayer, is viewed as an unnecessary extra and treated as such.

While a key to higher productivity might very well be the atomization of work, management must recognize that net or true productivity — that is, quality customer-pleasing goods and services — can best be provided by well-motivated human beings who understand the "big picture."

Of course, there's nothing really new about this. Von Steuben, a Prussian general on Washington's staff during the American Revolution, observed that, "In Europe, you tell a soldier to do something and he does it, but in the United States, he wants to know why."

Although wanting to know why is not necessarily peculiar to the United States, management often forgets just how important this is in developing individuals and organizations capable of excelling. When interest spawns inquiry, a sense of caring soon begets concerned commitment — and that leads to excellence. The challenge then, in a service-oriented society such as ours, is to make certain that such commitment flourishes.

Managing the "Touch" Factor

Grandfather turned to his grandson and said: "If two people tell you you're drunk, lie down." Grandson, a little perplexed, responded: "I don't drink." Grandfather replied: "It doesn't matter, they think you do. You'd better find out why." How many times must we walk away from transactions, battered and beaten, humiliated and humbled, but rarely (if ever) pleased?

It happened again last week. Customer walked into shoe store and requested a certain pump in a size 7. Salesperson walked into storage room and came back with three pairs of shoes: the requested pair in a 6½ and a different pair in a 7½ and an 8. Customer explains to salesperson that she wears a 7 and simply cannot fit into anything smaller. Manager happens to walk by, unaware of any of the specifics, but as if reading from a script remarks: "That style runs large." Manager had not seen "that style" nor been privy to the conversation, but insisted that if the customer "closed her eyes and pretended," a smaller size would surely fit.

An unusual situation? Not really. The salesperson, anxious to sell, insisting that smaller is better; the manager, anxious to close, supporting that proposition. The result: thousands of customers flocking to podiatrists to have their collective feet reshaped to their original size. Sorely lacking is the empathy, the concern, the "touch" factor that so many customers long for and so few get. Closets across North America and Europe are filled with shoes, shirts, pants and suits that *almost* fit at the time of purchase. Closets around the world are full of clothes that would stretch, shrink or magically mold to body shape. The resulting lack of touch has reached epidemic proportions and we, sometimes, thankfully accept it. Something is not right.

In a survey conducted by the ad agency of D'Arcy Masius Benton & Bowles, Inc., the sample responses of some two thousand people revealed interesting results. Three of the characteristics most admired in others included warmth, sense of humor and honesty. This should not come as a surprise to anyone. After all, this is what most of us want. What most of us get, however, is all too often quite the contrary. This is the bad news. The good news is that warmth, humor, honesty and compassion are not genetically transferred traits. They are, in fact, carefully developed characteristics fortified by organizations committed to the importance of the touch factor in buying and selling.

We are so surprised when we find ourselves confronted by one or all of these factors that we often go out of our way to buy and buy again. The touch factor reduces customer sensitivity to price and enhances the customer's desire to see the salesperson make a sale. Imagine letting customers work for you and your organization, leaving your business proclaiming to the world at large that their last transaction approached the pleasures of a Club Med vacation. Incubating the touch factor is no small feat, but in today's hypercompetitive business environment, there is a much greater risk in alienating just one or more potential buyers.

Today, the medical industry is, in most urban areas, confronting the basic economic dilemma of too much supply competing for too little demand. The result — fierce competition for your medical dollar. Enter American Medical International, Inc. (AMI).

AMI is a worldwide provider of quality health-care services. The company has experienced a great deal of growth because of the superlative quality of its health-care delivery and because of its commitment to the touch factor. In a particularly effective advertisement, Larry Hanan, executive director of a new AMI Regional Medical Center, said: "If you would like to know more about the changes made and the medical technology now available, feel free to call me at 221-8555. You can be sure there are people here who really care." We called. Larry Hanan answered and went on to explain the progress made by AMI. No secretaries, receptionists, music, or recordings — just Larry Hanan. The CEO of this Medical Center was sending an important message to his customers and employees. The touch factor is alive and well at AMI and will, in the long run, make a difference between winning and losing.

At Dixie Furniture Company in Charleston, South Carolina, the Kirshstein clan has transformed the importance of touch into a forty-year-old venture that is now servicing the third generation of customers from the same families. Known as the proprietors of "your happy family store," the Kirshsteins have been negotiating credit arrangements and cultivating customers in the same caring way since 1946. And the customers love it.

Be it furniture, clothes, or health care, many industries today are marketing commodities — no more, no less. What will make the difference in the long run is the care and feeding of customers.

George Baker of Texas-based Strawberry Communications points to a survey that indicated that seven of ten customers stopped doing business with companies because of the way they were treated on the telephone. This type of corporate attitude tramples over all other forms of good will and can leave customers disheartened and eager to shop elsewhere. It's that simple.

There is a considerable difference between being laid-back and being unconscious. If laid-back denotes cool, or hot, depending upon your orientation, and if this condition is generated by "the right stuff," it can be an admirable quality. True composure coupled with concern is hard to beat. Lack of concern coupled with ignorance will beat you almost every time.

Developing a service orientation as part of a touch-factor philosophy that pleases, as opposed to satisfies, is the difference between coming close and winning the cigar. Unfortunately, all too many transactions between buyers and sellers are close encounters of the imperfect kind. Correcting this is both possible and practical. In addition, it is certainly profitable for all involved.

Part of the touch factor is the first-time perspective. What this means is that we consciously strive for flawless service and perfect products the very first time around. We decide errors and flaws are unacceptable. This does not mean perfection will be attained. It does mean that near-misses are simply not acceptable. The first-time mentality is a characteristic of organizations that are proactionary: they recognize that there is always a better way and change is the status quo. In organizations of this nature, a premium is placed on individual performance through a system that truly recognizes and rewards the good things emanating from first-time results.

The couple had waited over two months for their new car. In effect, it was "custom-made" with a page full of options. They determined that this time they'd have one built just for them. (For those who have not ordered a car in this fashion, be assured it is not cheap.)

At long last, a call came from the dealer indicating the vehicle had arrived. It was beautiful, and as soon as it was cleaned, prepared and given a final inspection, it could be delivered.

Happily, the auto lived up to expectations. It was a beauty. The salesperson had the touch factor and did an excellent job of explaining each and every unique feature and option. He cared and represented a dealer who also cared.

Unfortunately, as the customers gave their brand-new purchase a one-more-time inspection, they noticed three indentations on the hood — visible blemishes that should not have been there and should have been detected and corrected by someone with a first-time mental set. The dealer was left with the car and the couple left with their check.

This was not what you might describe as a pleasing transaction. Admittedly, since the dealer is first-class, there was a happy ending, but how much happier it would have been if at least as much attention had been focused on high touch as on high tech.

Robert Leitstein

*Robert Leitstein, a graduate of Hobart
College, began his career in retailing at
Bloomingdale's, where he held various
buying positions. In 1968 he was named
vice-president of Neiman-Marcus in
Dallas, Texas. Leitstein joined Gump's as
president and chief executive officer in
1979.*

Success with Style and Action: The Evolution of the Gump's Tradition

During the early years of my career as a buyer for Bloomingdale's in New York and later as part of Neiman-Marcus' management in Dallas, I remember my associates speaking of Gump's
as if it were an entity against which we, as quality retailers, should
measure ourselves in terms of our success. Nothing has changed. I
must continue to remind myself and the staff at Gump's that a
reputation is hard to achieve but can be quickly destroyed. We must
always strive to maintain excellence.

There are scores of reasons why Gump's has been successful
since first opening its doors in 1861. Different things are important
to different people, but, basically, our clientele continue to visit
Gump's because we consistently present to them unique and beautiful merchandise in a very comfortable, familiar way.

The Gump's tradition was started by Solomon Gump, the son of a Heidelberg linen merchant, who purchased his brother-in-law's frame and mirror shop. As Solomon traveled about Europe collecting more unusual and beautiful merchandise for his San Francisco store, his clientele grew as rapidly as his desire to expand his unique merchandise base.

It is doubtful that anyone today would consider starting a new retail business with the Gump's merchandise assortment. Gump's holds an unusual position in retailing, as it is emulated by many but has been successfully copied by none. However, there are some principles of the "Gump's Philosophy" that could be applied to just about any type of business. I offer these to you.

Dare to be Different. There will inevitably be some similarities between you and your competitors, no matter what your business is. But the more you can differentiate yourself from the competition, the more you create and establish a style and image all your own. Keep your competition guessing.

At Gump's, we carry a collection of merchandise unequalled anywhere else in the world. We take great pride in the depth and breadth of products we carry. Nonexclusive merchandise we share with our competitors must be, at all times, in stock and in greater depth of assortment than anyone else's. Gump's is known to carry the largest assortment of fine quality china, crystal and silver. A Gump's patron knows that a visit to the store will expose him or her to as complete an assortment of goods as will be found anywhere in the United States.

Another striking difference is our jewelry department. Unlike our competitors, we offer no diamond rings or watches; we have chosen to specialize in those areas where we can maintain a dominant market position. Jade, pearls and semi-precious stones are our hallmark. Our collection of merchandise is unmatched by our competitors. Thus, we have an opportunity to maintain our price levels without constant sales, protecting our image as well as our margins.

Dramatize Your Merchandise. You can stock your store chock-full of beautiful merchandise and never move an item if it is not properly and creatively *presented*. We believe the mystique of our merchandise presentation is another element of our uniqueness, as Gump's has traditionally devoted special attention to the "theater" of our merchandise. It helps, of course, that the merchandise itself at Gump's is known for its superior design, quality and uniqueness.

In our stores, we strive to maintain an aura of sophisticated, refined luxury. Much of what we sell nobody really needs. We must therefore enhance their *desire*. We strive to create the feeling of being a guest in a gracious home. Our window displays are anticipated by the media and visited by thousands. And we create out-of-the-ordinary promotional themes, executed with the utmost style and attention to detail.

It has always been my philosophy to give back, in a cultural way, to the community that supports us. Each year we embark on a major promotional effort. One major event, "A Tribute to Italy," launched at Gump's by the Italian Ambassador to the U.S., featured the finest Italian merchandise created and showcased expressly for Gump's. Two very special exhibitions were highlighted: "Treasures of the Doccia Museum," 130 fine porcelains tracing the history of Italian porcelain, and "Treasures from the La Scala Museum," a collection of the personal possessions of Guiseppi Verdi. Neither collection had ever before left Italy. These important exhibits not only helped Gump's to make a cultural contribution but also reinforced our position as a store of style and taste.

On another occasion, we produced an English exhibition entitled "British Style." Again, much of the merchandise was made expressly for the exhibition, with special emphasis on the contributions of the Churchill family. Winston Churchill, M.P., attended the opening to host a major retrospective of his grandfather's oil paintings.

Let Your Managers Manage. When a customer enters Gump's, he not only feels comfortable but is also aware that his "host" is a tastemaker of some authority. Gump's is proud of its entrepreneurial sales staff, all of whom are hand-picked, authorized decision-makers. Gump's philosophy of management is to simplify the chain of command by making it short. There is no "going through layers" to get an answer. All players are kings and queens; there are no pawns. All communication is easy, efficient and professional.

Dot Your *I*s and Cross Your *T*s. Attention to detail is critical. In some businesses, this can be the single most important thing that distinguishes you from your competitors. At Gump's, we extend enormous attention to detail. Fresh flowers are continually replaced. Each item of merchandise is inspected and polished before the doors open in the morning. Visibility of senior management is important, and each of us spends some time during the day visiting the selling floors to greet customers and to monitor trends, opportunities and potential problems. At Christmas, for instance, we take turns manning an information booth at the store's entrance. To us, this is an investment in learning far more productive than second-hand reports, and it keeps us in constant communication with the sales staff.

Maintain Your Traditions — If They Work. You must know how to recognize what is working and what isn't. Don't make changes for the sake of making changes. Each time you introduce something new to your business mix, be sure you've analyzed how it will complement and how it could potentially damage the other aspects of your business.

Being with Gump's has been and continues to be a challenge for me personally as I continue to strive to maintain that Gump's mystique and style so well established by the Gump family over the years. The challenge is intensified by finding ways to stay ahead of the competition; we continue to introduce new ideas in merchandising and to provide our clientele with the best quality and extraordinary merchandise and selection. Each move forward is carefully considered.

The Gump's style lives on and is matched by no one. But it is the action and interaction of all these philosophies and principles of doing business that cause that style and grace to flourish.

More on "High Touch"

The roofer had been paid in full. The roof looked great — and then it rained. The roof still looked great, but the living-room ceiling looked horrible. (You can expect this when the roof leaks.) The roofer returned and fixed the original leak and then it rained again, and it leaked again. He came back a second time, gave the situation his personal seal of approval, and the rains and the leak returned. When the roofer was asked to return and repair, he commented in a highly agitated fashion that he "wasn't making any money on this job."

Small wonder! While he "wasn't making any money," the customer was stuck with a fine-looking roof that was porous and a living-room ceiling that looked like a relief map of the moon. The moral: if this nation is shifting to a service economy, why can't it be first-class service? While the manufacturing sector continues to shrink, it appears the philosophy and behavior that caused the shrinkage are often directed towards opportunities to make a fast buck in the service sector. Look for similar results.

In all too many instances, the same players are involved in this manufacturing-service transition. Only the names are changed to protect the innocent and/or guilty. Apparently, the essential philosophy remains the same, and this affects the output. It especially impacts the quality of the deliverables. We definitely don't need more of the same. More of the same further dulls our competitive edge, and today we are competing globally.

One of the truly great contemporary "heroes" of American manufacturing is Dr. Pat Carrigan, currently plant manager of the General Motors facility in Bay City, Michigan. What Carrigan realized, when she was plant manager at GM's Lakewood facility in Atlanta, was that more of the same simply would not do. Here she was in an industry that was loudly proclaiming to the world at large that it simply could not compete any more. But Pat Carrigan refused to give up.

For more than half a century, the Lakewood plant had been characterized by its disharmony. Today, despite industry-wide layoffs which also affect Lakewood, long-time employees who represent both management and labor recall Carrigan's tenure as a verifiable turning point in plant morale. What happened? The move towards greatness, starting with Carrigan as the catalyst, put top management and top labor in top-level meetings together. Recognizing the magnitude of the stakes involved and the fact that domestic competition had rapidly been replaced by global threats, the leadership team went to work. What evolved was a new, plant-wide commitment to change. Inscribed on a thirty-two-square-foot sign inside the plant is the dedication expressed by this team to change, risk-assumption, accountability, trust, pride, devotion to mission, dignity, honesty, respect and good communications. With form in place, joint efforts were expended on function. The results: productivity, labor efficiency and quality are way up. Absenteeism, sickness, workers' compensation and material costs are way down.

The bottom line: everyone wins. During the time that Pat Carrigan was at Lakewood, the skills of more than three thousand employees were enhanced via more than 400,000 hours of training. This was top-to-bottom management at work. Not at Honda, not at Nissan, but at General Motors . . . and that's good.

In the long run, quality service and products, produced and delivered by quality personnel, provide organizations of all types with their only significant competitive edge. The quick-fix, I've-got-you-now approach simply won't work; or if it does, it works only once.

In recent memory, NBC had not fared well in the ratings war. Change after change would ensue, but the ratings simply would not budge. Indeed, during the worst of times, some local affiliates around the country elected to drop their association with NBC and switched to another network. Too bad. Today, NBC has emerged as a powerhouse in the ratings. New management brought new ideas and a commitment to quality in program and service delivery that has successfully kept the rest of the industry at bay.

A great example: Theresa Potter, a hard-working professional in Miami, Florida, spends a great deal of time each day in her car, commuting to work. While local radio provides a menu of "drive-time" options to commuters nationwide, Potter missed the *Today* show. Rather than continue to lament the problem, she wrote to NBC News, asking, quite simply, if they ever considered broad-casting over the radio as well — and, if not, would they?

The executive producer of the *Today* show promptly responded to her request. In a handwritten, personalized response, he thanked Potter for the outstanding idea. Indeed, he wrote, NBC News had discussed this option, but the local radio stations simply would not provide the time. However, he said, they had not yet given up the quest.

This is the quality service delivered by quality personnel that makes up quality organizations. This handwritten response is the stuff of which great organizations are made.

Surprisingly, many business "experts" have discovered the difference people make. The true surprise is that the experts are surprised. Many of the new management and marketing theories are novel only to those who are not familiar with sound business basics or who haven't lived long enough to garner many of these basics through experience — or, if you'll pardon the old saw, the school of hard knocks.

Getting somewhere in the vicinity of the target often appears to suffice unless, of course, you are the customer — a.k.a., client, patient, taxpayer — to cite just a few of our roles and faces. The organization that sets about trying simply to satisfy customers will have a life span just a bit longer than the company that doesn't care too much one way or the other.

The organization that emphasizes the need merely to satisfy the ambition, fervor and commitment needed to deliver the best. Of course, the organization itself is inanimate. Therefore, it is its staff, from top to bottom, its human dimension, that lacks ambition, fervor, and commitment. Making an organization more effective means making its staff more effective. With an effective staff, homogenization becomes a condition of the past, and the organization, like heavy cream, rises to the top of its competition.

Rising to the top is what Douglas Varrieur, the chairman of Print Shack, is all about. Making staff more effective is one of the great accomplishments of this young, aggressive organization-builder.

For example, two of Print Shack's vice-presidents were engaged in a heated tête-a-tête regarding a mix-up between advertising and operations. Concerned about staff commitment and unity of focus, Varrieur stormed into the argument, sledgehammer in hand, and proceeded to bring down the wall separating the two vice-presidents' offices. Varrieur, drenched in sweat, calmly stated: "Now you can look and talk to each other every day." And look and talk they could — through the new designer eight-inch hole in the wall.

The point is that successful organizations are animate, touchable, and oriented to success — internally as well as externally. In just a few years, Varrieur has built this Tampa-based franchisor into one of the fastest-growing firms in the $4 billion-a-year quick-printing industry.

Every single staff member needs to understand the why of his or her job and should be familiar and comfortable with and committed to an organization's way of life. Further, it is the responsibility of the company to communicate formally its own unique way of doing business and of relating to people.

For example, the late Richard H. Rich of Atlanta-based Rich's department stores made absolutely certain that his customer-is-always-right ideology was more than rhetorical pap. To Rich's customers, it was a solid pledge you could take to the bank. The pledge and the behavior to back it up made Rich's a unique institution. Great organizations like Rich's build greatness in people. And the communication of these ideals permeates organizations committed to building an avenue for growth and development for all dedicated to the mission of success. Fortunately, Campeau Corporation, which in 1988 acquired Federated Department Stores, including Rich's, is such an organization.

Joseph E. Antonini is another great example of espousing and devoting oneself to an organization dedicated to excellence. Just two decades ago, Antonini assumed the not-so-glamorous position of store clerk in a not-so-glamorous organization with an eye on growth. Joseph Antonini and K-Mart Corporation soon embarked on a trek in the hypercompetitive world of retailing that would outdistance countless organizations. K-Mart held fast to its ideology and so did Antonini. Today, K-Mart is literally on the verge of becoming the largest retailer in the world, and Antonini, former clerk-par-excellence, is now president and chief operating officer.

What a team. What a story.

Cuddling Your Customers

The poster is brilliant. Above the desk is a magnificent scene of the Great American West, resplendent in color and detail. It is four-by-six feet and depicts a group of hard-riding cowhands galloping off into the sunset on their magnificent steeds. The picture is direct from *Arizona Highways* and vividly captures the beauty of the red-rock country. In small but clear print at the base of the picture, one finds not the name of the artist, but an unforgettable slogan that captures the essence of this vignette and the soul of the American spirit. The slogan reads: "If you don't make dust . . . you eat dust."

The picture hangs above Arthur Blank's desk. Blank, co-founder with Bernard Marcus of The Home Depot, Inc., lives and breathes with the pulse of this poster each and every day. Blank and Marcus are making a great deal of dust in an overpopulated, highly competitive marketplace and are doing it at the expense of tenderfoot adversaries who have grown fat and lazy back at the ranch. The dust made by Home Depot, which specializes in do-it-yourself building materials and home-improvement goods, is not in the area of superior products, location, or facilities — but in "cuddling" their customers.

When you walk into a Home Depot and scan the twenty-five thousand or so different items for just the right ceiling fan, telephone or two-by-four, you will most likely be served by an eager, ambitious salesperson who will not only talk the nuances of product with you but, perhaps more importantly, will also cuddle you until you buy and buy again. Blank credits the success of Home Depot to an enthusiasm and desire to help customers at each and every level of the organization. According to Blank, Home Depot strives to add to its team of sixty-six thousand professionals by recruiting team members who actually enjoy involving themselves with their customers' projects. The result: in seven years, Home Depot has achieved annual sales in excess of $1.5 billion, net earnings for the latest year reported were up 190 percent and average sales per square foot would make the weakhearted faint. Quite a track record for two executives who were fired from a competitive firm in 1979.

In order to frontally attack the cuddling of customers through a concerted team effort, one can follow some sage words of advice offered in *Effective Project Planning & Management,* a new and insightful book by professors Alan Randolph and Barry Posner. Specifically, they reinforced in theory what Blank and Marcus have done in practice:

• Direct people individually and as a project team. A cuddling "cult" must be created, built on individual commitment to team performance. There is no substitute.

• Reinforce the commitment and excitement of the project team. Clarity of your organization's goals helps to reinforce the commitment and energy expended by your employees. Home Depot describes a dedication to customers as the guidance system that drives its people regardless of position or job description.

• Keep everyone informed. There are few secrets in organizational life today. When customers have been successfully cuddled,

let everyone know. Likewise, when the experience is not such a delightful one, this, too, should be communicated. But, for goodness sake, don't dwell only on the bad stuff; this can be a killer.
• Take the risk of approaching problems creatively. One of the great customer responses engendered by Home Depot was the simple inclusion of decorator tiles in its inventory. Based on a hue and cry raised by salespeople from their observations of customers who could not find an adequate tile selection in stock, Home Depot has now become a major player in the tile business. Cuddling customers pays off for everyone involved.

Charlotte, North Carolina, is headquarters to a unique retailer that cuddles customers in innovative ways through 350 stores in sixteen states and more than thirty-five thousand employees. Belk Stores, founded in Monroe, North Carolina, one hundred years ago this year, has successfully localized its cuddling strategies from market to market through an unusual network of Belk and Leggett stores. The fact that the Belk family has retained strict ownership of the operation is a testimony to its commitment to a philosophy that will carry this successful company into its second century. A unique ownership program that allows the family to share equity with local owner/managers and a belief in the personalization of service to different customers in various regions has enabled this company to maintain its independence and unique way to doing business. The Belk/Leggett group gives as it gets within its stores, as well as to the communities it serves. This kind of cuddling of customers and markets makes good business sense and allows the company to add ten to fifteen new stores each year.

Making dust is far more desirable in almost any imaginable setting than eating dust. The making of dust in a competitive marketplace requires a commitment to product and service that must be relentless. The problem is that too many organizations would rather relent than rededicate. Making dust in the marketplace by an avowed dedication to cuddling and caring for customers has become the exception, not the rule, in organizational life today. It is all too easy for us to identify the failures, not the successes. It has become all to common to complain about the bad rather than praise the good because the bad is in too many instances far more common.

Consumers today will pay for first-class, relentless cuddling. Who wouldn't? However, too often we find ourselves snubbed, not snuggled. Whether your effective cuddling campaign espouses "I Care," "You Count," "Let's Get Warm," "Care to Cuddle?" or any other byword, it must be fortified by a top-to-bottom commitment that reinforces with action the promises made by mouth.

As you can see, the aim of customer service is to embrace with commitment, or cuddle — not to beat with indifference, or cudgel. Of course, we're extending to the limits the meaning of cuddle and cudgel, but all of us who have been cuddled and cudgeled understand. Further, in an era where the technologically impossible is often transformed into the readily possible, superior service is as elusive as ever because, unlike invention or innovation, it demands a daily toll, and this toll must be paid by the deliverers of service who feel the reward is in proportion to the investment. Creating this balance is an essential part of the position description of many who wear the mantle of managerial leadership. It might be the raison d'être for donning the mantle. Certainly, the Blanks, Marcuses and Bells give credence to this.

You study patterns of success, and the deeper you probe, the more convinced you become that the secret is there is no secret. This is precisely what makes the entire process both attainable and frustratingly elusive. It is well within the grasp of most, but having to ante up to stay in the game requires a commitment many are unwilling to make.

Having just revised a top-selling management text, one suddenly realizes that many of yesterday's corporate heroes and their organizations have fallen from grace, disappeared or joined the ranks of the ordinary. Becoming simply more of the same might be the saddest state of all.

As a customer, conduct your own study. What really differentiates the winning business from the also-ran? Happily, you don't need a business degree to develop the expertise to do this. What are you really looking for when you spend your money for goods or services? Isn't it true that we are all searching for quality and concern, whether we are spending a lot or a little? It certainly appears that those enterprises capable of standing the tests of time and the vagaries of investors are those that build on basics, pay attention to details, create a climate where everyone can get well and remember who ultimately pays the bills. This last point, as elementary as it might appear, is often forgotten. At least it was by one professional athlete, who opined, "The fans don't pay for my groceries." Unless endowed by a fairy godmother, this particular individual should give serious consideration to retaking Economics 101 or at least a quick course in common sense.

Winning organizations know who pays the bills. In turn, they recognize they are as good or as bad as their last transaction, and in order to be included in the next edition of someone's book, the winners ante up with quality and service for each person — each and every day. Winners cuddle, not cudgel, their customers. It's both the least and the most they can do for the folks who pick up the tab.

Joel R. Wells, Jr.

Joel R. Wells, Jr., grew up in Orlando, Florida, and received the B.A., B.S., and J.D. degrees from the University of Florida. He serves as chairman of the board and chief executive officer of SunTrust Banks, Inc., and as chairman and chief executive officer of SunTrust's Florida subsidiary, Sun Banks, Inc.

Building Success Through Productivity, Innovation and Quality Service

SunTrust Banks, Inc., today represents an assemblage of what, until recently, were six separate bank-holding companies owning an aggregate of over fifty banks in three different states. Many people have asked about how you successfully bring together, in one organization, such a disparate group.

The key ingredient, based upon our experience, is to look for banks that have a common approach. In our case that's a pragmatic belief that the way for a bank to succeed is to service its market rather than to market its services. While is has always been true in a more subtle sense, today, in an era of deregulation, it is absolutely clear that a bank's greatest asset — its franchise, if you please — is its customer base. Banks that have excellent customers succeed. Banks that have mediocre customers have problems.

We are a highly decentralized company because our strategy is a market strategy rather than a product strategy. What the market needs and what the role of the bank should be varies from market to market. Orlando varies from Atlanta. Macon varies from Miami. Pensacola varies from Nashville. What doesn't vary is the attitude a customer appreciates from a bank: an attitude of commitment to the customer's success.

The role played by Atlanta's Trust Company Bank in the original public underwriting of the Coca-Cola Company in 1919 not only launched that hugely successful worldwide enterprise but also contributed significantly to the locating of the corporate headquarters for "The Real Thing" in Atlanta and to the selection of Trust Company Bank, and now SunTrust Banks, Inc., as "The Coca-Cola Bank."

There can be such an identification of a bank with its community that the founder of our Orlando bank, Linton Allen, used to say, "Build your community, and you build your bank." Mr. Allen always practiced what he preached. In 1956, he played the key role in assembling land (personally optioning eight thousand acres with his own funds) to persuade Martin-Marietta to build a huge defense plant in Orlando. This transaction propelled Orlando and Central Florida into its first era of explosive economic development and also permanently established Mr. Allen's bank, which became Sun Bank, as Central Florida's dominant bank.

In our company, tangible results like these not only have had a great influence on our current strategy and structure but also are inexorably tied in with issues such as productivity, quality, service and innovation. Our history greatly influences our present management philosophy, which, in turn, we feel, influences all of the career people working for our banks, diverse as they are. Our career people, in turn, are the ones who really "serve the markets," "build the communities," and tend to the maximum support of our customers' success. It's really an application of the Mescon axiom, "Top to bottom, inside out."

If bankers really want to serve their markets and build their communities, it requires innovation. If bankers, or anyone else engaged in a service business, are really committed to pleasing customers, it requires productivity and quality.

All managers want their businesses to grow. However, many focus on growth through "new" business. New business is welcome, but it's only an aspect of what really counts, and that's "more" business. More business encapsulates the idea of paying attention to present customers and growing through the expansion and success of an excellent customer base.

One of the things we try to guard against is focusing on issues from the bank's point of view to the exclusion of the customer's point of view.

A few years ago, we were one of the first banks in Florida to introduce automatic teller machines. Our first machines were installed with a belief that they would reduce expenses as an alternative to employing traditional tellers. We marketed the machines as twenty-four-hour banking. Quite honestly, I believe that we failed to rationalize the machines from the customer's viewpoint. I doubt that we had too many requests for banking at 4:30 A.M. on Sunday mornings.

Initially, our ATMs were a flop. I resolved to find out why, so I got an access card, memorized my personal identification number and learned to use the machine. Immediately, I appreciated the phenomenal utility of immediate cash access as an alternative to cashing a check. A few days later, it was a holiday, and the banks were closed, but I was having a staff meeting at the office. At the meeting, one of our staff people told us about having just heard some folks talking on a CB radio band, and one party asking whether the banks were open. Upon being told by a "radio buddy" that the banks were closed, the intial party expressed, with some vehemence, frustration about needing to cash a check, to which someone responded, "If you bank at Sun Bank, they've got a machine where you can cash a check any time."

This incident caused us suddenly to recognize the point for the customer, and we changed our marketing approach for our ATMs from twenty-four-hour banking to "Open the bank any time." From the customer's point of view, the idea of being able to access his or her funds at any time, rather than at the bank's convenience, was tremendous, and our idle ATMs almost overnight sprang into tremendous popularity.

Speaking of ATMs, a few years later, Florida's premier supermarket chain decided to install, at their expense, ATMs in all of their stores. This development met a very frigid response from many of Florida's banks, who gave a cold shoulder to cooperating in order to allow their customer base access to their accounts through an alien machine network. We took a contrary view for a very simple reason: we thought our customers, many of whom patronized the stores in the chain, would appreciate the additional convenience of being able to use the machines at the stores as well as the ones at the bank. The decision paid off.

We believe our career people enjoy building the community. We believe they enjoy pleasing customers. We believe these objectives not only require productivity, quality and innovation, but also produce productivity, quality and innovation.

In the mid-1970s, the State of Florida suffered its first severe economic downturn since World War II. Since banks reflect their communities, loan losses mounted and bank profits plummeted. Obviously, we were concerned about restoring our positive momentum, and one day we sat down to discuss new marketing strategies with our advertising agent. The agency had prepared a number of creative twists on the conventional bank product advertising for loans and deposits. None of them suited me. I told the agency I wanted something more basic — something that would project our attitude and our positive feeling about the long-term prospects of our markets. After scratching their heads for a few days, the agency brought back one of the most unconventional campaigns ever undertaken by a bank — a campaign that said "Thumbs Up!"

"Thumbs Up" soon became "Thumbs Up, Florida," and then "Thumbs Up, Orlando," "Thumbs Up, Tampa," "Thumbs Up, Ocala." It became T-shirts with a big thumb up. It became decals. It became lapel pins. We practically became the "Thumb Bank" rather than Sun Bank. "Thumbs Up" was by far the most successful advertising campaign we ever did. It may be the best campaign ever done by a bank. The secret of its success was its impact on our own people. It transformed pessimism into optimism and projected those positive feelings out to our customers and to our communities.

We believe our career people are proud of their bank. We believe our customers are proud of their bank. We believe our banks are special to their communities. This mutual love affair creates special effort to do a good job, to be innovative, to deliver quality service, and the bank prospers from the success of the customer and the market. The glue that today binds together our fifty separate banks, operating across a breadth of varied markets in three different states, with over six hundred offices and twenty thousand employees, is our belief that we are in an exciting service business with an opportunity to create real value for our customers and for our communities.

Since we are proud of our customers and our communities, we don't want to let them down. We believe we are a quality company, and we want to show it through innovation and productivity. It's really like the old story of the three workmen — one said he was laying brick, the next that he was making a living and the third that he was building a cathedral. I believe our people see themselves as builders. As such, productivity, innovation and quality service become natural means toward that end.

3

THE POWER OF PEOPLE: The Competitive Edge

Being There: A Basic Need

A story: Once there was a young man who attended school in a large urban university as a part-time student while holding down a full-time job. After nine arduous years of work and study, study and work, he completed his studies. He went to his professor and said, "I'm ready to graduate. I want to be successful. I need your advice."

The professor looked at him for a moment and asked, "Are you absolutely certain you want to be a success?"

The student assured the professor that "After nine years of being a second-class citizen, I am committed to the idea of success," and repeated his request for advice.

"In that case, I will advise you," said the professor. "Show up."

The student was stunned. "Do you mean to say that after nine years of paying tuition, attending classes, passing exams and studying, you're saying all I have to do to succeed is to show up?"

"Well," said the professor, "that's actually the truth only about 70 percent of the time. But if you want to increase your odds, show up *on time*. And if you want to devastate virtually all competition, show up on time, dressed to play. Chances are, you won't even have to break a sweat."

This is a true story; it happened in my own classroom. More important, it illustrates a major reality of life in American enterprise. During a time when some in this nation are loudly proclaiming to the world at large that we can't compete, the fact is that too few of us even bother to show up, fewer show up on time and it's a unique and hardy minority that show up on time and dressed to play.

Simply being there puts you ahead of most of the pack. But being there when you're supposed to be there and being ready for the action almost guarantees victory and success. All of that may seem obvious to the enlightened reader, even a bit too much so, but as advertising genius Leo Burnett once said: "Never overlook the obvious."

In recent years, a virtual fetish has developed about what is known as the "laid-back" style, and fondness for this casual, easy-going approach to life has penetrated our working as well as our private lives. But there is a significant difference between composure under pressure and simply not caring. The latter attitude produces negative results, and, to a great extent, our society today suffers from those results. There are people who don't show up when or where they are supposed to, products that don't work, and service-oriented organizations which provide a great deal of service but very little which can be classified as first-class.

As consumers, we all too often find ourselves walking away from a transaction grateful that we weren't abused, humiliated or ripped off — in short, settling for mediocrity when we ought to be demanding excellence. This is not a situation restricted to the public or private sector, but a rather common denominator in a nation which still defines a standard as the average amount of work an average individual, working at an average rate, can produce. If this is to be our norm in terms of expectation, we may be able to build a great society in terms of sheer size — but we will not achieve greatness in terms of productivity or quality.

Keeping this in mind, consider the self-imposed inflexibility and rigidity existent in many organizations. Much management today is nearly obsessed with rules, policies, regulations, SOPs and guidelines which essentially promote, encourage and reward merely average performance. Aside from the disservice done to those who excel in such an environment, that philosophy automatically establishes a ceiling for expectations which is not far from ground level and can often result in apparent approval of below-average performance.

In a discussion of reward systems with a student enrolled in an executive development course, this negative backlash effect was sharply illustrated. The student, a mid-level manager with a multibillion-dollar, multi-national organization, expressed his dismay at being unable to terminate a staff member whose performance was, at best, unsatisfactory and, at worst, debilitating to the operation. A quagmire of corporate regulations and policies had neutralized the manager's options; only after twelve months of appeals and counter-appeals had he been given the approval to fire the employee — provided he gave the man thirty days' notice.

Two weeks prior to the employee's release, the manager received a memo from Personnel, advising that corporate policy mandated that the exiting staff member was to be given a raise. The raise could be minimal but had to be awarded. In essence, this manager was forced to reward a terminated employee for sub-standard performance.

Recalling the impact of the laid-back approach to life and business, it is ironic that some of the strongest advocates of the casual look are prone to perceive it as unfair, unjust and underhanded when they find themselves on the receiving end. Usually, this is a fairly natural reaction to the abdication of responsibility *by another*. But it is also, in a way, recognition that making the system work is truly everyone's business. In short, the professional spectator doesn't contribute much to an operation.

Living a purposeful life is not a specator sport. A free and productive society cannot afford the questionable luxury of too many observers; there must be a sense of responsibility among the majority.

Carrying this over to a practical setting in the classroom, consider the honor system. I recall making the routine announcement prior to an examination that anyone caught cheating would receive a failing grade for the entire course and hearing a protest from a student who indicated that he was offended because he didn't cheat. He had missed the point, largely because he received it from a self-oriented perspective. What about the behavior of others? The heart of an honor system is to accept responsibility for making sure that others don't cheat. One has the duty to see to it that all play by the same set of rules and carry their share of the load. This is not to suggest classrooms or societies populated by either informants or Samaritans. Rather, it's a simple statement that one's responsibility does not always end with one's self. If only to protect against having to shoulder an unequal burden or be placed at a disadvantage by an unethical competitor, the individual has a duty to himself first and then to his society or group to demand that standards be upheld and met.

This, in fact, is the fundamental theme of our current drive for reindustrialization, and this issue may be more important than retooling, financing or foreign competition. How can our nation expect to regain its leadership position unless all of us recognize and accept our individual responsibility?

Perhaps we need to step back and reassess the relationship among expectations, demands and rewards, and face the fact that we are mired in *mediocrity*. We expect it; we tolerate it; we encourage it; we even reward it.

The risk-taking character of our society — that vibrant entrepreneurial spirit which vaulted our nation to economic prominence — has slowly been replaced with a kind of bureaucratic bliss, and form instead of function has become the driving factor in our way of life.

Our contentment with sameness and our endorsement of mediocrity are no longer acceptable or appropriate in a global market populated by aggressive, innovative and ambitious competitors. Perhaps we are not "hungry" enough; certainly, we are not as hungry as they are.

Where there is little risk, there is little reward, and where there is no risk, the best possible outcome is breaking even. If productivity and performance are to improve, all organizations must reestablish the link between performance and reward, from top to bottom; we must regain the understanding that if you don't "do," you can't "get."

After all, in the material world, unlike the spiritual, the meek inherit . . . nothing.

S. Truett Cathy

S. Truett Cathy opened his first restaurant, The Dwarf House, in 1946. In 1967 he began the Chick-fil-A chain in shopping malls. Today, the chain includes 360 restaurants in thirty-one states and five new versions of Chick-fil-A that are outside malls. He has also recently begun a second chain in Atlanta. It is named The Dwarf House, for that first restaurant he owned.

Innovation Based on Sound Values — A Formula for Success

In 1946, my brother Ben and I raised a little over $10,500, bought a small piece of property in south Atlanta and constructed the restaurant that would one day launch the national chain called Chick-fil-A.

We christened the ten-stool, four-table grill "The Dwarf House" because of its small size and opened the doors for business. Open six days per week, twenty-four hours per day, the Dwarf House quickly became a popular neighborhood spot for socializing and enjoying a good meal.

In the beginning, the Dwarf House menu featured primarily beef items and breakfast. But soon I began experimenting with ways to serve chicken. However, I found it difficult to cook the chicken fast enough to offer quick service, so I began looking for ways to shorten the cooking time. My experimentation paid off when I found that removing the skin and bones of the chicken allowed a faster cooking time and allowed us to serve our customers quicker.

As the Chick-fil-A boneless breast of chicken sandwich gained popularity and carved a place for itself in the market, I saw an opportunity to take the business a step farther. In 1967, I opened a Chick-fil-A restaurant in Greenbriar Mall, Atlanta's first enclosed shopping mall. The restaurant was an instant success and laid the groundwork for our mall operations. Since that first mall restaurant opened, Chick-fil-A has become one of the nation's largest privately held restaurant chains and has experienced above average sales growth over the years.

Today, we have over 350 restaurants nationwide, more than one hundred of which have opened in the past five years, and I believe the momentum of our success will continue as we embark upon an aggressive national expansion program in upcoming years. Approximately twenty-five mall restaurants are planned for each of the next five years, in addition to our continuing expansion into the free-standing restaurant arena.

While still committed to our in-mall concept, we have begun to broaden our market potential by opening Chick-fil-A restaurants outside of malls. Customer acceptance of the new restaurants in Atlanta has been overwhelming and plans now call for us to continue active expansion of the concept in Atlanta in 1988.

Another growth opportunity for Chick-fil-A is our full-service Dwarf House restaurant. Patterned after the original restaurant where I created and launched the Chick-fil-A sandwich, our new Chick-fil-A Dwarf House is a full-service restaurant concept offering table and counter waitress service, self-service and a drive-through window.

I believe much of Chick-fil-A's growth and success can be traced to innovative business decisions that have given us a competitive edge. Three of these decisions are business principles that have been at the very core of the business since its inception:

• A unique entrepreneurial relationship with our restaurant operators. Chick-fil-A operators are independent business contractors. They can concentrate their attention on sales because they are free from the additional business issues faced by franchised restaurant owners.

• A commitment to quality products. Our boneless breast of chicken sandwich and our nuggets are consistently rated number one in taste and quality over all major fast-food competitors.

• A commitment to creating a business atmosphere that attracts and keeps good people. We are recognized as having one of the best operator and crew incentive programs in the fast-food industry, resulting in perhaps the lowest turnover rate in the business.

A unique entrepreneurial relationship. At Chick-fil-A we attribute much of our success to our unique entrepreneurial relationship with our restaurant operators. As independent business contractors, not franchisees, Chick-fil-A operators represent a cross section of diverse backgrounds and work experiences joined by a common thread that forms the foundation of our success — the vision and desire to build their own business.

This entrepreneurial spirit thrives in an atmosphere that is unique in the fast-food industry because the Chick-fil-A concept is a departure from franchise arrangements. For a financial commitment of only five thousand dollars, a Chick-fil-A operator subleases a fully stocked and equipped restaurant worth more than $250,000 and shares that restaurant's profits fifty-fifty with the home office.

This entrepreneurial opportunity allows operators to concentrate their efforts on building their sales and income potential while receiving support in marketing, promotions, operations, accounting and training from Chick-fil-A, Inc. That's why we say our operators "are in business for themselves, but not by themselves."

Most operators come to Chick-fil-A with no prior restaurant experience. That's because we want people with the character, proven ability and desire to achieve, rather than those with restaurant experience. I believe we can teach anyone to cook chicken and make coleslaw, but seldom can you teach a person the motivation needed to lead others and to succeed in the operation of a business.

A commitment to quality products. Our commitment to quality products goes back to the original decision to serve only the best part of the chicken — all-white, boneless breast meat — in our Chick-fil-A sandwich and Chick-fil-A Nuggets, Hearty Breast of Chicken Soup and chicken salad. This commitment carries through to all Chick-fil-A products and is instilled as one of our primary missions in all our restaurant operators and employees.

Consumers show their preference for Chick-fil-A menu items time and time again by rating Chick-fil-A chicken sandwich and nuggets number one in taste and overall quality over all major fast-food competitors. Consumer research, conducted semi-annually since 1982 by Marketing and Research Counselors, Inc., shows consumers rank our products highest for overall food quality.

Consumers tell us they can also taste the quality difference in our other food — including coleslaw, potato salad and carrot-and-raisin salad — all made entirely from fresh ingredients in each restaurant. Our lemon pies and lemonade are also made fresh from lemons squeezed on the premises.

Customer loyalty can also be traced to our ability to serve food fast and efficiently — an attribute lost by many fast-food chains that have extended the wait in line along with their menus. But at Chick-fil-A we have not fotgotten who we are: a chain dedicated to serving good food quickly. By keeping the menu simple, we can serve food rapidly while maintaining quality.

A commitment to creating atmosphere. Chick-fil-A has traditionally been a company with strong commitments — a commitment to our store operators, a commitment to our young people and a commitment to our customers and future customers. This tradition of commitment has grown from an even greater purpose that reflects our dedication to people and our incorporation of Biblical values into our business philosophy.

At Chick-fil-A, the corporate purpose was written by our employees and is engraved on a plaque that stands at the front of the corporate offices as a daily reminder of our organization's two-part goal: "To glorify God by being a faithful steward of all that is entrusted to us, and to have a positive influence on all who come in contact with Chick-fil-A."

I've always believed people are our most important asset. This belief, at the very heart of my business philosophies, is one that is reflected in innovative incentive programs that help us maintain one of the lowest turnover rates in the fast-food industry. While the specific incentive programs are easily described, our commitment to people extends beyond specifics to something less easy to put into words. As Len Gay, Chick-fil-A operator at Annapolis Mall in Annapolis, Maryland, put it, "It's hard to describe, but Chick-fil-A has a people-oriented atmosphere. From top management down, you're given the feeling that you're important."

The primary incentive is the operator's ability to directly affect his/her income by aggressively working to increase the restaurant's sales. Incentives include the opportunity for operators to earn Mark VII Lincoln Continental's in Chick-fil-A's *Symbol of Success* program. All restaurant operators who increase their restaurant sales by 40 percent (or $200,000 for higher volume locations) over the previous year receive a new Mark VII to drive the next year. If they repeat this growth the following year, they are awarded the title to the car. More than one hundred operators have reached the *Symbol of Success* goal since the program began in 1975.

Another popular benefit is our annual seminar — an all-expense-paid, four-day business meeting at a luxury resort. At the seminar, we host nearly one thousand members of the Chick-fil-A family, including operators, staff, their spouses and guests, at locations such as The Southampton Princess Hotel in Bermuda.

Our incentives and low turnover rate have created an impressive career longevity among operators — in 1987, 155 operators had five years of operator service with Chick-fil-A, forty operators had reached the ten-year mark and four operators had been with Chick-fil-A fifteen years.

We also have a strong commitment to the young people who work for us. Each year, hundreds of our younger workers benefit from this dedication to their development as crew members. One of the most visible signs of this commitment is our scholarship program. Restaurant employees who work twenty hours per week for two years or more and who are recommended by their operators receive a one-thousand-dollar scholarship to the college of their choice. Since 1973, we have awarded nearly $4.5 million in college scholarships to nearly forty-five hundred crew members across the country.

Restaurant employees are also eligible for a four-year scholarship worth up to ten thousand dollars to WinShape Centre at Berry College in Rome, Georgia. The program began in 1984 under a private foundation (WinShape Centre, Inc.) with Chick-fil-A, Inc., as the major supporter. Since its inception, there have been more than 112 students from twenty-nine states and Mexico who have attended Berry College under the WinShape program.

In addition to our scholarship programs, we have demonstrated our commitment to youth in a variety of other ways. In the summer of 1984, the WinShape Foundation also established Camp WinShape at Berry College. Created to develop the boys and girls of today into the men and women of tomorrow, the camping program is operated during the summer months on the WinShape Centre complex in the north Georgia mountains.

Designed to promote the growth and education of young people through an experience that will last a lifetime, the camp offers two-week sessions with recreational activities including horseback riding, swimming, bicycling, puppetry, singing and crafts, as well as inspirational activities such as morning and evening devotionals.

WinShape Centre has also established a foster home for underprivileged children. Aimed at helping a group of young people who might otherwise face an uncertain future, the current foster home, Huddleston House, is designed to house up to twelve children and two foster parents and is the first of several that I hope to build. The opportunity given me to establish programs such as these has been one of the most rewarding aspects of Chick-fil-A's success.

Where do we go from here? Chick-fil-A is still a young company committed to continued growth and innovation. Even after forty years in the restaurant business, I see myself and the company as just shifting into second gear.

People Make the Difference

It happens. The customer had recently completed his weekly trek to the grocery store. Another significant deposit had been placed in the coffers of that establishment. Unpacking the groceries at home, he realized that the true mission of the week was unfulfilled. While he was certain that the latest flavor of Ben & Jerry's ice cream (chocolate fudge) had been purchased and bagged, it simply did not make it home. The family would be heartbroken.

The customer frantically returned to the store, where the manager graciously responded with not one but two pints of the frozen delight from Vermont. No excuses were offered, no alternatives suggested. The manager, one of the front-line representatives of that organization, helped retain a customer who left the store satisfied, pleased and loyal.

At Publix Supermarkets, this is the rule, not the exception. Groceries are groceries — except at Publix. There, founder George Jenkins has created a work ethic that is truly people-oriented. The stores are immaculately clean and polished. Purchases are pleasantly delivered to your car, and tipping is strictly forbidden. What Jenkins has realized is that, as more and more industries are peddling strictly commodities, it is the people who make the difference. Loyal employees foster loyal customers, and it is this very brand of loyalty that keeps the buyer pleased and the seller profitable.

Toward that end, Ben & Jerry's is a special company. Ice cream is ice cream, right? Well, not quite. Today, if you don't give your ice cream a lofty, exotic name, it just won't sell, right? Wrong. As Ben and Jerry say: "This carton contains some of the finest ice cream available anywhere. We know, because we're the guys who make it. . . . It costs more, and it's worth it!" These two have taken an average, everyday commodity and humanized it, improved on it and created a winner. We all identify with Ben and Jerry. There is no secret to success in the marketplace today. It is truly the people, the Bens and the Jerrys, who make the difference.

Mattel, Inc., the billion-dollar manufacturer of toys, unlocked the secret to people and product development when over forty-eight thousand children across the country submitted entries for Mattel's Masters of the Universe competition. This innovative promotion allowed the ultimate consumer, the kid, to submit the ultimate new-product idea. The five winners shared $300,000 in scholarship monies. A great idea? Since 1982, Mattel has sold more than 125 million plastic action figures — to kids. It is people who make the difference. To Mattel, it is little people, but people, nevertheless.

Many times, infectious enthusiasm for and by the people, both employee and customer, reveals itself in organization performance.

Ryder Systems, Inc., is a multinational, multibillion-dollar corporation that is wowing its competition. Guided by the spirited leadership of Tony Burns, Ryder has evolved from a position as a dominant force in truck leasing to a major player in airline maintenance, insurance, bus transportation (in 1985, Ryder saved the Dallas Area Transit Authority $9 million by operating five hundred buses) and other transportation-related businesses. Burns does all of this with twenty-six thousand team members managed by a scant three hundred. The prevailing attitude at Ryder has changed dramatically over the past few years. According to Burns, in days gone by Ryder approached customers with: "This is the product, this is the service, take it or leave it." Today, the customer approach is: "How can we help you solve your problems?" Burns has espoused a reinvigorated commitment to quality and leadership.

One day, the CEO of a multibillion-dollar organization was visiting Ryder headquarters. The executive veered from the main path, strolled onto the lawn and picked up a candy wrapper. Why? He said that the sign of a quality organization is symbolic. It is cleanliness, having products face buyers with the name clearly visible, greeting the customer with a smile and simply saying thank you. To Burns, this is the goal of Ryder, of the company, but more importantly of the people who make up the company. It is practical, and it is real.

To say there is nothing new in building and running a successful organization is not quite accurate. Conversely, it is not overly *in*accurate. A decade of new leaders, and thank goodness for those leaders, has suddenly discovered that in effective organizations, managers are visible and interact with those who make things happen, and those who make things happen are people, period. Not so incidentally, this truism applies to all organizations, large or small, public or private. Simply stated, in the long run it is basics, basics, basics — rather than location, location, location.

First of all, let's recognize that building a customer is always good business. The Jesse James approach leads to a few quick kills and bankruptcy. Hence, and we've cited this on many occasions, handle each transaction with each customer as if you had to live with him or her in a very small room for the rest of your life. Chances are the customer will be pleased and the business will prosper. It is therefore a plus for the consumer and a plus for the organization. A logical deduction would be to strive for the double-"plus" in dealing with others, rather than the double-cross.

Since people make the difference, one might conclude that you can attract the best and then watch good things happen. Alas, there is more to it than that. You can go for the best, but cultivation makes the difference. Corporate cultivation, among other things, involves training and development, recognition and rewards, and a climate conducive to growing and winning. Fortunately, accomplishing this is not only possible — it is profitable.

John Sloan, Jr.

John Sloan, Jr. is president and chief executive officer of the National Federation of Independent Business, the largest small-business organization in the United States. Prior to joining NFIB in 1983, he was president and chief executive officer of First Tennessee Bank in Nashville. A native of that city, Sloan was reared on an operating farm in Williamson County, Tennessee. He has received degrees from Vanderbilt University and the Stonier Graduate School of Banking at Rutgers University. He served as an officer in the U.S. Navy.

The Corporate Culture Tells Much About a Business

Having had experience in government (military service), business and now with a nonprofit organization, I find myself able to draw similarities and contrasts among the management techniques required in each of the sectors. However, the emphasis in this essay will be on similarities, because I believe that whether we are discussing a business, a school or a government agency, there is one important ingredient that can cause the organization to excel, to fail or to plod along in mediocrity. That ingredient is people.

We need only reflect on our most recent pleasant or unpleasant experience with an airline, a department store or our bank to be reminded how important that ingredient is. What remains fixed in our memory is the ticket agent who, despite a hectic hour of flight delays, took a moment to offer a friendly suggestion or an extra service. Or we might recall waiting in a slow moving line at the bank only to be treated rudely by a teller when it was finally our turn for "service."

Customer service is the most important aspect of any business. Building a quality product or delivering a unique service will not produce repeat business if the link between the organization and the consumer is flawed by the person with whom we deal.

Building quality consumer service is a challenge not easily met. It starts with the person at the top. The chief executive — the individual charged with the overall success of the organization — must have the vision for quality service and the ability to communicate this vision to the organization's people. Those traits should be among the top criteria for selecting an individual to run the show.

The CEO must relate first to the people within the organization, but it is not enough to have mastered that challenge. The CEO must also relate to the customer, supplier, regulator, competitor and myriad of other individuals who interact with the organization. The leader of any organization can begin to relate to the people within and without the organization by creating a "corporate culture." Most large organizations have a distinguishable corporate culture. It sets the tone for everything the organization does. It reflects the corporate values. Those values define what is important to the organization.

The corporate culture is a reflection of the general attitudes that prevail within the organization — attitudes about management, attitudes about customers or clients. That is why the CEO must be people-oriented first. Attitudes must flow from the top down. A positive attitude toward the customer must be fostered in the executive suite. The various levels of management must be imbued with it. It must arrive in its purest form at the point of contact with the customer.

Having mastered the "people factor," the successful CEO can begin to address organizational structure. There is no hard and fast rule with regard to that structure. Nevertheless, the most effective organizations are those in which the leadership has made a determined effort to understand the people who must fit into the corporate structure and tailor the structure to accommodate the capabilities and shortcomings of the people who are working in the organization.

Of course, in an ideal world, people could be hired to fit the structure, but for those who do not have the luxury (and considerable challenge) of starting from scratch, it makes sense to work with people already in place, augment them as necessary and shape the structure to make the most of the available talent. My preference, therefore, is a fluid organizational structure, one that makes the most of the people on board but is flexible enough to change as people, talents and corporate needs and market conditions change.

Once the corporate culture has been established and the people melded into a suitable organizational structure, attention should focus on the product. It matters not at all whether this "product" is hospital care, lobbying or aubomobiles — the key to the success of the organization will be the quality of the product. Again, the CEO — the people person — must motivate all employees to strive for quality. The corporate culture must encourage, must motivate, employees to appreciate the significance of a quality product. Quality is an outgrowth of pride. When management successfully instills pride in the employees, quality products are more likely to result. Management must create a sense of self-worth among employees and recognize them for a job well done.

The attributes of a successful company are no secret: people, organization and quality. The difficulty is bringing the ingredients together in a successful mix, placing the right emphasis on each ingredient and in the proper sequence.

People Power

In a May 1982 column, Urban C. Lehner, as *The Wall Street Journal*'s Tokyo representative, shared the following joke, one which bears repeating: A Frenchman, a Japanese and an American face a firing squad. Offered a last wish, the Frenchman asks to hear *La Marseillaise*. The Japanese asks to give one more lecture on Japanese management. The American asks to be shot first. "I can't stand one more lecture on Japanese management," he says.

Many of us are up to here about the "miracle in Japan." Don't misread this: There's much to admire and emulate, but there's certainly nothing new. As a matter of plain, simple fact, even the sometime student of management history recognizes that the emergence of Japan as a quantity and quality pace-setter is no miracle at all, but rather, the highly successful application of some of the earlier findings of such organizational theorists as Robert Owen, F. W. Taylor, Elton May and a score of others who built upon the known, the assumed and the hoped-for.

In the United States, our quest for quality is not thwarted by others and not by lack of technical expertise; for the most part, the enemy is from within. Simply stated, we've forgotten how we got as good as we are; we've not heeded Satchel Paige's admonition not to look back; and we appear to be suffering from a type of national narcissism. Each of the above could be fatal. But, happily, we can prevail if we are prepared to do what must be done.

In 1813, Robert Owen's *Address to the Superintendents of Manufactories* demonstrated unique insight into the reallocation of management efforts from the "inanimate" machines of production to the "vital" machines — the people involved. Owen is considered by many to be the father of personnel management. One hundred and seventy years ago, in *New View of Society*, Owen wrote:

> If then due care as to the state of your inanimate machines can produce such beneficial results, what may not be expected if you devote *equal* attention to your vital machines, which are far more wonderfully constructed?
> Here then is an object which truly deserves your attention; and instead of devoting all your faculties to invent improved inanimate mechanism, let your thoughts be, at least in part, directed to discover how to combine the more excellent materials of body and mind, which by a well-devised experiment, will be found capable of progressive improvement.

People, not machines, Owen argued, were, are, and will forever be the key to the long-term success of the organization. One hundred years after Owens' discourse on the importance of people in organizations, Frederick Winslow Taylor delivered a speech to a committee of the U.S. House of Representatives on the Workings of Scientific Management. What Taylor, the father of modern management, focused on is the top-to-bottom, bottom-to-top mental revolution that reorients management and labor toward corporate performance, thereby substituting peace for war and replacing cooperation for antagonism within the organization. Once again, however, the burden is placed squarely on management's shoulders. In his testimony to the committee, Taylor said:

Now in its essence, scientific management involves a
complete mental revolution on the part of the workingman
engaged in any particular establishment or industry — a
complete mental revolution on the part of these men as to
their duties toward their work, toward their fellow men,
and toward their employees. And it involves the equally
complete mental revolution on the part of those on the
management side — a complete mental revolution on their
part as to their duties toward their fellow workers in management, toward their workmen, and toward all their daily
problems.

Taylor argued and successfully implemented a "we" rather than
a "me" ethos in organizations. His scientific management theories
revolutionized industrialized organizations by refocusing business
efforts on producing and, more importantly, rewarding quality
performance.

Finally, what review of management would be complete without
a brief look at the insight of George Elton Mayo? Mayo's work at
Western Electric nearly sixty years ago established him as the
father of the human relations school of management. His years of
research and study concluded that a strong sense of group par-
ticipation and involvement, along with teamwork, is a stronger
motivator than many of the material rewards that we too often take
for granted. Mayo synthesized his efforts into some very basic
conslusions that even today should haunt us, and in *The Social
Problems of an Industrial Civilization*, he wrote:

In modern large-scale industry the three persistent problems of management are:
1.The application of science and technical skill to some
  material good or product.
2.The systematic ordering of operations.
3.The organization of teamwork — that is, of sustained
  cooperation.
  . . . It remains true that if these three are out of balance
the industry will not be successful. The first two operate to
make an industry effective . . . . the third to make it
efficient.

Striving for quality means we're going to build on basics, but on basics that work and are still applicable. To paraphrase Peter Drucker, it requires we do the right things, and what's right today might not have been applicable yesterday and might be obsolete tomorrow. This should not be interpreted as an approach permeated by a situational ethic and attitude. With excellence our goal, organizations should adopt a proactionary perspective and constantly search for a better way.

The search is for perfection, and this search has no end. For example, we must put to rest the notion that paying one's dues is a one-time affair. In reality, it simply means you're eligible to get back in line tomorrow. That's the bad news.

The good news is that the line is short. Today's best can, however, very well become tomorrow's historical oddity, and the organization that forgets this might join the ranks of those who forgot what kind of business they were in and failed to recall how they got as good as they were. Corporate cases in point range from W. T. Grant to the smallest fine restaurant which lost its quality when it expanded its menu; the lesson is there for the learning.

If you cited civilization's great concepts and inventions, near the top of the list would appear the division of labor. Without division of labor, mass production would be impossible, and our much heralded standard of living wouldn't be much to herald. However, along with the division, or perhaps, atomization of labor, has developed a keyhole view of work and responsibility.

Without question, that staunch private enterpriser Adam Smith would be appalled at the impact his research into the manufacture of pins has had. While Smith formally introduced us to the concept of division of labor by examining the manufacturing of straight pins, he would be intrigued at our peculiar ability to stick it to ourselves by specializing production to the point where we are now at a level of diminishing returns.

We have so fragmented and diffused the talents of management that, in far too many instances, the pieces simply do not fall together into an effective and efficient organization. In essence, "If it's not part of my job description, it's not my responsibility. Let someone else worry about it.'' We are creating a society of knowledgeable ignoramuses. We are producing employees capable of functioning quite well at a specific task, but few, if any, are capable of integrating and coordinating the various organizational forces. Have you ever tried to order a hamburger without pickles or mustard in a fast-food restaurant? Not only might you disrupt the entire system; you may also receive a package containing *only* pickles and mustard! If we're to compete *successfully* on an international basis, this jaundiced, jurisdictional way of viewing work must be put to rest, and quality must become a way of life.

There was a CEO who would check daily on the number of units his factory produced. After observing this ritual for the better part of a month, it was suggested he might be better off asking other questions. How many perfect units were produced? How many units were manufactured that would stay in the customers' homes? How many units were shipped that would require no premature service calls or adjustments? How many units were, by the most demanding standards, absolutely first class? How many units literally reeked of quality?

The point is that we are so obsessed with quantity that the quality factor is systematically ignored. Even the most elementary analysis of profits indicates that two basic factors are involved: revenues and costs. Historically, our mindset has focused on the revenue component of the equation. Current economic factors have forced us into examining the costs, or what we argue is the quality component. By concentrating on efficiency through cost containment, not only is a better product or service delivered, but that great intangible, customer loyalty, is also fostered.

In recent years, there has been a great deal of interest in quality circles. Hopefully, this interest will be translated into action. It should be understood that there is nothing either mystical or magical about quality circles. Essentially, the entire concept is structured around the belief that if you want to improve an operation, talk to the person doing it.

Chances are this person knows more about it than anyone else, but in all likelihood he or she is the last one ever asked about anything pertaining to quality or productivity. In all too many instances, productivity and quality issues have been handled by management in the traditional mind-over-matter fashion, i.e., we don't mind and you don't matter. Robert Patchin, as Northrop's Director of Productivity Improvement Programs, suggested that the employee of the 1980s is usually better educated and more sophisticated than his earlier counterpart and that the individual actually wants to be involved. In Patchin's judgment, the old, authoritarian management philosophy is not equipped to deal with the 1980s employee, who is usually more inquisitive and less willing to accept the unexplained than yesterday's worker.

On several occasions, former bank president Joseph E. Birnie would talk about the need for pleased rather than merely satisfied customers. Birnie would constantly indicate that superior service provided the most significant competitive edge, and that when a customer was pleased, you added another salesperson to your staff at no additional cost. However, pleasing the customer requires a quality orientation from the top down, and it is pleased employees who please customers.

Bluntly, deal with customers as if you had to live with them for the rest of your life. If you operate in this fashion, each transaction represents a plus for both the customer and the business, and in the process, everyone profits. This is what quality is all about.

Occasionally, step back and examine your own responses as a quality-conscious consumer. How did you respond when your suit was delivered from the dry cleaner minus a button? Were you a trifle perturbed when you returned your car for repairs on the same problem for the third time in a month? Remember when you attempted to discuss intelligently a billing error with the department store?

Management theories from Z to A deal with human, not material resources. Products, performance and productivity are primarily human-manipulated issues. We have the expertise, the resources, and now the challenge. Why not meet it?

Ronald W. Allen

Chairman of the board and chief executive officer of Delta Air Lines since 1987, Ronald W. Allen first joined Delta in 1963 as a part-time methods analyst. A native of Atlanta, Allen is a 1964 graduate of the Georgia Institute of Technology, where he received the Bachelor of Industrial Engineering degree. He serves on the boards of directors of the Atlanta Chamber of Commerce, National Service Industries, Inc. and the Citizens and Southern Corporation.

The Evolution of the Delta Family Spirit

On June 17, 1929, flying a five-passenger aircraft called a Travel Air, Delta Air Service inaugurated scheduled passenger service with a flight from Dallas, Texas to Jackson, Mississippi. 1929 was not a very good year to launch a new company, especially an airline. Four months after Delta opened for business, the stock market collapsed and began the worst depression our country has ever known. To complicate matters, Delta was doing business in the most poverty-stricken part of the nation — the Deep South. Delta was surrounded on all sides by adversity and by competitors who were far wealthier and larger. Yet, with an extraordinary application of hard work and common sense, Delta survived and grew from obscurity to world prominence by offering, simply, the best customer service possible.

Today, Delta Air Lines is a seven-billion-dollar corporation, flying 375 of the world's most modern, fuel-efficient jet aircraft, employing over 52,000 people and serving 154 cities in the United States, Puerto Rico and ten foreign countries. Delta has been profitable for thirty-eight of the last thirty-nine years and has paid dividends spanning thirty-nine consecutive years — a record unparalleled by any other airline. In 1987, Delta carried more than 53 million passengers.

Competition in the airline industry is very intense, particularly in today's deregulated environment, wherein the primary focus is often on price alone. While price is certainly an important competitive tool, it is not the only consideration. Many customers are willing to fly a low-cost operation one time because of the fare, but when they notice the "difference" in Delta people and service, they come back to the airline they can count on. Delta sells superior customer service, and offers competitive fares, as part of its air transportation package. Moreover, Delta believes a large part of the traveling public will remember the "Delta Difference" — people who care about customers.

Delta's superior customer service does not go unnoticed by the traveling public. In 1987, for the fourteenth consecutive year, official government records show Delta received the fewest number of passenger complaints per 100,000 passengers boarded. Also in 1987, for the fifth consecutive year, the readers of *Travel Holiday* Magazine voted Delta their preferred domestic air carrier.

Superior customer service has paid off in continued growth and profitability for Delta Air Lines, but the questions that we continue to hear are, "What does Delta do differently? Where does the 'Delta Family Spirit' originate?" Well, it really isn't much of a secret; it has been talked about, researched and written about for almost sixty years. It's the Delta people — indeed, the Delta family. C. E. Woolman, Delta's founder, began a tradition based on a grass-roots philosophy toward customer service: Take care of your people, and they will take care of your customers. Mr. Woolman was a caring, compassionate, people-oriented individual with a genuine concern for the customer and for the people of Delta. The traditions begun by Mr. Woolman have set Delta apart from most airlines and, indeed, most corporations in this country. Since Delta's inception in the depths of The Depression in 1929, it has operated on the premise that people make the difference in any enterprise. During those early years, some basic beliefs were formed about the meaning of our company and the people who were a part of that company. Those basic beliefs have sustained our company through all of the challenges we have faced since 1929 and are still the central core of Delta.

The axioms we live by, simply stated, are:

Hire individuals who enjoy being of service to others — those who have the technical skills to perform in many complex positions needed to support the airline — and

Hire individuals who have the ability to take on increasing responsibility in the future.

Maintain a firm "Promote from within" policy. With few exceptions, Delta personnel begin their careers at entry-level positions with the opportunity to advance on individual initiative, performance and personal ability.

For almost sixty years, Delta has had consistency of corporate leadership and business philosophy. By the time an individual reaches a position of supervision and management, he or she is well-versed in company policies and business philosophy and has a thorough knowledge of our company and the airline industry. There is, too, a strong and continuing communication between management and all personnel groups. Communication between managers and the people who work for them is an on-going process at several different levels. Every effort is made to create an environment of approval so that each employee feels confident in taking that affirmative step needed to solve a problem or please a customer.

Since management personnel have all come up through the ranks, the majority of our people know their managers on a first-name basis. There are also regular meetings between top management and employee groups. Because we operate on an open door policy, anyone who works for Delta can, and often does, speak personally with members of top management on a confidential basis.

Delta believes that achievement should be recognized and has a number of recognition programs in all divisions of the company. One policy especially appreciated by Delta personnel is the company's effort to retain all permanent personnel through periods of economic turbulence. In an industry characterized by peaks and valleys of growth, Delta works hard to avoid the furlough of permanent personnel. One of Delta's highest priorities is to keep the team together — through the bad times as well as the good. Delta has not released one permanent person in over thirty years.

Further, Delta's wage and compensation package has always compared very favorably to industry levels, and the company has always shared profits with its people through pay increases or additional benefits. Vacation benefits are generous, and company-funded medical and dental insurance and retirement programs are excellent. The Delta people feel that the company assigns a top priority to their well-being.

If these traditions sound idealistic with regard to people, where do the hard business factors of productivity, innovation, initiative and customer service come into the picture? That's an easy question at Delta. All of those things are closely related. Productivity is very important in any industry. At Delta we are thoughtful when we talk about productivity. Our people work very hard and are very proud of the designation "Delta Professional." Since productivity is one of the most important characteristics of a professional, the search for productivity gains at Delta typically falls in the area of automation and technological improvements. You see, from the very beginning our public contact people know that productivity — when it comes to customer service — is responding to customers' needs. So each person "grows up" feeling a personal commitment and responsibility to the customer. These are the people who have, on countless occasions, opened their homes to stranded passengers, driven passengers to their destinations when they were not met at the airport, saved lives through CPR, accompanied passengers to the hospital on their own time on their own initiative, and stopped and assisted people who have had car trouble. Such acts of concern and generosity are a daily occurrence.

Then, too, Delta people are constantly looking for a better way to get things done. For instance, when a Delta maintenance crew undertook a job which an outside contractor would have required six months to complete, they refined the process until they could do the same job, but better, in a little over four weeks. Another group of individuals decided to spearhead a project to purchase a thirty-million-dollar airplane for the company, one which soon became the flagship of Delta's B-767 fleet, aptly named "The Spirit of Delta." A retiring flight captain took out a full-page advertisement in the Atlanta newspaper to say "thank you" to the company he had been a part of for over thirty years.

The "Spirit of Delta" — which manifests itself in customer service — is a state of mind at Delta. It is a state of mind that cannot be legislated. Delta people have it because they love their jobs, believe in their company's mission and want to protect the legacy they have earned.

For me, personally, it is truly an honor to work with such an outstanding team-oriented group of professionals. It is a humbling experience to watch the team in action and be responsible for maintaining the uniqueness of Delta Air Lines. That uniqueness — that Delta Family Spirit in our people — is a joy to behold.

The Best, No Less

The customer had one of those days. A grueling day at the office, followed by a number of the errands required of any working couple. Last stop: the dry cleaner. The ticket was presented to the clerk, who promptly handed over a beautiful pair of canary yellow designer jeans. The problem: the jeans were peach the day before. Nice crease, lightly starched, but the wrong color.

The customer explained the dilemma to the clerk, who displayed the sympathy of Conan the Barbarian. The clerk remarked that she was in no position to make a hasty judgment on a cleaning error. In fact, she intimated, there might indeed be a question about the original color of the pants. It was suggested that the customer return on Saturday to discuss the matter with the boss. The customer was a trifle perturbed. Nevertheless, with dinner in the crockpot and a dog to be walked, there was little choice, but to return to the cleaner's on Saturday.

Saturday arrived. A beautiful day (wouldn't you know it?). This time, depending on teamwork, the couple returns to meet manager. Manager greets couple with the gentility and warmth of The Terminator. Couple explains situation, citing obvious cleaning error, and waits patiently for remedy to arrive. No chance. Manager explains to customers that this is obviously a manufacturing defect, and they should definitely, at their convenience, return the pants to the retailer (pants were bought on vacation in the Dry Tortugas). Couple explains that during the past three years they have contributed an average monthly payment of two hundred dollars to manager's cash flow and would appreciate his remedying the situation. The manager replied: "It's not my store, and they're not my pants." Stonewalled again.

The customers exited this place of business fantasizing about the myriad uses of the dry-cleaning press on both Conan and The Terminator. They also left the store frustrated, disenchanted, disheartened and disgusted . . . . and this was the good news. The bad news was that a mutually beneficial three-year relationship was abruptly halted. They were mad!

An uncommon story? Hardly. A unique occurrence? Not really. The fact of the matter is that behavior like that exhibited by Conan and The Terminator is becoming more the rule than the exception in organizational life today. This is the good news. The bad news is that, all too often, we sit back and take it. At least, we argue, it's better than being physically attacked. In all too many organizations there's a commitment to complacency that has reached epidemic proportions. There is a mission of mediocrity that has become endemic in situations pitting seller against buyer. There is an anti-performance dictum that has, in all too many instances, become the rule — not the exception — in organizational life today.

Some management theorists argue that too many businesses are customer-oriented instead of being attuned to the machinations of the competition. The fact is, if you truly cater to the customer, you will win almost by default. In most instances, it is the implementation rather than the strategy that does you in.

As both player and manager, the great Pete Rose has become an anachronism in contemporary baseball. Rose arrives at the ballpark more than six hours before each game. In fact, he goes to the ballpark on off days, vacations, and holidays. His obsession, dedication and commitment are viewed as freakish, absurd and outdated. He is a perfectionist, a dedicated professional who will not settle for second best. He is an overachiever, and that scares us. Pete Rose is a rate-buster, something that frightens his colleagues and friends. Rate-busting, first-class performance has been replaced with a bureaucratic bliss that espouses form, not function. In too many organizations, there's no room for Roses. How do you handle the overachiever? How do you manage a rate-buster who makes peers uncomfortable? Pete Rose is great . . . . but is it greatness we want?

Contentment leads to mediocrity, and mediocrity leads to disaster. In today's marketplace, there is little room for mediocrity and contentment. There is too much competition, and the competition is simply too hungry. Customers, owners, managers and employees must get mad. Aren't we all tired of second best? Wouldn't it be nice to win once? Why should we settle for canary when what we really want is peach? We constantly need to reassess what we order, get and give. No longer is average, mundane or the usual acceptable. This goes for products, services and the way we care for and feed our employees and customers. What a terrific managerial problem to manage an organization of Roses. What an incredible managerial dilemma to manage an organization of rate-busters who come early and stay late. In 1912, Leon Leonwood Bean (founder of L. L. Bean) mailed out his first circulars. They read:

> I do not consider a sale complete until goods are worn out and the customer still satisfied.
> We will thank anyone to return goods that are not perfectly satisfactory.
> Should the person reading this notice know of anyone who is not satisfied with our goods, I will consider it a favor to be notified.
> Above all things we wish to avoid having a dissatisfied customer.

L. L. Bean wanted customers to get mad. This infectious madness keeps everyone on his or her toes and, consequently, *everyone* wins.

A survey conducted in 1983 by Daniel Yankelovich showed only 23 percent of U.S. workers said they were working as hard as they could. The real problem is that in all too many instances this is true for management and customers as well. We have factored this inefficiency into our organizational behavior, and it shows. Why not settle for nothing less than the best? Buyer or seller, manager or employee, owner or customer — everyone gains from first-class performance. We all need to get a little mad and a little uncomfortable. Hypercompetitive global markets threaten our comfort and convenience. There is no substitute for the best. There is no competition against the best. The best is, quite simply, the best.

We should finish the saga of the peach/canary designer jeans. The customer returned the pants to a local Ann Taylor outlet. Ann Taylor, a division of Campeau Corporation, is a high-quality retailer of women's clothing. Before the customer could relate half the tale, the manager, a dedicated professional, simply said that it would be her "pleasure" to return the jeans to the manufacturer and credit the customer. No excuses were offered; no alternatives suggested. The customer left the store satisfied, pleased and loyal. The best was expected, and the best was delivered . . . . no more, no less.

Herman J. Russell

Herman J. Russell is a graduate of the Tuskegee Institute and president and chairman of the board of H. J. Russell and Company, H. J. Russell Construction Company, Paradise Apartments Management, City Beverage Company, Inc., Interstate Construction Company, Inc., and Georgia Southeastern Land Company. He is chairman of the board of Concessions International, Inc., Gibraltar Land, Inc., Diversified Project Management and Russell-Rowe Communications, Inc. He lives in Atlanta, Georgia.

Competing with the Biggest and the Best

It is considered fashionable to claim that "Our commitment to excellence is the cornerstone of our success"; it is also in vogue to cite "Quality service will yield increased business." Few businesses, however, have actually put these principles to work. At H. J. Russell & Company we have, and we will. From the days as a small, family-owned plastering company to the era of the diverse corporate structure that exists today, the same guiding principle of striving for excellence has governed H. J. Russell & Company and the way it does business.

Any small black company located in the South during the 1950s faced an enormous challenge just to survive. We were no different, save for our desire to be competitive and our belief in maximizing productivity. These were not just words. We lived by those rules daily. I was a one-man Executive Committee, Chief Operating

Officer, Chief Purchasing Officer, Chief Estimator and Job Foreman. The philosophy of getting the most out of myself logically transfers to others within the H. J. Russell organization, and the results, I believe, are apparent.

The H. J. Russell organization is close-knit, lean and very deliberate in its acquisition of human resources. Those who do join our organization are apt to be bright, aggressive self-starters who respond well to challenges and are not afraid to take risks. Such persons rise within the organization by hard, dedicated work, great attention to detail and an intensity found in only a few successful companies. These individuals are the type who will chart the future of this organization or some other company. For that is also a large part of my philosophy. Not only must I promote quality service and excellence of performance within H. J. Russell & Company; I also have a responsibility to make those goals the objectives of future generations as well. The true measure of success for me and the H. J. Russell organization will be our ability to inspire future businessmen and women to apply the principles of hard work, discipline and integrity en route to achieving success.

In the daily operation of the varied divisions of my company, I urge my managers to exercise their judgment over the full spectrum of their area of responsibility. While I am always available to aid in the resolution of problems, I believe that real growth and development of managers comes with the experience of making tough business decisions and seeing them through. Out of this environment will emerge strong, capable leadership that is committed to the same quest for quality that the H. J. Russell Company was founded upon.

By maintaining an attitude that "We can compete with the biggest and the best," we have earned a reputation for quality workmanship that has propelled us to our current status in the construction industry. The lesson of regard for performing well on small tasks was not lost on me. Excellence of performance on small jobs soon resulted in the larger contractors and builders of Atlanta seeking us out on major projects. All of these opportunities reinforced our belief in providing quality service at every level.

That was our goal as well when we landed our first major project in 1967, the Equitable Building in downtown Atlanta. As the low bidder on the job, I was questioned by the project's Development Director as to whether or not I had underbid the work. I responded, without hesitation, that I was fully prepared to stand behind the bid as submitted. I knew that quality work had gone into its preparation, and quality should result. I was right. The job turned out to be one of the Company's most profitable early efforts. Because we had emphasized quality early on in the bid preparation, we were able to attract highly skilled workers, acquaint them with the latest technology and provide them with the tools necessary to complete their tasks efficiently. That combination, that formula, still works for our company — quality in preparation and skilled, highly motivated people equipped with the proper tools equal success. In order to apply this formula for success effectively, we have resisted the temptation of rapid expansion. If quality is to be sustained, growth must be managed, and managed conscientiously. As in our early years of development, the commitment is still to that end — to develop an organization that will always stand for quality in its work, integrity in all its dealings and the maximum effort from its people. Those elements are the underpinnings of our successful past . . . . and future.

Quality = Products + People

Let's face it: there are certain products that make quality statements. There is that select group of entities that evoke a unanimous chorus of voices proclaiming them to be the very best. There are a collection of products that, beyond the most exacting, the most demanding standards, are absolutely first-class.

What comes to mind? Mont Blanc pens, IBM-PCs, Nikon lenses, Fabergé eggs, Steuben crystal and De Beers diamonds — to name a few. Products like these, produced by companies with long and glorious histories, carry with them a unique, overwhelming momentum. Traditionally, the marketplace reserved a hallowed position for the excellent, while others seemed content to slug it out for the remaining shares. Today, the rules have changed.

The emergence of non-U.S. competitors as both quality and quantity pace-setters in a global setting has instigated a rash of domestic challenges that makes the buying of goods and services more fun than it has been in years. The gauntlet has been dropped, and many American companies have collectively responded with a "Yes, we can!" attitude. Suddenly, we are confronted with domestically produced cars that are every bit as economical, sporty, fast, aerodynamic and inexpensive as those from abroad. Remarkably, U.S. manufacturers in a variety of industries find themselves rising to a challenge that was perceived for years as insurmountable.

And, to what we must imagine would be the the glee of Adam Smith (and the chagrin of the remaining xenophobic few), competitors from around the globe are rising to heightened levels of competition. It's much like professional wrestling giants Hulk Hogan and Rowdy Roddy Piper slugging it out in a winner-take-all bout in Madison Square Garden. Frankly, without a scorecard, it's a bit difficult to keep track of the competitors. If they look, smell and handle alike, and run the same, differences are subtle at best. Competition is a wonder to behold. What seems to be emerging, at last, is one very important assumption: the quality that emerges in the marketplace is not a function of product alone, but of product and people. It is relatively feasible in the long-run to produce quality products, but quality people don't just happen, don't just randomly occur. Rather, quality people are carefully selected, trained and rewarded by organizations that are themselves committed to quality.

Joel Wells, the brilliant strategist who, as chairman of the board and CEO of SunTrust Banks, helped orchestrate mergers first with Flagship Bank and then with Trust Company of Georgia, ascribes the success of this rapidly emerging giant to three simple factors. These include quality financial products, quality people and quality service. There is no mystery to the equation. Quality as perceived by the marketplace equals product and people — no more, no less.

One of the truly great by-products of our rededication to competition is our eagerness to reject the easy way out. No longer is "no" the immediate response. Responding to numerous detractors, an effective promotion for Goodyear, a company better known for its tires and blimps, celebrated the company's production of a supercomputer for NASA rated among the fastest in the world. Take a great company with great people and watch the great products emerge. The winners and the new champions are the millions of consumers who demand quality in both products and people. After all, if you don't ask, you don't get.

On a trip to Japan, an American tourist was enthralled with the thousands of Japanese children wearing Mickey Mouse ears, Donald Duck shirts and Goofy smiles. What the folks at Walt Disney have demonstrated is that a uniquely American product coupled with a commitment to selecting and training unique Japanese employees can produce quality that is, in fact, universal. Simple, isn't it?

The fact is, quality service provided by quality people really does make the difference. Location, product and a host of other variables can generate a competitive edge in the short run. The long-term winners always strive to deliver the best in the best possible way. Two examples:

The automobile, an expensive one, was brand new and had to be towed back to the shop in Atlanta four times in less than one month. It had probably traveled more miles backwards than forwards. While the customer was unhappy and disappointed, he noticed that in each instance the dealer's staff responded with a sense of immediacy and concern. They appeared to be as upset with the situation as the customer was. On the fourth occasion, the dealer, Robert Hennessy, told the customer they would eventually determine the cause of the breakdowns, but the customer had already been inconvenienced far too much. Therefore, Hennessy suggested the customer select another brand-new automobile from his inventory. The customer did, the replacement was trouble-free, and Hennessy and his personnel added a pleased patron to their sales force at no additional cost. While this incident occurred several years ago, the customer has never forgotten, a plus for both the dealer and the customer.

The Sengos in California sell delicious dried fruit. So do a lot of other folks. However, the Sengos seem to do it with a special sense of dedication and purpose. They appear to have a real handle on the quality formula. Recently, a pleased, not satisfied, customer received this note with his order: "Enclosed is a $1.00 refund for overpayment. Our new prices are lower. Thank you, The Sengos."

As far as our customer is concerned, The Sengos now have a monopoly on shipping dried fruit to him — and whomever else he can contact.

Again, quality equals products plus people. This formula assures that everyone can get well together. After all, whether it's transportation or food, a couple of bucks or several thousand dollars — isn't this what excellence is all about?

Rainmakers, Changemakers, and Parade-Watchers

If you believe organizations have a life of their own, think again. No matter how carefully crafted it is, a company won't go anywhere without people. It is this human element that transforms a good-looking organization into a top entity, and it is performance that generates profits.

In his classic book *Strategy and Structure*, which examined the growth and development of some of America's largest industrial organizations, famed business historian Alfred Chandler hammered home the point that changing company strategies must be accompanied by a subsequent evaluation and analysis of company structures. A radical alteration in the strategic direction of a firm must, in most instances, be matched with a radical redesign of the firm's organizational setup. While strategy and structure may, indeed, impact on the performance of the business, a far greater — and indeed more sustaining — imprint is made by the people involved. It is the people, top to bottom, that alter strategy, redesign structure and make the new strategic plan a functioning reality. Strategy and structure are the vehicles, the mechanisms, through which people make things happen. And it is the people who make the ultimate difference in the performance and productivity of the business.

Some may recall the enormously popular Art Linkletter program *People Are Funny*. In retrospect, the show might have been entitled *People Are Always Different — And Sometimes Funny*. For example, when people come together to achieve a common purpose, an organization is formed. This organization can be large or small, public or private, for profit or not. No matter what the mission, it is people, all kinds of people, who score goals and make profits. Therefore, the role of a good manager is one of melding goals, structures and people into accomplishment-attaining vehicles capable of benefiting a wide range of constituencies. Simply stated, management is a long-term process that continually transforms diverse elements into supportive relationships. Ideally, this process should also lead to a positive situation for all involved. When the minuses exceed the pluses, adjustments are in order. Good management is not a given. In fact, good management must recognize that employees today have radically altered their demands and their expectations. It is the great organizations that recognize these changes and respond accordingly.

A study conducted by *The Miami Herald* examined the changing expectations of graduates from the 1980s versus graduates of the 1970s. Specifically, today's graduates think making lots of money is important, as is marriage (though not in the foreseeable future), and in spite of relatively average-paying jobs, many enjoy affluent lifestyles characterized by skiing trips, new cars and expensive sound systems.

Perhaps more importantly, this lifestyle is being augmented by an overwhelming number of young adults aged twenty-two to thirty-two who are still living at home. The other major demographic change: almost two-thirds of all women aged twenty-two are single — two and one-half times the same figure in 1960. The people, the newcomers in the world of work, our world, have changed . . . . but the bigger question is: has management changed as well?

Good managers have great challenges before them. The workplace is populated by the most affluent and educated work force ever, motivated by different goals, different aspirations and a different set of expectations. The challenge is onerous. Changing organizations with changing strategies, structures and people in a hypercompetitive global environment are but a handful of the new demands placed on managers at all levels.

To the experienced practitioner, this is nothing new. To the neophyte, student or sometime observer, Peggy Lee's song *"Is That All There Is?"* might be apropos. Each is partially correct.

From the beginning, and the beginning was really long ago, management has been viewed as a process where goals are attained through the efforts of other human beings. The process itself is made up of functions traditionally categorized as planning, organizing, motivating and controlling. The person who wears the mantle of administrative leadership should master the above and do his or her best to get lucky along the way. Usually, luck often accompanies proficiency, while knowledge, hard work and a penchant for chipping away appear to provide a sturdy foundation for organizations capable of converting the impossible into the ordinary.

More than ever before, today's winning manager must serve as the maestro coordinating the organization's strategy, structure and people like a great orchestra conductor. Production, finance, marketing and human resources must complement each other like the woodwinds, percussion and brass in pursuit of a great symphony. The winners: the consuming public. It can be a winning scenario for all, but the burden is on management to make the system work.

Organizations tend to be more similar than dissimilar. Likewise, managers often exhibit behaviors and styles that make classification a relatively simple matter. For example, who has not experienced the rainmaker? Typically, the rainmaker generates thunder and lighting — and everyone gets soaked. Other than this, not much happens in terms of tangible results or progress toward pre-determined goals. Rainmakers rarely provide umbrellas but almost always generate an adverse climate where even potential winners become certain losers. Further, since the rainmaker rarely sows the seed needed for individual and organizational growth and development, what emerges after the rain would often be better buried.

Management by intimidation will not work in today's workplace. Management by fear, innuendo or threats will result in short-term gains and long-term disaster. Rainmakers *will* rain on your parade if given half a chance, and the resulting lack of commitment and loyalty can be devastating even for the hardiest of organizations.

Many years ago, a management expert suggested that the role of a catalyst is a luxury that can no longer be afforded. Yet, we've often been urged to function as catalysts by commencement speakers, motivational experts and the like.

Generally speaking, as a catalyst you may alter the behaviors of others without changing your own actions. No wonder so many aspire to be catalysts. To be creatively competitive, you might very well affect and alter the behaviors of others, but in doing so, be prepared to change your own modus operandi. Changemaker managers understand this concept and view change as essential — as basic as eating or breathing. Improvement through consciously developed consensus stamps the changemaker as a winner and his or her organization as profitable and effective.

Who doesn't love a parade? Parade-watching can be exciting, enjoyable and entertaining. With a seat in the first row, it can be downright thrilling. However, put a parade-watcher in charge and the result is a spectacle of another variety. Clinging to the past and present, the only movement emanating from the parade-watcher is one of treading water. Generally, the parade-watcher is so busy staying afloat or making time that he or she neglects what must be done — and sooner than one might imagine, the organization becomes an artifact and the parade-watcher a fossil.

John Sherman, previously a megacommercial developer in Kentucky and, more recently, mayor of upscale Bal Harbour, Florida, was sick and tired of too many parade-watchers and not enough changemakers, of too much mouth and not enough movement. Specifically, Sherman ws troubled by the moribund response to helping bright, deserving but underfinanced kids go to college. His answer: a special scholarship endowment fund, seeded with his own capital, to guarantee financial support to outstanding graduates of elementary schools upon successful completion of high school five years later. The incentive had to be provided early in the process. Sherman, counting the number of parade-watchers, assumed the role of drum major, of changemaker, and got the parade moving.

Change can be managed only when management has the desire and willingness to do what must be done. When management works in concert with a strategy, structure and its people, the great things will inevitably happen.

Samuel H. Turner

Samuel H. Turner joined the Life Insurance Company of Virginia in Richmond as president and chief executive officer in 1980. Previously, Turner had been a principal and member of the board of directors of Tillinghast, Nelson and Warren, Inc., an international insurance and actuarial consulting firm. A native of Atlanta, Georgia, Turner received his bachelor's and master's degrees from Georgia State University.

Quest for Survival: Essentials for Being There

By almost any measure, the last five years had been successful. Strategies developed and executed had worked. Momentum had been generated. A sense of urgency had emerged. Yet, there was the stark reality that the "competitive race" is one which has no finish line. There was no comfort in assuming that current strategies would continue to work. Too many things seemed to have changed and be changing. It was time for reassessment of direction and strategies.

With that shared conclusion by our management team, the issue was then one of how to go about it. I'd felt uncomfortable relying on elaborate strategic and business planning processes ever since I spent a few years with ITT in the early 1970s and saw the planning process totally consume substance. So we decided to concentrate on thinking. Our consultant (Having been a consultant, I had nothing against consultants!) had provided a valuable academic and practical framework for our discussions and artfully guided us with "lecturettes" and penetrating questions. We'd been at it for several days, and it had all been enlightening, maybe even fun. Then he put the big one on the table — "Where do you want this company to be five years, ten years, from now?" The least he could have done was be specific on the date! No fuzzy answers were acceptable. He wanted us to come up with something we could go public with as a vision statement of sorts.

How in the hell are you supposed to answer that sort of question, when no one could begin to describe (at least in a way anybody would believe) what our future operating environment would look like five or ten years out? Would interest rates be 6 percent or 16 percent, stable or volatile? Would tax laws change as much over the next five years as the last five years (and in our business, those changes were like showing up to play the game and finding out somebody had changed the rules)? Would "playing fields" really be level, or just unlevel in a different way? In what we suspected would be a period of intense price competition, would a major competitor take pricing to an irrational level? Reality then struck. No one had faced a more uncertain, threatening future.

Where did we want to be? The honest answer was that we wanted to be there, you know, really . . . *be* there! Even though we meant more than mere existence and sought to be there as a strong, viable and decisive competitor, it was still not the sort of statement that motivates employees. It nevertheless provided a sufficient challenge for us given the future we faced. So that's the issue I would like to address — the quest for survival, or essentials for "being there."

Change for change's sake. If the perception of future operating environment is dominated by uncertainty and the likelihood of change, perhaps radical change, it seemed obvious that companies will also have to be prepared to change, dramatically at times, if they are going to "be there." Because any change initiative creates anxiety, if not resistance, within an organization, we were seemingly faced with quite a management challenge — how do we create an organization, a collective of individuals, which is comfortable with change?

We could never come up with a better answer to that question than this one — you change, then change again, then change again, and then change again. Comfort with change could be realized only by having experienced it and survived it. The thesis was that anxiety created by change would reach successively lower levels of intensity with each round of change experienced. We couldn't eliminate anxiety, but we believed we could lessen it and shorten it. We couldn't eliminate casualties, but we could reduce them.

As a management team, we endorsed change for change's sake. Internally induced change was controllable; externally induced was not. Without preconditioning to change, the enterprise exposure to risk of change would be unacceptably high. So we set about to create change, almost constant change, as a form of organizational conditioning. For example, we probably haven't gone more than twelve or so months without significant structural changes to the organization. And there have been other self-inflicted changes. And, yes, when externally driven changes have occurred, we believe we've responded to them a lot more positively and effectively, and with many fewer casualties, than would have otherwise been the case.

Change for change's sake . . . one of the essentials for "being there."

Small is beautiful. It was an exciting, almost electric atmosphere. There was an observable intensity, but employees appeared actually to enjoy what they were doing. There was an air of camaraderie. They seemed to share a commitment and identity of purpose. Perhaps it was a small company or an office or smaller division in a larger company.

Most managers have felt or observed the kind of work environment just described. It's one in which the seemingly impossible becomes possible, and ordinary people do extraordinary things. In a sense, it is enterprise in its highest form. But it has repeatedly proven difficult (if not definitively impossible) to achieve within a massive structure on a top-down basis.

Most managers would like to have the kind of atmosphere described. We did. But more than "like to have," we had to have it if we were going to be an effective competitor. How does one turn large into small? We sought to keep the organization broken up into smaller units than had existed previously. That structural positioning, alone, wasn't sufficient to be sure, but it was, we thought, necessary. Not only did it facilitate development of a "small is beautiful" work environment; it also provided the degree of structural flexibility essential for organizational responsiveness to change.

Small is beautiful . . . . another essential for "being there."

Pressure release valves. Time is of the essence. Something has happened, an opportunity or threat has emerged. The company must be repositioned, and fast. Many managers have faced this sort of circumstance. We did. We had to reposition the company, establish a new momentum, and fast. But we sure as hell couldn't afford to let the wheels run off the wagon just as we got it rolling. The first time we had to go through this, we were lucky in one respect — the ex-CEO was still accessible — (ex-CEOs are useful at times, especially if they are on your side). Because people were likely to turn to him anyway and tell him how the new management team was screwing things up and because he was on our side, he was positioned as a "monitor." He, better than almost anyone within the organization, could assess individual and collective inputs (*e.g.*, "Oh that's just Joe, he always complains"). Then it finally happened. The whistle went off. The structure was vibrating; the wheels were about to go. What to do?

We did what any good management team would do in the circumstances: we backed off to let things settle down. But we could afford that for only a short while. Backing off was neither a permanent solution nor one we wished to resort to in the future. Then the notion of "pressure relief valves" struck us, and they have since become a part of our culture.

Pressure relief valves have been those sometimes crazy things done to keep it all Fun (spelled with a big *F*), things such as "Dress-a-Banana" Day; "Dress Down from the Waist Up" Day; shutting down an hour or so early and going out on the lawn for beer, popcorn, corn dogs and music; "Fifties" Day with free hot dogs and Cokes at lunch. The list is almost endless. We also added a fitness center and have, because of an enthusiastic (if not zealous) director, maintained about 20 percent of the employee population involved in its activities. Not only have all of these things acted to keep the pressure tolerable, but they also fit right in with the kind of work environment that we wanted to develop.

Pressure release valves . . . another essential for "being there."

Organization is not a matter of preference. Organization structure either enables and reinforces strategy, or it inhibits and obstructs strategy. It's next to impossible for a tightly controlled, highly centralized, bureaucratic organization effectively to survive new opportunity-driven activities. That requires flexibility and speed. On the other hand, it's next to impossible for a loosely controlled, highly decentralized, entrepreneurial organization effectively to pursue activities requiring total operational focus and maximum efficiency. One thing seems clear — there is an inextricable linkage between structure and strategy. This would suggest that organization structure is, therefore, dynamic. For each structure, there is a time and place.

With such a perspective, it has been particularly amusing, if not disappointing, to observe so many instances in practice where organization structure clearly appears to be more reflective of the CEO's personality or personal preference than strategic design. Some CEOs have even said it, *e.g.*, "I believe in a highly decentralized . . ." When the day comes in such companies for a significant shift in strategies, organization structure may end up being a major impediment to survival.

Organization structure is, to a large degree, a function of strategy; it is dynamic and interactive. We've tried to maintain an organization structure that is consistent with prevailing strategies.

Organization is not a matter of preference . . . . another essential for "being there."

Hustle as strategy. Winning strategies in business essentially deal with the way a company seeks to gain and hold some sort of meaningful advantage against other players in the game, their competitors. There are obviously quite a number of ways to gain a competitive advantage, but some advantages are harder to gain than others and some are harder to hold. There are also some which the marketplace does not highly value; therefore, they are not meaningful. The "right" ones are obviously unique to each industry and company for each set of circumstances and each set of customer/buyer preferences.

Within various industry segments of what I refer to as the financial services sector (comprised of banks, life insurance companies, stockbrokerage firms and the like), sustainable advantages in product are almost nonexistent. And product life cycles have shortened dramatically. For example, in each of the last six years in our company, something like 65 percent to 75 percent of sales have been on products introduced in that or the previous calendar year.

Advantages in service are not likely to be of meaningful value at the customer level, at least within a wide range of tolerable service levels. Advantages in distribution, although perhaps historically meaningful, have eroded and continue to erode due to lack of channel control (*e.g.*, mobility of sales forces) and/or ease of duplication.

Further, there appear to be no significant barriers today between various industry segments of the financial services sector. For example, stockbrokerage firms can and do own insurance companies and non-bank banks, banks are selling mutual funds and all forms of insurance — regulations or not, insurance companies own stockbrokerage firms and/or non-bank banks, etc. This creates an environment in which individual industry segments are characterized by relative ease of entry.

The environment described is substantially reflective of that within which we have had to operate. In that sort of environment and against competitors who were often a multiple of our size, we

Samuel H. Turner 199

have had to be aggressive and fast. A few years ago, a consultant even described our dominant strength as speed.

Although aggressiveness and speed were judged by us to be essential, we had — until recently — classified such attributes as matters of style, not strategy. In late 1986, we were tempted to change our classification. Specifically, it was an article by Amar Bhide in the September-October 1986 issue of *Harvard Business Review* that created this temptation. In this article, entitled "Hustle as Strategy," he says:

> Businesses characterized by ease of entry, fast action and service intensity (such as those comprising the financial services sector) are like poker, not chess. . . . you play each hand as it is dealt and quickly vary tactics to suit conditions. The way a firm hustles . . . [and] takes advantage of transitory opportunities makes a real difference in how consistently it wins.

Hustle as strategy . . . another essential for "being there."

The supreme calling for any management is the survival of the enterprise it directs, and from that calling emerges the "quest for survival." Not surprisingly, the conscious risk tolerance of most managers falls short of any life-threatening risk to the enterprise. There is certainly no peer reinforcement for managers who are willing to "bet the company."

Yet, enterprises do die! They are acquired and sold off in pieces. They find themselves trapped in obsolescence or strapped with unsupportable cost structures. They get caught going left when their industry or market (their operating environment) is going right. Some die slowly; some suddenly. In all ways and times, enterprises die — and often at the hands of well-intentioned management.

The particular cause of death which is of concern here — and one which I suspect is a leading cause of enterprise mortality — is incongruence between an enterprise and the environment within which it operates. Maintaining that congruence represents the foundation of strategic management.

Against this background, I will conclude with an analogy. Within *natural* ecological systems, organisms must meet their environment's conditions for existence in order to survive and prosper; they must adapt and conform to their environment or they perish. Further, to adapt and conform, to achieve congruence, an organism must cope not only with the physical aspects of its environment but also with other environmental factors such as competitors, predators and the escape tactics of its prey. Finally, because environments are dynamic and change, an organism must — within its capability to do so — also change to maintain congruence.

The notion suggested here is that these fundamental tenants are equally true within an ecological system comprised of enterprise structures (business organisms), business sectors or industries (species) and their operating environments. This essay has addressed some of the essentials for improving an enterprise's continuing capability to adapt and conform to a turbulent and threatening operating environment.

4

THE
SIMPLE
THINGS

The Yellow Brick Road

You can't do it with mirrors, bells, whistles or sleight of hand. At least, you can't on a long-run basis. Eventually, you'll either have to step in front of the curtain or, for one reason or another, the curtain will open.

Remember the Wizard of Oz? A sometimes well-motivated person with a penchant for the peculiar. Behind the glitz, an ordinary sort who probably would have benefited more from a good public-speaking course than audio-visual effects. Sending Dorothy to do the hard stuff (and then failing to deliver) shot the Wiz's credibility but did a world of good for Dorothy and her pals. Now, if you adopt an "All's well that ends well" perspective, you might condone the Wizard's behavior, but with Dorothy and company, it could just as easily have gone the other way — and, in real life, it often does.

In the 1970s, Trammell Crow Company could have gone the other way. Up to its developments in debt, the eyes of Texas were looking askance. Trammell Crow hung in, and the resulting success story is an example of stepping out from behind the curtain, putting the gloves on and saying to Dorothy: "You want to go to Kansas? I'll take you."

Septuagenarian Crow has built an organization that has a top-to-bottom, inside-out belief in ownership. About one out of every ten MBAs interviewed by Crow each year is invited to join the team. Their reward? In most cases, a generous salary and a piece of the action — specifically, a limited equity share in various Crow projects. Crow has effectively built his own yellow brick road that follows a rough and arduous path, inhabited by lions, tigers, bears — and lots of perks for those who make the grade.

Management is a reflective process. Subordinates tend to behave the way they think their superiors expect them to behave. With a manager who is a solid, visible role model, good things can occur: productivity, quality, commitment, a willingness to do whatever has to be done. Subordinates identify with this type of person, and winning becomes an organizational way of life.

Conversely, management by word, not reinforced by behavior, can result in lowered productivity, quality by accident, commitment to self only and a keyhole view of one's role, resulting in "It's-not-my-job"-type thinking. Hence, it takes only role models in key positions to generate a good-things-are-happening climate. Unlike the Wizard, those role models must be where things are produced or where customers are served. Being behind the scenes simply won't create the magic, and even effective delegation has limits.

Let's talk chicken. Salisbury, Maryland, is a great place to do just that; you see, this lovely community situated on the eastern shore, just minutes from the tumult and crowds in Ocean City, is headquarters of Perdue Farms, the parent of Perdue Chickens. The beautiful landscape of the Delmarva Peninsula is not marred by a glistening, towering headquarters building. In fact, it isn't disturbed by a glistening, compact central office. The headquarters of Perdue Farms is more nondescript than the convenience stores in Bel Air.

This simple, two-story structure surrounded by coops filled with fat chickens is the nerve center of one of the most aggressive, exciting "high-tech" agribusinesses in the world. New research labs brag about "low-fat" chickens and genetic engineering. The catalyst for this energetic, enthusiastic group that commands 30-plus percent of the industry is Frank Perdue. Simply, Perdue loves chickens. So, too, does company president and CEO Don Mabe. As a matter of fact, everyone at Perdue loves chickens. What we see at Perdue is management by word and by deed, by rhetoric and by substance.

When everyone in an organization is committed to quality in product and performance, the work force becomes the greatest marketing power imaginable. People love Perdue, and Perdue people love Perdue Chickens. What a wonderful place to watch.

Few would quarrel with the importance of understanding the big picture or how all the various pieces fit. Before attempting to put a puzzle together, it is usually helpful to look at the picture on the box so that you know you're assembling the Statue of Liberty, not Mt. McKinley.

In providing organizational leadership, knowing how the pieces fit is essential, and demonstrating a willingness to assist in putting them together can often add the magic of role-model motivation.

Knowing how the pieces fit and demonstrating a commitment to building a better puzzle is not solely in the province of mainstream management. Take Huntsville, Alabama, as an example. This city, which prefers to be identified with the Tennessee Valley, has become one of the greatest new-venture and high-tech incubators in the western world. The City of Huntsville has done everything possible to accommodate and attract prospective businesses. The city fathers of Huntsville U.S.A. (the preferred nomenclature) have constructed a better puzzle, and everyone in Huntsville is motivated to sell it. In recent years, more than $600 million in federal research monies has poured into Huntsville. The NASA Space Camp has captured the imagination of young and old alike. The symphony, ballet and museum are all part of the grand plan to entice and solidify deal after deal. Magic is indeed taking place in Huntsville, and this act uses no mirrors.

Real charisma is durable. It holds up under pressure and inspires people to live up to their potentials and to exceed their own perceived expectations. Real charisma can transform a collection of individuals into a powerful, goal-attaining unit. Real charisma may even be learned by observing and emulating. We are not describing brainless, follow-the-leader patter, but a careful analysis of, for example, what makes the Lee Iacoccas of the world tick. In essence, real charisma generates real results. You can't do this with mirrors.

Victor Kiam does not believe in mirrors. Everybody knows what Kiam has done for Remington. Kiam took a moribund electric-shaver manufacturing company that had lost thirty million dollars during the five-year period prior to takeover, shook it up, dazzled it and managed it to the point that saw 1985 sales hit $160 million and Remington capture between 40 and 50 percent of the market. Kiam's book, *Going For It! How To Succeed As An Entrepreneur*, is a series of personal revelations on ingredients for success. More importantly, Kiam has invested more than four million dollars of his own money to promote his gospel. This is what great management is all about. The bells and whistles have been replaced by hard work, dedication and unwavering commitment. This is the Great American Dream.

In this sequel, Oz makes a great comeback. The curtain has lifted, and Oz has become a true wizard. Through inspiration, motivation and a great deal of perspiration, the entire organization is now squarely secured on the yellow brick road. All special effects aside, what has transformed this organization is a commitment to building an entity full of role models dedicated to nothing short of ultimate victory over the next wicked witch.

The Power of Pride

Hello, John. One moment, Bill. Can you hold, Jane? I'll see if I can locate him, Alex.

The overfamiliarity of greetings in all too many organizations has reached epidemic proportions. Today, telephone operators, receptionists and customer-service representatives across the corporate community express a familiarity with customers that makes the meek blush and the bold bluster.

Customer calls the Acme Company and asks: "May I please speak to Ms. Davidoff?" Receptionist responds: "Who may I say is calling?" Caller replies: "George Clark." Operator answers, "George, I'll see if I can locate her." George retorts: "Are we related?"

Now, George is a nice name. As a matter of fact, as names go, it ranks right up there with the nicest. But what bothered George bothers all too many today. The receptionist, who meant well, doesn't know George, never has known George and may never have the pleasure of meeting him. To wit, the Georges of the world should be *Mr. Clark* — no questions asked, no familiarity intended. Pride is at stake. Those receptionists, operators, customer-service representatives and others on the first-line contact crew make the critical — and maybe the final — impression with current and prospective customers. All of those people wear the Acme Company name emblazoned on their outfits. Regardless of whom George intended to call, he got an individual who expressed pride and concern in a way that would encourage many customers to run and hide. Pride, the reflection of company culture and care, expresses itself in many ways. But whether George was a butcher, a baker or a broker is of no concern. George was a prospective customer deserving better — and in most instances settling for much less. Pride should permeate the organization, and customers in this hypercompetitive business climate of ours will, in the long run, settle for no less.

A casual and admittedly personal study has indicated a high degree of correlation between the first-name opening and the no-problem response. If you get either one, proceed with caution. While some contend "first-naming" customers or potential customers is simply a friendly approach, others consider it rude and offensive, preferring top-notch service to one more pal. Nothing builds customer loyalty and friendship quicker than extraordinary service. Of course, extraordinary service is generally a characteristic of people and organizations that do it right the very first time. This builds legitimate pride, and in this there is power.

Although the sample is limited, the no-problem reaction usually heralds an approach that ranges from apathy to incompetence. Specifically, it often signifies that while it is no problem for the person making the statement, the individual requesting assistance is in deep trouble. It is the old mind-over-matter relationship, where "I don't mind, and you don't matter." Hence, no problem!

St. Marys, Georgia, is perhaps an unlikely place to look for a bastion of corporate pride. But that's because you might have overlooked Gilman Paper Company. Whether you're munching on muffins in Macon, dining on doughnuts in Detroit or chewing on croissants in Charlotte, there is a possibility they were delivered to you in a paper bag manufactured by Gilman. As you finish your muffin, you might notice that the bag has inscribed on its bottom, "A Quality Product by Ronnie O'Quinn and Crew 61." O'Quinn and his crew put their mark, their signature, on every bag and sack they produce. More importantly, what they are in fact communicating is a sense of pride and concern, not for your muffin or croissant but for you as a customer. O'Quinn and Crew wear the Gilman Paper Company name with pride.

The health care industry is slugging it out for our business. Too many hospital beds in some cities, too many physicians in others, make for a demanding demonstration of private enterprise at work. Recently, a newcomer to South Florida needed some minor surgery. Not knowing who or where to call, he contacted the Physician Referral Service at South Miami Hospital. He was in luck. Not only was the surgeon he visited a first-class professional, but the referral service at South Miami also called back three weeks later to see how he was doing and to inquire as to whether he was satisfied with the service. We're not talking about a brake job here. This is a medical service that reflected a special kind of pride and concern that will ensure the vitality and growth of a special kind of hospital. The lesson: You can win and win again.

Emphasizing customer service, Portland, Oregon-based Fred Meyer has emerged as a formidable retail operation. Established in 1922, Fred Meyer's customer-service policies have remained constant. Specifically, "Always give the customer Quality, Value, Selection and Service" and "If any customer is ever dissatisfied with any product we have sold, they are welcome to return it, or the unused portion, and we will gladly replace it with a comparable item or return their money." Now, that is a legitimate approach.

Cy Green, president of Fred Meyer, observed that "We need to continue to change and offer better service and prices and merchandise to customers. What we do today will have to be better tomorrow." Green's statement, coupled with the founder's customer-service policies, is the foundation for the basics of good business, legitimate pride and profits for all.

Richard A. Henson

Henson Aviation was founded by Richard A. Henson, an aviation pioneer and Fairchild Aircraft test pilot, in 1931. His company has become one of the nation's foremost regional airlines, and Henson has been a leader in the concept of the commuter airline industry. Now affiliated with Piedmont Airlines, Henson's company employs more than one thousand people and has annual revenues of approximately one-hundred million dollars.

On Time Means On Time: The Importance of Detail

Management's biggest weakness today is in leadership. Top management can be passive or active, and I see too much passive management today. Instead of active, "digging-down-deep-and-looking-under-the-cover" top management, I look at our industry and see weaknesses everywhere. Somehow, we have to convince the new breed that entering the world of work with a college degree doesn't give you the license to sit up in an office and expect that fellow under you to do everything without your being involved. What I see going on in today's world, compared with the world that my generation initiated and made happen, matured in, is dreadful. Managers today don't make it happen the way they should, and that's my biggest problem. I'm chairman now, a role I think it proper that I move into, but I find myself day-to-day, out of necessity, getting involved in details.

All major carriers have a fifteen minute grace period within which they claim you're not late; as long as you're within that fifteen-minute window, you're on time. That's horribly wrong. I boarded a major airline twice in the last week. Twelve minutes after departure time, we were still sitting on the ground. I said, "I wonder what they're fooling around about?" Here was a ramp agent in coveralls up at the galley, filling out a form, *leisurely*. They pushed back just within the fifteen-minute time period. They won't report that flight as late, but if such minor delays accumulate on down the line, you've got problems.

We put in a competitive program in all of the thirty-six cities we serve. *One minute* off of that gate is late, and the staff reports the one minute delay. Why do the major carriers have a fifteen-minute grace period? That's crazy! Either you're late or you're on time. We're going to give two plaques every six months — one for the station with the best on-time performance and another to the runner-up. We have an on-time competition going on while our parent company, Piedmont Airlines, gives fifteen minutes — that's where they're wrong. This is detail, and they aren't attending to it.

The total comes from the little things. I have a brigadier general as president and a Navy commander as vice-president; everybody in management is a college graduate except me. I think managers today do need this formal education. But perhaps we should all stress our ideas more than our backgrounds. Don't lose the common touch. Don't lose the common sense approach to problems. If you put those two factors together, boy, do you have a winner! The employee with both is going right to the top. I wish I could find a fellow that had education and common sense both. Son of a gun, he'd go up in our company so fast. I'm looking for him.

My management style is contrary to what the airline industry looks for. As a matter of fact, I have been soundly criticized by Piedmont. When I was out to select a president, I rejected a good many Piedmont sent to me, so many they finally said Jesus Christ himself wouldn't please me! I can delegate responsibility, but when the outcome does not meet the standards that I set, I get back into detail again.

Seeking, Succeeding—and Listening

At a time when many detractors were loudly proclaiming to the world at large that someone, somewhere, atop some grand tower in Atlanta had erred, the Coca-Cola Company responded with a swiftness and a completeness that not only demonstrated profound respect for the market place with the reintroduction of Classic Coke but also garnered so much praise for roughriding CEO Roberto Goizueta that accolades for his innovation, creativity and action became legion.

After all, the winning process of see, seek and succeed is not necessarily a linear one. In Coke's case, great fortunes had been spent on market research which unequivocally argued that the new was better than the old. Indeed, numerous blind taste tests seemed to bear this out. However, there was a greater force at work. A force that all too many market researchers ignore. A force that few textbooks effectively identify and examine. A force that in all too many organizations today has become more myth than reality, more fiction than fact. The force is the simplest and at times the most elusive. The force is, quite simply, what people want, no more, no less.

As far as Coke is concerned, what the customer longed for was not a soft drink in a bottle; it was a slice of history, of Americana, of something stable and precious. In this instance, the customer, not the Coke, was king. And guess what? This is the only true "formula" for long-term success.

We have for many years probed the importance of listening with "three" ears. With ear one, you listen to what people are saying (this is easy). With ear two, you listen to what people are not saying (this is a little more difficult). And with ear number three you listen to what people *want* to say but just don't know how to (this is the most difficult form of listening). In effect, when you throw a party, you want people to show up. When you introduce a product or a service, you want people to buy. If you don't listen with three ears, people will show but not stay. People may buy, but not twice. Stroking, grooming and cultivating customers is a timely, taxing process. Straining to listen with that third ear can be tiring. Not straining can be deadly.

At a Cuban restaurant situated in Miami's exotic Little Havana section, the owners have learned to listen with three ears. Following a grand feast, a customer, on the way out, decided to take one more longing glance at the dessert table. He stood and stared (and maybe drooled) over a kiwi fruit cheesecake. The proprietor literally rushed over, cut a piece of the cake, handed it to the customer and simply said: "For you." The customer walked away truly satisfied, truly pleased, and with cake in hand. Everyone was a winner.

Some may remember a commercial produced by GTE/Sprint which claimed that the company spent one billion dollars in 1985 for new technology. That was impressive. What is even more impressive and, indeed, much more important is the claim made by GTE that in that year, the company spent five hundred dollars (on the average) for each and every Sprint customer. That new line in Dubuque, the new switching box in Tempe and the new electrical work in Wellesley were not for the company. They were for you. And that's the way it should be.

Regardless of the organization, regardless of the size, companies remain in business and prosper because of a unique ability to listen with three ears — no matter what the product or service.

Nick Fiorello, for example, is a relatively young man who came to the United States from the old country. Mr. Fiorello, who works for Brooks Brothers in Atlanta, knows fabric and style, but, more importantly, he knows people. His understanding of each is such that customers become friends who in turn recommend, without reservation, other friends who become customers. Fiorello sees, seeks and succeeds because he listens with all his ears. There is no surer way to prosper, regardless of your position or job description.

In 1985, *Industry Week* featured a report conducted by the renowned management recruitment firm, Robert Half. The article reviewed a survey of 320 U.S. executives. These managers esti- mated that their employees "stole" an average of four hours and twenty-two minutes a week by getting to work late, leaving work early, socializing, making personal telephone calls and conducting personal business on company time. The study concluded that all too many employees don't care about the company, so why should the company care about them? That's an horrendously expensive cycle. You see, listening with three ears involves the cultivation of customers and the examination of employees. When you throw a party, you want guests and hosts. If you don't listen, you get neither.

Interestingly enough, the so-called "little things" have done in more than one business. While the big ones monopolize your thought and time, the little ones sneak up and wipe you out.

A few weeks ago, two business people scheduled a 7 A.M. breakfast meeting. Right after they placed their orders, a restaurant employee decided to (or was told to) vacuum the carpet. The carpet got cleaned, the noise was unbearable and the meeting a waste, and two more paying customers decided to take their money to quieter environs. Incidentally, when it was suggested that this general cleaning might best be accomplished after the restaurant closed or before it opened, the manager responded by saying "that just isn't a convenient arrangement."

A sound operational principle might be that convenience should best be viewed through the eyes of the customer. Too often, as we have previously indicated, the customer is treated in a mind-over-matter fashion: the employee doesn't mind, and the customer doesn't matter. When this is the case, the employee is often treating the customer the way the organization is treating the employee. Again, organizational effectiveness is a top-to-bottom, inside-out situation.

Customer sensitivity is a matter that embraces all organizations dealing with external publics. Schools, governmental agencies, hospitals and religious institutions, to cite just a few, have customers and constituencies who must and should be served. Therefore, hosting a party and having no one show up is definitely not just a private-sector concern. More than one public or not-for-profit entity has recognized this the hard way: playing to an empty house just isn't much fun.

On Promises Kept and Deadlines Met

It was a 7 A.M. undergraduate course in management. For almost all of the students, it was their first exposure to the subject. The professor, in explaining his expectations, indicated that the class would begin at 7 A.M. sharp, and tardy students would not be allowed to enter. He further explained that he would repeat this announcement for three straight classes, giving each student an opportunity to weather the shock, adjust or simply make other arrangements. In presenting his rationale, the professor stated the class would be studying management, and managers should not expect others to do what they won't or can't do themselves. Simply stated, the manager is a role model whose behavior is watched and often emulated. The manager should lead by deed.

To many of the students, the on-time or no-admittance policy was perceived as being unfair, improper, un-American or just plain crazy. Some indicated they lived long distances from campus. The professor suggested they leave home earlier. Others stated they were working or had families with whom to contend. This generated even less sympathy, since the average age of the undergraduate student in the class was twenty-eight, and 85 percent worked either full- or part-time.

Still, a few felt compelled to test the on-time or no-admittance policy and were left out, looking in. Some of the younger students had parents call the professor to find out why, if they were paying tuition, their children couldn't enter class whenever they arrived. To these parents, the professor explained not only the nature of the course but also his desire to make certain their children developed a winning and responsible habit. Not one parent contested the policy after that explanation.

Actually, after the first three warnings, not only was tardiness *not* a problem, but attendance was unusually high and very few students dropped the class.

Now, the real shock was the view expressed by many of the students that this was the very first time they were ever held accountable in this fashion. Remember, 85 percent were employed, yet promises-kept-and-deadlines-met behavior was initially considered off-the-wall, out-of-this-world. However, once they understood the rationale, virtually all students showed up and succeeded — further demonstrating that most of us do exactly what we want to do, have time for those things we want to have time for and remember what we truly consider to be important. Of course, there are factors we can't control. Happily, they seldom affect productivity, quality and attitudinal issues. When they do, folks are generally both sympathetic and empathetic.

"The problem is lack of communication." In classroom-case analysis and in the "real" world, lack of communication is cited as the villain more often than any other factor. In reality, lack of communication is more often symptomatic of factors deeply (and sometimes not so deeply) buried in the organization.

Dr. Keith Davis, a legendary communication guru, argues that one of the greatest obstacles to effective communication is our gross inability to listen, to stop talking. Our commitment to effective communication must start with a belief, from the highest levels of the organization, that customers, employees and suppliers have valuable insights to offer. Davis argues that nature gave people two ears, but only one tongue — a gentle hint that we should listen more than we talk. The listening is a reflection that the people within the firm care about you and your ideas or concerns. In a similar vein, tardiness (or the repair person who promises but doesn't appear) is often merely a symptom of something else. The something else may be rooted in either the organization or the individual. Whichever, the results are the same — the alienation of some other human being and the resulting loss of sales.

The failure to show is symptomatic of the belief that you don't matter. Failing to show or showing up late is a reflection of an ethos, a belief that the company doesn't care.

Domino's Pizza has revolutionized the food-delivery business by simply committing itself to the philosophy that each and every customer, regardless of position, status or standing, will receive his or her pizza within thirty minutes . . . . guaranteed. This simple policy communicates to the public at large that each individual order, with or without anchovies, is important to the health and welfare of the company. This two-way communication sends an important message to everyone coming in contact with the organization: the company listens to its customers.

Outstanding service is no fad, nor is it an accident. Underlying technological advancement, innovation or the most carefully conceived and crafted corporate strategy must be the realization that the raison d'être is quality in product and service. Through this realization, profits, the manna of private enterprise, are generated, profits for the organization, its owners and staff, and profits for consumers who are pleased.

One of the truly all-American, gold-medal-winning examples of the belief in product and service is exemplified by a grocery chain founded in Richmond, Virginia, a half-century ago. Ukrop's Super Markets, the $250 million, nineteen-store chain, has a lock on the hypercompetitive grocery market in Richmond. Customers love the stores, employees love to go to work, and Joe Ukrop, the founder and chairman, still walks the aisles. President Jim Ukrop claims that besides great produce, spotless aprons and niceties throughout, the company takes care of its customers and employees and is fair with its vendors. These simple ethics are fortified by an unusual, unwavering commitment by the Ukrops to remain closed on Sundays and to sell no beer or wine.

And performance, the bottom line? In the last four years, company revenues have increased more than 40 percent, while the company's market share now exceeds 25 percent. Profits for all. Everyone has fun. The system really works.

Too many see technology, innovation and location as a killer cluster, poised to devastate competition. Be assured, if the cluster is not built on quality, at best the edge will be short-lived.

A financial institution had all the right tools. It had researched investment instruments thoroughly. Competitors' products had been exhaustively reviewed and an innovative investment certificate was ultimately developed. A slick marketing campaign was planned with a high-flying Madison Avenue firm to tout the merits of this option to prospective customers. The stage was set, and management sat back to reap the inevitable rewards.

The problem? No one on the front lines of the organization, no one dealing with the consuming public had been given one bit of insight into the product. No one on those most important front lines had been trained in the care and feeding of prospective customers in the use of this innovative investment product. The result: a mob scene in many branches the day after the ad campaign started and only a handful of employees who knew more than the prospective customers. The killer cluster strikes again. Great technology, innovation and location built on form, not function. Another great idea bites the dust.

Another example, the flip side: Oil-changing, a single service in a multi-billion-dollar industry. Every automobile needs one, lots of people do it themselves — but no single company had a grip on the industry until Jiffy Lube cornered the market on fluid maintenance. This simple idea, backed by a commitment to quality and service (including vacuuming interiors) has helped this company open almost nine hundred units worldwide and grow at an annual rate of 70 percent over the last several years. In responding to Jiffy Lube's competitive reaction to Texaco and Exxon's entry into the market, founder W. J. Hindman says that if you have a quality product, quality service and quality people serving as the eyes and ears of Jiffy Lube in the community, you grow a winner. No dogs, no ponies, just a stock selling for more than fifty times earnings. Why worry about competition under these circumstances?

There is no escaping the fact that quality is a consciously developed attribute. It is never the permanent possession of any organization, but must be constantly and continually earned.

While many portend rough times for the fast-food industry in the near future, the business continues to prosper. In aspiring towards a corporate goal of more than twelve thousand stores worldwide by 1992, McDonald's retains a dedication to simple family values that has enabled it to dominate the industry for more than three decades. The company's vice president for individuality promotes the belief, in this four-billion-dollar enterprise, that what really counts is the interface between buyer and seller at each and every counter system-wide. The level of commitment to quality at McDonald's is reflective of a culture built one-by-one on individual employees. McDonald's knows what it took to get where it is and will not relinquish the basic tenet that its success was built on promises kept and deadlines met.

Today's best can very quickly become an also-ran the very instant the best forgets how it got that way. There isn't enough space to list the "invincibles" of yesterday that are barely remembered today simply because of a failure to understand that being the best necessitates both a conscious approach to excellence and a never-ending search to do things better. This requires leadership which recognizes that change *is* the status quo.

Harold V. Haverty

In 1954 Harold V. Haverty began his career with Deluxe Checks. He was named plant manager in 1963 and regional manager in 1966. He was appointed vice-president in 1969 and was elected to the board of directors in 1970. Haverty moved to St. Paul in 1971 to join the corporate administration staff as vice-president-general manager. He became executive vice-president and chief operating officer in 1976, and president and chief operating officer in 1983. He was elected chief executive officer in May of 1986.

The Two-Box System and Other Details That Produce Quality

Founded in 1915, Deluxe Check Printers, Inc., is a leader in the U.S. payment systems market. Within this market, Deluxe has four primary businesses. The first is printing checks and related transaction forms for financial institutions. As the company's core business, printing checks and related transaction forms accounted for 86 percent of Deluxe's 1986 sales. Deluxe's share of this $1.5 billion market exceeds 50 percent. The company's second area of business is electronic funds transfer (EFT). Deluxe supplies software and processing services for automated teller machine (ATM) and point-of-sale equipment. The third area of business for Deluxe is business systems — record-keeping systems for small businesses and medical and dental practices. This area includes short-run computer forms, pegboard accounting systems, unit sets, medical and dental forms and other business forms. The fourth and final area of Deluxe's business is identification systems. In the new-accounts verification market, Deluxe assists financial institutions in identifying people whose accounts have been closed for good reason.

Productivity. One day back in the early 1930s, a young pressman in the Deluxe Chicago plant learned a valuable lesson. While his press was busy printing an order of Deluxe business checks, the pressman decided he could relax for a moment and gaze out the window at the Chicago scenery. As he enjoyed the view, the pressman didn't notice the approaching plant superintendent, who noticed him. The superintendent stopped and asked the young man for a dollar bill. The pressman dutifully took out a dollar and handed it to the superintendent, who then tossed it out the window. As the dollar floated off into the Chicago day, the superintendent told the startled pressman, "That's what you're doing with company money."

Losing a dollar made a lasting impression on that young pressman. In his fifty-two-year Deluxe career, he eventually became the company senior vice-president of production and was responsible for many innovations that improved company productivity. He became known, as one co-worker put it, as the one "who didn't waste any time. He was always improving everything he did."

The story of the young pressman illustrates an important point about Deluxe productivity: it is only when people and technology work together that the greatest productivity is achieved. Over the years, Deluxe has witnessed just such a blend of people and technology working together to attain impressive results. Because it has installed the latest technology in its plants and because its work force has learned to use that technology as efficiently as possible, Deluxe has enjoyed steady growth in productivity. As one business analyst noted, "A walk through a [Deluxe] printing plant is no gee-whiz high-tech tour. Not that Deluxe has stinted on automation. The point is, high tech has not replaced human creativity and accountability."

A case in point appears in Deluxe's check orders, which continue to increase each year. On average, the more than sixty nationwide Deluxe production plants process about 400,000 check orders each work day and ship more than 97 percent of these orders within two days. Many orders are actually shipped the same day they are received. Our strong commitment to advanced production and communication technology has enabled us to handle the nearly 47 percent increase in order units printed since 1976 without proportional increases in staff or plant area. This indicates that we are clearly benefiting from high levels of productivity throughout all levels of the corporation.

Technology is an important reason for Deluxe's productivity gains in handling check orders, but we also credit our accomplishments to our employees. Although the phrase "Our people are our greatest asset" may sound like a cliché to some, we say it with great sincerity — because at Deluxe, our employees are the key to our success and we recognize that their willingness to invent, adapt and use technology ensures our success.

Visitors to Deluxe plants often notice this successful blend of people and technology. After touring a Deluxe plant and examining its advanced technology, one recent visitor — an officer from an English bank — remarked, "Your technology is very impressive, but what really amazed me is your people. I've seen a great number of printing operations in this country and in the United Kingdom, but I've never seen people work so efficiently. Your productivity must be fantastic."

Service. When it comes to customer satisfaction, we are proud to consider the following:

It is certainly a pleasure to deal with a firm that takes the extreme personal interest in their customers that you people do.
                                        — A Midwestern Deluxe customer

I have always been impressed and amazed at times with the things that Deluxe does for its customers. The positive, friendly attitude of all your employees — from the sales representatives in the field to the customer service representatives at your many offices — certainly does make our job

a lot easier and much more pleasant any time we do have a
problem and need your help.
                          — A Southern Deluxe customer

In addition to coming from different locations of the country, these comments from satisfied Deluxe customers share another distinction — time. Deluxe received the first in 1924 and the second in 1986. The many supportive comments Deluxe receives each year — whether in 1924 or 1986 — attest to our excellent service record. We believe excellent service is one of the primary reasons that we have become the nation's largest supplier of checks and related transaction forms to the financial industry. Deluxe founder W. R. Hotchkiss, once a country newspaper publisher from Wisconsin, established the company in 1915 by providing financial institutions service that was unavailable at the time. "The matter of service is of vital importance to our company," Hotchkiss wrote in 1936. "It is one of the main reasons for the success of our company. In it we take pride. Deluxe service is more than common service. It is unusual service — the kind that surprises and pleases customers."

Today, Deluxe's reputation for excellent service has drawn national attention. Such service is a constant goal — just because we produced good service last time doesn't mean we don't have our reputation on the line this time. You have to set the service clock back to zero on every order.

There are three distinguishable components to Deluxe service. The first is product service. Here, Deluxe's goal is to produce its products quickly and accurately. For example, Deluxe's two-days-or-less service schedule for catalog check products and its high accuracy rate are industry standards. In 1986, in producing more than half of the nation's 42 billion checks, we shipped 97.1 percent of our check orders within our two-day service schedule, and we produced 99.6 percent of our orders without error. We believe this level of service is unmatched in our industry.

To eliminate delays in the delivery system, Deluxe has plants in every region of the country. Each plant has an in-house detached postal operation, where Deluxe employees label, sort and sack customer orders by five-digit ZIP codes before sending them to the postal service for final delivery. Although this procedure takes extra time we believe it is justified because it eliminates all the primary and secondary handling normally connected with sending mail through the postal system.

Customer service is the second component of Deluxe service. Deluxe's obligation to its customers doesn't end once it has sold a product. Instead, teams of Deluxe customer service representatives (CSRs) across the nation provide the continuing service customers need. Whether working in a national office or a local plant, the goal of each CSR is to answer all of a customer's questions during one telephone conversation. To do this, Deluxe CSRs receive extensive training to learn about products and order information and how to serve customers. They also learn how to give value-added customer service — service that exceeds a customer's expectations. CSRs tend to extend extra service naturally, but our goal is to identify and reinforce this service behavior so that it can be consciously applied to every customer's call. We want to take that extra step every time.

Sales service is the third component of Deluxe service. The goal of Deluxe's field sales representatives is to work as partners with financial institution customers. This includes identifying their needs and providing all the products and services they require, from checkbook covers and accessories to new-account verification services and EFT processing services. In addition, Deluxe sales representatives offer a range of sales support services and materials to help financial institutions promote their own services to their customers. These sales support services include customizing and personalizing catalogs, offering cross-selling guides and providing special brochures for financial institutions. In sales, Deluxe's strong emphasis on service is the main reason why the company can help financial institutions serve and satisfy their customers.

Innovation. "Be it known that I, William R. Hotchkiss, a citizen of the United States, residing at St. Paul, in the county of Ramsey and the State of Minnesota, have invented new and useful

Improvements in Printing Presses." So begins Deluxe founder W.
R. Hotchkiss's patent application, dated June 15, 1923. "The object
of this invention is to provide an unusually high-speed and efficient
press particularly adapted for check printing and other work usually performed on platen presses."

After tinkering in his workshop for nearly ten years, Hotchkiss
had invented a specialized press that printed checks three-on-
a-page at more than twice the speed of any other press. Hotchkiss's
press may have sounded good on paper, but there were a few kinks
to be worked out before it transformed the check-printing industry.
As one retired Deluxe employee recalls, "The first Hotchkiss press
jumped almost one foot off the floor when they started it up, it was
so out of balance. They had to weight the flywheel to counteract
the cylinder coming down." Once its initial problems were corrected, the Hotchkiss Imprinting Press, which was granted a patent
in 1925, represented the most advanced check-printing technology
of its time. It gave Deluxe a distince advantage over its
competitors.

During its history, Deluxe has often been the leader in check-
printing innovations. In its early years, for example, Deluxe printed
the first check catalog of bank checks and was instrumental in
introducing consumers to checks as a means of payment. Later on,
the company took the lead in promoting personalized pocket
checks, which eventually became the most popular product in
check-printing history. In the late 1950s, Deluxe worked with the
American Bankers Association to develop the machine language
that today appears as the code line on the bottom of every check.

Today, Deluxe continues to develop innovations that ensure its
success. In production, for example, Deluxe has developed the
most advanced system in its industry. Since 1980, we have committed more than $170 million to develop and install state-of-the-art
equipment in our plants. As a result, we are now producing the
majority of our personalized check volume with an advanced and
proprietary computer-driven technology that has given us a competitive edge in quality and speed. This technology has gone into
all phases of production — from optical character readers that enter

customer orders to computer-controlled presses that print those orders and automated binders that pack them for shipping.

In 1985, Deluxe finished linking its nationwide facilities with a computerized information network that uses more than 225 computers and two thousand terminals. This network — a prime example of how Deluxe uses technology to better serve customers — enables Deluxe to process reorders more quickly and accurately than before. Deluxe's data base — called DataSave — stores an average of twenty million customer records on active file in any Deluxe plant, and each record lists all the order history information for each financial institution account. As a result, Deluxe CSRs usually have all the information they need to answer customers' questions.

Quality. Gregarious, dynamic and witty, George McSweeney, Deluxe's second president, was the consummate salesman. Fellow employees called him "Mac," and during his thirty years with Deluxe, McSweeney was ultimately responsible for transforming the small mail-order business into one relying on a nationwide sales force. Despite concentrating on increasing Deluxe's sales, McSweeney was just as concerned with improving product quality. Two important McSweeney contributions to quality took place nearly fifty years ago.

The first occurred in January 1939, when McSweeney saw it wasn't enough for Deluxe just to send perfect checks to its customers. They had to arrive that way. "Our responsibility ends," McSweeney said, "only when we place in the hands of the bank, customers' checks which are not only perfect insofar as the checks themselves are concerned, but also in perfect condition." As a result of McSweeney's directive, Deluxe began mailing its pocket checks in small, attractive boxes that protected checks from damage.

McSweeney's second contribution took place in 1940. His idea this time was to insert the check box into a special mailing box. This box would provide even more protection for Deluxe checks. "We want to continue to place in the hands of the depositors a box which will be attractive in appearance and in good condition,"

McSweeney said. "If [checks are] crushed in the mails, the customer does not have an attractive package. We want to avoid this, and, therefore, we will pack the checks in two boxes." Deluxe still uses the two-box system McSweeney devised for mailing its finished checks.

McSweeney's concern for improving a small part in Deluxe's production process produced great results. Today, that concern for the minor details in improving production continues at Deluxe and has earned the company a reputation for the best quality products in its industry. To measure quality, Deluxe uses one important gauge — the accuracy of its printed orders. The company values accuracy so highly that it publishes its accuracy rate each year in its annual report. Since we began reporting those percentages soon after becoming a publicly held company in 1965, the company has printed more than 99 percent of its check orders without error every year. The accuracy figure is an important one for Deluxe employees. They want to know how they did the preceding year, and we want them to know. For us to omit the accuracy figure would lead our people to question whether we mean what we say about our commitment to quality.

The secret behind Deluxe's quality is a tightly controlled production process that minimizes the possibility of error. On one hand, technology — such as a computerized pre-validation system that eliminates errors *before* they enter production — plays an important role in the quality of Deluxe products. One the other hand, Deluxe employees — such as proofreaders, inspectors and process control specialists — are also important. Each employee is responsible for quality, from those who monitor the quality of our documents to those who examine each piece of machinery.

As a result of these controls, less than one-tenth of 1 percent of Deluxe documents are rejected during the in-plant tests it conducts. This figure is important because mistakes and poor quality are expensive to Deluxe and to our financial institution customers, who can't afford to jeopardize relationships with their own customers.

Listening Our Way To Quality

There is an old construction-industry story about a project super-intendent who was so effective he could yell things into place. Like all old stories, there is at least a scintilla of truth in this tale. That's probably why some stories last long enough to become old. Admit-tedly, on a short-run basis, some can still yell things into place, and, occasionally, this is necessary. However, if we're looking for the type of permanence and excellence that characterizes long-run relationships, a sounder communications link must be forged. Spe-cifically, why not consider the exciting and profitable possibility of listening your way to quality?

Quality in products and service is both a state of mind and an end result. Obtaining quality is realistic and well within the grasp of most individuals and organizations. Actually, the price paid to achieve quality is less than that involved in "alibi-ing" your way to second-best. As producers and consumers, we are ultimately and simultaneously on both ends of the stick. We understand quality because we have too often experienced lack of quality, but when this occurs, we sometimes forget that what we are receiving is a function of what we produce. Too often, however, communicating the quality connection is taken too lightly, and, by the way, this is a problem for both producer and consumer.

On the delivery end, all too many firms ignore completely the quality of their own products. Certainly, quality is often neglected in price or in packaging. But how often does the organization try to communicate effectively the quality of that product to the buying public? Quite simply, quality is frequently taken for granted. Most of us are truly smart shoppers. When prompted, we can and do recognize the trade-off between price and quality and will seek the "better" product. The moral: don't stew; *tell*, and listen to your customers.

On the receiving end (and we are all guilty of this), too often we walk away from a transaction grateful that we weren't hurt too badly. Our failure to express our occasional dissatisfaction to producers communicates complacency and a contentment with mediocrity. Unfortunately, mediocrity spreads rapidly. When we encounter products that don't work, service that is second-class and treatment that is unacceptable, we rationalize that it could be worse. The moral: it *could* be worse, but it could be better. Stew and tell. Producers will listen.

In understanding organizational behavior, keep foremost in mind what we refer to as the reflective phenomenon, i.e., that subordinates tend to behave the way they think their superiors expect them to behave. Bluntly, if you don't like what you see at the bottom, take a careful look at what's going on at the top.

Characteristically, the effective manager listens to his organization's two primary groups: specifically, employees and customers. They generally know more about what's right and wrong with the organization, its products and services. Unfortunately, these constituencies are rarely tapped. Hence, the quality quest is hampered by the listening lag.

Recently, while a customer browsed through a large department store, an encouraging event unfolded. After hours and hours of searching for the right dress, a female shopped spotted what she had been looking for. She asked the salesperson if the dress was available in a size ten. The salesperson said no but then quickly relented and said, "Yes, but the last size ten is on the display mannequin." The shopper then asked the inevitable: "Can I have it?" The salesperson, still somewhat hesitant, thought it advisable to ask the department manager.

"After all," she said, "only display personnel are allowed to handle mannequins."

The department manager came over, spoke briefly with the salesperson, rolled up her sleeves, and told the anxious shopper, "The dress is yours."

For the next thirty minutes, one of the most entertaining events ever witnessed in that department store unfolded. Mark our word, it is not easy either to dress or undress a mannequin. As the department manager wrestled with the dummy, a crowd gathered. A jazz band that had been strolling the mall stopped in the store and provided musical interludes to the great undressing. The mannequin simply refused to cooperate. The manager, undaunted in her quest to deliver the product, persisted.

Finally, after a half-hour struggle, to the cheers of hundreds who had gathered to watch the manager's efforts, the shopper was rewarded for her patience. She obtained the only size ten dress in that style in that store. Simply, the manager had listened to the customer. No excuses had been offered, no alternatives had been suggested. The manager, the corporate role model, had set an important example for her subordinates. She listened and responded to a prospective customer who left the store a truly satisfied, happy customer.

At a large metropolitan furniture store, customer dissatisfaction was getting out of hand. It simply could not continue. Five million in furniture sold and one million returned. From a dollar perspective, 20 percent of everything that went out came back in. It was more like a revolving door than a sales transaction.

In attempting to find out why, management talked with the sales-people and was assured the problem resided in warehousing and delivery.

Management then talked to personnel in those areas and was informed in no uncertain terms that the blame rested with the salespeople.

At this point, you have the not-so-unusual situation of one segment of an organization attempting to build its status on the ruins of another. When this becomes the primary business of a business, everyone loses.

After examining the return problem with those who sold and those who delivered, it was recommended by a company maverick that it might be good to talk to those returning the merchandise. Specifically, she suggested that listening to the consumer might prove more fruitful than talking to others.

The results were both interesting and beneficial. According to customers, over 89 percent of the returns originated on the sales floor and were generated by lack of product knowledge coupled with a failure to comprehend customer needs. For example, a one-hundred-inch sofa simply won't do for an eighty-nine inch wall. It may be purchased, but it will come back.

By listening, the company pinpointed the true causes of customer dissatisfaction and — with the help of sales, warehouse and delivery personnel — developed policies, programs and procedures that effectively treated the causes. The result was a gratifying and profitable 87-percent reduction in returns.

If management more often requested that the real expert "come on down," chances are that almost all employees would step forward.

Employees represent a formidable resource and are too expensive to be viewed as mere hired hands. Why not, then, get your money's worth and utilize not only the hands but also the total being? Ask, then listen! You'll discover the employee usually knows more about his or her job than anyone else but is rarely asked about it or about how to improve things. Listen to the employees and watch for a definite improvement in quality.

Our sudden fascination with Japanese management and quality circles is, to a great extent, simply no more than the development of and commitment to a comprehensive listening program. A wise man once said, "When two people say you're drunk, lie down." Likewise, when two employees say there is a better way, listen! When salespeople offer design modification suggestions, listen. When more than one customer complains, listen. Our obsession with action ignores the importance of listening first. And action without thought will usually turn out to be counterproductive.

Quality is not the result of a command performance. It is a function of an organization that listens to and cares about all its various constituencies. In the 1920s, one segment of the famous Hawthorne investigation was built around a mass depth interviewing program involving literally thousands of employees. Emerging from this landmark study came not only valuable employee relations data but also a "three-eared" methodology for collecting the data.

It was suggested that interviewers learn to listen with "three" ears. Specifically, with ear number one you were to listen to what the other person was saying; with ear number two you were expected to listen to what the other person was not saying, which can be more important than what is expressed; and with ear number three you were instructed to listen to what the other person wanted to say but simply did not know how to express.

And this is what all of the popular "how-to-listen-more-effectively" courses always ignore. You can, with little training, learn to listen better with ear number one, but using ears two and three effectively is no easy task. Listening with all three ears demands a tremendous amount of effort. You will find, however, that the quality of information received from ears two and three far exceeds that "heard" by ear one.

There's little doubt that quality is not a command performance. It cannot be demanded. Rather, quality is a consciously developed characteristic that helps provide a powerful competitive edge for those organizations that listen — with three ears.

Perfection: The Possible Dream

Perfection. When was the last time you observed, experienced or participated in an act of perfection? When was the last time you witnessed a flawless performance, purchased a flawless product or were treated with flawless service? Can you recollect receiving excellent treatment or accurate delivery in the past week, month or year?

Perfection, flawlessness, excellence and accuracy are words that don't easily come to mind. Indeed, terms like these are difficult for many of us to vocalize. We have for all too long accepted the mundane, promoted the average and rewarded the mediocre.

Perfection and the pursuit thereof represents to all too many businesses what the fountain of youth represented to Ponce de Leon — the impossible dream. Flawlessness to all too many organizations implies almost, not quite, and within reason. Excellence is something that we can read about, explore and discuss but never pursue or demand. The pursuit of perfection is a challenge and a chase that must be won. The pursuit of perfection must be vigorously and relentlessly incorporated into everything we think, say and do.

In a global business community populated by aggressive, hungry, ambitious competitors, nothing short of perfection will do. We must put to rest the notion that excellence represents fantasy, not fact, in organizational life today. The gauntlet has been dropped; the challenge has been made. In the game of winners and losers, losing is no fun. And in business there is just no such thing as a good loser.

Nothing but perfection is acceptable. *Nothing* but perfection should be rewarded.

At Motorola, the worldwide electronics company, employees are deeply committed to the pursuit of perfection. Motorola's Participative Management Program (PMP) is a system that allows labor and management to pursue excellence at work collectively. At Motorola semiconductor plants in Mesa, Arizona, and Austin, Texas, PMP participants have established awards that are granted for achieving a single standard: 100 percent, unequivocable perfection. Several thousand Perfection Awards have been won at the Mesa facility. A Perfection Award was awarded to twenty production employees in Austin who delivered 2.1 million units without a single defect. The success of PMP and the Perfection Awards are a result of an effective top-to-bottom commitment to perfection that is encouraged and reinforced throughout Motorola.

It is the little things that count on the road to perfection. But too often it is the little things that we all too often simply forget.

A particularly effective IBM ad read as follows: *If your failure rate is one in a million, what do you tell that one customer?* The ad went on to examine the simple precept that governs all production and service delivery at IBM: defect-free performance. But, the ad concluded, if an IBM computer or office system ever needs attention, it is the mission of IBM to provide flawless and accurate service. Perfection, even for that one customer, is an ideal that must never be forgotten, an aspiration that must never be lost.

Defect-free performance is pursued by *all* employees at IBM. This is perfection at work.

In a recent classroom discussion focusing on the relationship between perfection and profitability, a graduate business student wondered: "How, in our pursuit of profit, can we realistically incorporate a passion for perfection?"

After all, many who view relationships of all kinds from a short-range perspective operate from an "I've got mine, too bad for you" philosophical framework. Evidently, there's no place for perfection in this model. However, there is ample clearance for perfection in a system that prizes the best at any level or price. This sentiment served as a basis for responding to the student by recommending that in a system of private enterprise you should handle each and every transaction as if you had to live with the buyer in a very small room for the rest of your life. Do this and the buyer will be pleased, and chances are excellent that the seller will prosper.

Perfection and the pursuit thereof are not exclusively private-sector properties. All organizations, large or small, public or private, profit or nonprofit, should aim for perfection 100 percent of the time. In all too many instances, discussions of quality and first-class service are limited primarily to private-sector organizations and strictly business transactions. This keyhole perspective misses the mark by miles. What of perfection in student-teacher, patient-physician or client-social worker relationships? Why not excellence here, just as we expect excellence in products or services from our automobile manufacturers, restaurants or financial institutions?

Harding Young and Norman Harbaugh are consummate professionals. They take great pride in their work. Each is experienced and knowledgeable. They are Georgia State University professors of management who approach each class with missionary zeal and leave each student (a.k.a. customer) with the distinct sense that he or she has acquired knowledge by being exposed to a human being who loves learning and who welcomes the opportunity to share a storehouse of facts, theories and principles with others.

Even in classes that overflow, excellence begets excellence. Young and Harbaugh provide each student/customer with the kind of attention delivered only when you are routinely prepared to go beyond the call of duty. The result of this commitment, this striving for perfection, is a bonus for everyone involved. Further, this striving is highly contagious and can ultimately lead to an organization culture or personality where winning is expected and heroic behavior is recognized, rewarded and reinforced.

This is the stuff of perfection, and this stuff isn't bad at all.

Sam Turner, the innovative chief executive officer of Life of Virginia, has maintained creative momentum in that organization by emphasizing not only products but service of the highest quality, delivered by people who are willing to do whatever it is that must be done to please the customer. You see, in the insurance industry (as in many industries), products don't differ significantly. What does differ is the people. Perfection is not possible without people. And a commitment to pursuing perfection doesn't just randomly occur. Doing whatever it is that must be done requires an ongoing attitude that is initiated and maintained by top management, who continuously recruit and reward individuals who are also committed to perfection.

People pursuing perfection represent a wonderful sight to behold. People pursuing perfection, representing organizations pursuing perfection, are the catalysts so desperately needed to vault this nation back to its preeminent position in a world marketplace insistent on excellence.

Robert P. Forrestal

In 1983 Robert P. Forrestal became the twelfth chief executive of the Federal Reserve Bank of Atlanta. Born in New York City, he received his B.A. from St. John's University and his law degree from Georgetown University Law Center. He has also studied at the University of Virginia, the University of London, and the Administrative Staff College in England. He was a Fulbright scholar in France and served as an officer in the U.S. Navy in Morocco, Italy and Great Britain.

Challenges of Management at the Federal Reserve Bank of Atlanta

The Federal Reserve Bank of Atlanta, like its counterparts around the country, actually conducts three distinct businesses. One is the provision of financial services such as check-clearing, the processing of cash and electronic funds transfers to banks, savings and loan associations and other depository institutions. A second "business" is supervising the activities of bank-holding companies and state-chartered member banks to ensure that they conform to those laws and regulations set forth by Congress and the Federal Reserve Board of Governors to assure the safety and soundness of the banking system. The Fed's third undertaking, which is to shape national monetary policy, entails evaluating current economic conditions both in the Southeast and the country as a whole. The output of this "conglomerate" of businesses ranges from selling certain services at market prices to providing unpriced "public goods" such as regulation and monetary policy. Running an organization with such disparate concerns is a challenge faced by a growing number of businesses and one that is not unique to a quasi-public institution.

In American business generally, conglomerates have proven more difficult to operate in practice than on paper. Many of the conglomerates assembled in the 1960s and 1970s have been vulnerable to takeover and dismantling by corporate raiders in the 1980s. In part, changing economic conditions account for this weakness, but the chief cause lies in the difficulty of managing a concatenation of diverse enterprises once the pieces have been put together. Whereas conglomerates have tended to falter in the 1980s, Federal Reserve Banks have successfully weathered substantial economic changes over the same period, including a rather turbulent storm in the banking industry. Simultaneously, they have managed to strengthen the bonds among their component operations. To a large extent, this accomplishment springs from crossfertilization among the three businesses that Reserve Banks perform.

Although the Fed has some basic characteristics that are not shared by purely private corporations, several elements of our experience suggest fruitful approaches to management problems in other settings. A brief review of the profound changes in the market for our products and the ways we responded will serve to highlight these elements.

The Fed under Fire. From the inception of the Federal Reserve System in 1913 until the passage of the Depository Institutions Deregulation and Monetary Control Act of 1980, or MCA 80 as it came to be known, the three businesses of Federal Reserve Banks were on a fairly equal footing. Their products — payments functions, bank supervision and regulation and monetary policy — each served the public policy goal of promoting more stable, real economic growth. They served this end by bringing order to a payments mechanism that was marked by uncertainty prior to the Fed's creation, by formulating and enforcing regulations designed to reduce the risk of disruptions to the banking system and by influencing the amount of money and credit available in the economy.

Aside from this commonality of purpose, which was not changed by MCA 80, there were two additional similarities; the products of the district banks were provided free to members, and all three "businesses" focused on the commercial banking system as the central — and largest — part of the nation's financial system. Bank examiners monitored member banks' adherence to Fed regulations. Payments services like check-clearing were offered only to member institutions. Monetary policy, too, was implemented through commercial banks. By raising or lowering the amount of deposits banks were required to hold in reserve, the Fed could influence the amount of money and credit available. Altering the discount rate, the rate at which banks borrow from the Fed, had a similar effect. Beginning in the 1930s, open market operations were increasingly used to further the same goal by changing the amount of pressure on bank reserves. In each case monetary policy was effected through the reserve position of member banks.

The economic and price stability that prevailed in the post-World War II era helped sustain this common framework. However, the steady rise in interest rates from the late 1960s through the 1970s, along with technological advances that made it easier to transfer funds over great distances, gave rise to competitors for services that banks alone had long provided. Nonbank firms, for example, began offering higher rates for savings instruments, some of which also carried check-writing privileges. Some large banks, restricted by the Federal Reserve System's reserve requirements, interest-rate ceilings and prohibitions on interest-bearing transaction accounts, threatened to give up their bank charters, feeling they would be better able to compete outside the regulatory structure governing depository institutions. To prevent the disruption to monetary policy such a defection would have entailed, Congress passed the Depository Institutions Deregulation and Monetary Control Act of 1980. Among its other provisions, the Act required *all* depository institutions to maintain a reserve account with the Fed. Furthermore, it mandated the Fed to offer its financial services to all depository institutions, but at a price adjusted to ensure that market competition would not be disturbed.

Charging competitive prices for services called for thorough reorganization of the operations end of the Fed's business. Of course, this necessity was not unanticipated, since the supervisory and monetary policy arms of the System's banks, as well as the Board of Governors, had been studying how the changes in the banking industry might affect the Fed. One consequence of this investigation had been a move to emphasize efficiency in the Reserve Banks' financial services. In the mid-1970s, the System had instituted a method for more accurately monitoring the cost-effectiveness of those operations which, like check processing, could be measured in a per-unit fashion. This innovation catalyzed shifts in management style across the board at the Atlanta Fed following MCA 80, because the measures and rankings introduced in the 1970s prompted employees and managers alike to think in competitive terms. Someone had begun to keep score, and those whose actions were being tallied wanted to play to win.

Coping with a Changed Environment. The Atlanta Fed's management had always prided itself on running a lean shop. Therefore, we welcomed the chance to establish that claim in a head-to-head contest. What needed to be done, we felt, was obvious. We set about assessing every detail of our operation with an eye to keeping the efficient elements intact and scrapping or modifying the rest. Once more we did the obvious by asking our line employees their opinions out the ways their assignments were organized and how they might be made more appropriate.

This emphasis on the obvious is not meant to be facetious. Rather, it points up the fact that there are no secret formulas for achieving better results. Regardless of how good an organization's managers are, those who actually perform each task on a day-to-day basis have a unique perspective on all its aspects, including inefficiencies in current procedures and means to improve operations. As we analyzed the details of production with the help of our employees, a highly refined internal measurement system evolved. This, in turn, permitted us to keep score among ourselves — a development that brought about the competitive tendencies among managers in our six branches vis-à-vis one another as well as in relation to the other Reserve Banks. Furthermore, the Atlanta Fed let it be known that one way to advance in the organization was to come in with the best numbers. Rather than specifying a particular path toward this end, we gave managers effective "ownership" of their individual operations, indicating our acceptance of a diversity of management styles. This freedom in concert with our demonstrated confidence in employee creativity at all levels fostered a team spirit that reinforced the competitive culture. The bank's effort met with success, and after a relatively short period the System-wide rankings of all twenty-five payments offices showed Atlanta's branches routinely holding spots one through six.

Having achieved this goal, we began to realize how different our other two businesses now seemed compared with the payments operation's competitive environment. Of course, there was room to increase efficiency in our other businesses — supervision and regulation of banking and the monetary policy information generated by our Research Department — and the extension of System-wide ratings to these areas accelerated this process. For example, the Supervision and Regulation Department, which had not yet automated at the time of MCA 80, took the step of converting from typewriters and calculators to word processors and personal computers. Bank applications and other business are now handled with greater efficiency than in the past by the department's latest configuration of computers. The Research Department not only automated but also attempted to raise the quality and depth of its work, both in conjunction with informing policy decisions and enhancing the public's understanding of important policy issues.

By their very nature, the Fed's supervision and regulation and research areas were far less amenable to the quantification of output that is intrinsic to our "factory-like" financial services operations. Moreover, while cooperation is important in all three of our "businesses" — System-wide task forces continue to address problems of broad concern in the payments network — we found it to be essential in the monetary policy and supervision and regulation functions. Research, for example, is often furthered by collaboration between scholars with different areas of expertise. In the regulatory area, inter-Bank sharing of ideas and even personnel can be extremely useful when particular banking industry problems arise.

It is true, of course, that MCA 80, in effect, precluded the financial services departments from having access to information about specific depository institutions that our regulatory or research divisions have since it would be an unfair advantage over private providers of financial services. Notwithstanding this "Chinese wall" between the Fed's payments services and its regulatory and monetary policy activities, research as well as supervision and regulation can benefit greatly from the interchange of information, not only with each other but also with operational departments. This is particularly true in regard to new technologies, financial instruments and methods that might affect the structure and flexibility of the financial services industry and, hence, the effectiveness of monetary and regulatory policies. By the same token, those departments that provide financial services can plan better for the future by knowing more about the economic outlook and industry changes that economists and examiners foresee. Thus, the cultural disparity that we came to recognize in our three divisions taught us an important lesson — one that applies to many other companies as well. We learned that the goal of efficiency can be carried too far if not balanced by a broader sense of an institution's basic purposes.

Clarifying Corporate Values. This lesson in balance was brought home to the Bank in a definitive way when we began to articulate our corporate values, an exercise that many companies have carried out in recent years. To identify "core values" that would be woven into a statement of corporate philosophy, management once again asked employees to help. By an overwhelming majority, the staff singled out integrity as the most important value, variously defining it as scrupulous fairness, honesty and impartiality, as well as conduct that is governed by the highest standards of professionalism. The theme underlying all of these definitions was the need to maintain strong public confidence in our Bank and the Federal Reserve System. On management's part, integrity connoted considering employees' needs, listening to their ideas, treating them with respect and enhancing their career satisfaction. Thus, integrity at once expresses the outward-reaching relationship between the Bank and the public and the internal compact between management and employees.

The value employees next most frequently cited was cost-effectiveness, followed by quality service. In framing the corporate philosophy, however, management chose to reverse these two. Their feeling was that while a competitive culture naturally favors the score-keeping inherent in cost-effectiveness, service — even at the expense of absolute efficiency — better follows the theme of integrity. The employees' perception that economizing came before service suggested that we as managers might have been emphasizing the bottom line a bit too strenuously in our attempt to be the best. With this realization, we stepped back and reexamined our objectives, drawing upon our traditional public service orientation to work out a balance in both theory and practice.

While the bottom line is crucial, stressing quantity too forcefully can overload an organization in ways that cause workplace morale to deteriorate and ultimately diminish the quality of output. The entire corporation can become driven as by an engine without a governor; in such a situation, employee dedication to the goals of the corporation serves only to stoke the fire. This inexorable pressure eventually causes cracks to open. Internally, the pressure may take the form of a slippage in benefits that engenders resentment and lessens employees' desire to represent the company in a positive manner. Toward the outside, stresses may surface in a lack of attention to customers' individualized requests, in the discontinuation of certain specialized services that do not lend themselves to economies of scale or in other ways. In the end, the bottom line must suffer under such an excessively productivity-focused corporate philosophy, for it becomes self-defeating. Hence, when arranging core values in a conceptual hierarchy, we aimed for balance by giving precedence to quality service and highlighting the importance of consideration for the needs of people inside and outside our corporate walls.

Communicating these lessons in balance from senior management was facilitated by the Bank's management structure, which fosters interchange at all levels among employees in different divisions. At the top, a management committee composed of six of the Bank's senior officers convenes regularly. This meeting enables officers to share the perspectives of their different areas when considering problems and solutions. Likewise, officers and middle managers meet separately and in joint conference to be kept abreast of developments in the Bank and the System. Information is relayed from these meetings to other personnel in department and team meetings. Such interchanges are doubly valuable: they keep staff aware of potential new directions, while nurturing employees' identification with our corporate purpose and the Federal Reserve's vital role in the economy. In the current environment, interdepartmental communication also reinforces the need to temper the competitive spirit and drive for efficiency with a commitment to quality.

Conclusion. Ordering priorities and balancing the need for greater efficiency with the value of offering quality products and services are challenges left unaddressed all too frequently in today's business environment of mergers and takeovers. When companies are forced to pare down staffs, overhead segments of their operations — analytical and human resource services, for instance — are often the first to go, since their contribution to the bottom line is not apparent. What too many companies do not seem to realize, however, is that any shrinkage in internal support services may lead to a corresponding drop in morale and productivity, which in the long run cuts into profit margins.

The experience of the Atlanta Federal Reserve Bank in treating the question of priorities has been instructive to me because our response was shaped by the entire organization, management and line employees together, and reflects a consensus that is well-suited to the contemporary marketplace in general. As I have noted, the Atlanta Fed was presented with a challenge from the banking community, the Congress, and the economy — a simultaneous restructuring of the financial industry and a rewriting of the basic rules under which the System had traditionally operated. This challenge changed the relationship among the Bank's three businesses, bringing market dynamics — the competitive pricing of financial services — to bear on an operation that had been conceived of primarily as a public service. The ensuing process of adjustment yielded a management philosophy that maintains the element of service while consciously transforming it into a counterweight to bottom-line concerns.

The Atlanta Fed's reliance on open discussion among management and staff was the key ingredient in achieving an approach to production that is subscribed to from bottom to top in our organization. In my view, free expression works best as a management methodology because, more thoroughly than any other way of encouraging people to work together for a common goal, it embodies the fundamental values of America's democratic society. Both open communication and democracy rest on the belief that the people themselves best govern their own collective affairs when they are given a voice along with their responsibilities. Since our democratic system underwrites the business community's ability to provide goods and services in the free market, it follows that our corporate structures should more fully reflect the same belief.

5

INNOVATION GENERATION

Breeding the Corporate "Intrapreneur," Part I

In examining the interests of today's college students, one is almost immediately impressed by the large number of young men and women who want to go into business for themselves. The reasons for this trend are varied and at times difficult to isolate, but the underlying theme seems to be one of "I'd rather do it myself."

In 1987, new business incorporations rose by a record 700,000, indicating that more and more Americans want to — and are — going into business for themselves. Across the country today, more than one hundred colleges and universities offer formal programs in innovation and entrepreneurship at the undergraduate and graduate levels. That same uniquely ambitious spirit that Alexis de Tocqueville recognized among Americans during his travels in the 1880s seems to be as active as ever in the 1980s.

Interest in entrepreneurship should not be automatically perceived as an anti-big organization movement, although this is a small but potent factor. Rather, we're dealing with a reaffirmation of the American dream, a recognition that Horatio Alger is not only alive, but also prospering.

The challenge to corporate America is not to suppress or discourage the entrepreneur but, rather, to create an ambiance, an organizational climate, that nurtures, encourages and incubates entrepreneurs within. This process of *intrapreneurship* requires a top-to-bottom commitment in organizations intent on competing in today's hypercompetitive global marketplace. Providing an intrapreneur with sufficient resources and authority to innovate and create from within is somewhat foreign to the bureaucratic pattern, which generally seeks more form than function. Providing an intrapreneur with the flexibility and mobility to respond to market threats and opportunities when rapid response is requisite is not the modus operandi for the bureaucratic style, which encourages more illusion than substance. Providing the intrapreneur with the vehicle to develop his or her creative enterprise to the outermost limits is a foreboding risk to all too many organizations. We insist, however, that a much greater risk is that of losing. For in the material world, unlike the spiritual, the meek shall inherit nothing.

If you can remember the 1930s, chances are the notion of limited options had a powerful influence on your attitude, perspective and behavior. For millions, young and old alike, times were tough and getting by became a passion, not a style. Options were limited and there was a tendency to take what came along and to hang on for dear life. The adventure was survival. It was a bit like going to the corner drugstore for an ice cream cone. (At that time, the druggist was also the ice cream vendor.) Deciding on a flavor was a relatively simple task. There was vanilla or chocolate. If you wished to splurge, you could get a dip of each. Options or choices were limited.

Compare this with a trip to a modern-day Baskin-Robbins. The options are awesome; walking out with thirty-one dips on a single cone is not a practical alternative.

The message is relatively simple. Happily, this is a thirty-one-dip era. While coping with an abundance of options has proven too much of a challenge for some, others have successfully solved the dilemma of knowing how to prosper when the cup runneth over.

While the 1960s and 1970s placed a premium on doing one's own thing, many failed to recognize that self-actualization as a vocation was a pretty tough way to make a living. Ours is a society of individuals and organizations, and economic success is usually tied directly to providing needed goods and services to other human beings. More than ever before, many have decided they'd rather do it themselves and are performing the role of the entrepreneur instead of donning the mantle of the professional manager. Again, while a basic motivational factor might be doing one's own thing, this time around there appears to be an understanding that there are indeed strings attached and success involves *quid pro quo* relationships; or, to paraphase the popular commercial, you're going to have to make money the old-fashioned way — by earning it!

Of course, the budding entrepreneur soon recognizes that in terms of hours, effort and commitment, working for yourself means accounting to a tough taskmaster. The difference, according to Horatio Alger-types, is that the locus of control, or the shot-calling system, resides primarily within yourself rather than originating from someone else in a formal organization structure.

It is this inner drive, coupled with an ability to function with a minimum of outside direction, that differentiates the organization person from the classical risk-taker.

The process of intrapreneurship attempts to incorporate the inner drive with minimum outside direction within the traditional organizational setting. Harnessing the collective energies of intrapreneurs can create monumental problems for organizations. Not harnessing these energies can be fatal. A brief look at some superlative organizations that have instilled the enthusiasm of entrepreneurship within the classical organizational setting illustrates the power and the potential success of intrapreneurship.

Historically, one CEO who early on embraced the concept of intrapreneurship is Roberto Goizueta, CEO of Coca-Cola. In 1984, at a luncheon in Miami, Goizueta heaped kudos upon entrepreneurs: "Entrepreneurs are the ones restoring the vitality of this country's economy, a country that for a short while seemed to be content with trailing in the wake of other nations rather than exerting its competitive might. Entrepreneurs, large and small, are the true modern American heroes. Entrepreneurs are the people who choose not to follow the crowd, but rather to move forward on their own, to fulfill their dreams and to create for themselves a better future. The Spanish poet Antonio Machado described this vital spirit beautifully when he wrote, 'Traveler, there is no path. Paths are made by walking.'"

At Coke, Goizueta has encouraged the spirit of entrepreneurship in short order. He and his intrapreneurial management team have made so many aggressive (and successful) changes at Coke that some analysts worry that the company is taking unnecessary risks. But in reflecting on his years at the helm at Coke, Goizueta succinctly responds: "Not to take the risks was an even bigger risk. We had to do it to regain the company's momentum."

IBM is yet another shining star among the corporate supporters of intrapreneurship. IBM freed a group of employees from traditional bureaucratic bonds, moved them to Boca Raton, Florida, provided them with the necessary resources and authority and asked them to design and develop a personal computer in 12 months. We will let history speak for itself.

When Sanford Weill received the 1984 Entrepreneur of the Year Award from his alma mater, Cornell University, some wondered why. Why would the president of American Express receive an award generally restricted to "independent" business owners? Now chairman, president and CEO of Commercial Credit Company, Weill is the penultimate "deal-maker," who had teamed with the innovative CEO at AMEX, James Robinson, to foster an innovative, aggressive organization. According to Weill, "Most people think of entrepreneurship with small companies. I think it is a key in major industries to have entrepreneurship in the corporate soul.

Obviously you need more bureaucracy, but that bureaucracy needs to be cut through.''

At Flowers Industries, a rapidly growing specialty foods company operating out of Thomasville, Georgia, that has acquired thirty-five bakeries in twenty-four years, the emphasis is on decentralized decision-making and rapid deployment of resources. Says Martin Wood, senior vice-president: "The people in the trenches make the decisions. We encourage and have a spirit of entrepreneurship with decision-making at the action level. We also encourage dissent and diversity of opinion until the quarterback calls the signals. Then we all join together.''

It should be understood that the spirit of entrepreneurship is not solely the possession of the lone entrepreneur. In many large organizations of all types, innovative behavior is fostered by a philosophy and reward system that places a premium on creativity, innovation and rate-busting performance. Unfortunately, while the philosophy is widely held and loudly spoken, it is too seldom implemented. Hence, many ineffective organizations have spawned the most successful entrepreneurs, a dubious distinction indeed.

Encouraging the intrapreneur is a challenge for all organizations intent on pursuing and achieving excellence in these competitive times. Winning organizations staff winners throughout.

Directing the energies and efforts of entrepreneurs to corporate ends is a provocative challenge to management. This spirit of entrepreneurship is communicable within organizational settings. While it is difficult to manage and difficult to control the payoff, the proverbial bottom line can yield impressive, long-term rewards. The competition won't wait to capture this spirit. Will you?

Breeding the Corporate "Intrapreneur," Part II

Nurturing the rate busters, a.k.a. the producers, innovators and corporate entrepreneurs, must become an essential ingredient of the way we run our large organizations, public or private.

There is nothing new about the notion that work should be a satisfying and rewarding experience. The late Abraham Maslow even talked about the self-actualizing possibilities of an occupation where employment of a meaningful nature could become an end in itself rather than a means to an end or, worse, an unpleasant interval between weekends.

In building this climate, incentives — both economic and social — play a critical part. Essentially, there must be a proper balance between pay and performance, between personal commitment and external reward. (It should be noted that while money and motivation are not necessarily inextricably bound to each other, money is still a universally acceptable way of saying, "I like you and your work.") Interestingly enough, paying for performance as an incentive for productivity and quality is more often preached than practiced.

There is a lesson to be learned from the Olympics: going for the gold, and what this means individually *and* collectively, can become as habit-forming, and be far more beneficial, than opting for "also ran" or, worse, "never ran" status. Building a winning climate is often more easily done than said. Getting decision-makers to try it, however, is more easily said than done.

Entrepreneurial activities within organizations don't just happen. Innovation and creativity within organizations don't just occur. Entrepreneurs within the corporate environment, "intrapreneurs," don't fall like manna from heaven. Rather, they are carefully cultivated and nurtured by a management team committed to excellence. This pursuit is guided by five simple factors that characterize a first C.L.A.S.S. organization. Let's briefly examine each of these components.

Customer. Talk to your customers. What you will quickly discover is that your customers probably know more than anyone else about their own needs but are rarely (if ever) directly asked. Don't be surprised if your customers provide some of the most innovative suggestions and options that you've heard of late.

Leadership. Confucius once suggested that while the advisers of a great leader should be as cold as ice, the leader should have fire and a spark of divine inspiration. The leadership of innovation and entrepreneurship is a top-to-bottom proposition. The great organizational leader-manager must impart optimism and enthusiasm that is communicable throughout the organization. Strength, dedication and optimism in the upper echelons make employees strong, dedicated and optimistic. This is at the heart of the reflective phenomenon of management. Heroes at the top beget heroes throughout. Simple, isn't it?

Attack. The process of intrapreneurship requires a full-fledged, dedicated frontal attack. Your blitzkrieg requires a specific performance expectation. Be it three, six or nine months, your attack must be swift and complete. Build it, make it, develop it — use pins, needles, glue or rubber cement, but have it there in front of you, to examine, probe and refine. If you are truly committed, then this powerful offensive must be financially buttressed. You won't know if you don't try. And if you don't try, you will never know and will always wonder. You need to care for *and* feed the entrepreneur. The nurturing and development process must have the right financial ingredients. This is critical if your attack forces are to have a fighting chance.

Size. In order for your attack to be successful, your team of entrepreneurs at work on any given project must be of a manageable size. Our experiences suggest the use of no more than thirty-five dedicated, driven professionals at work on a project at any one time. Limiting the size improves the flexibility and response time of the team. Smaller clusters of intrapreneurs are generally more cohesive and coordinated and far more task-oriented.

Support. It is easy to vocalize support and encouragement; it's much more difficult to mean it. Support comes in all shapes and sizes, but it's particularly important in maintaining the momentum and enthusiasm of the team, particularly if the attack is unsuccessful. Success breeds confidence; failure must be effectively managed and strategically redirected to transform a problem into an opportunity. The intrapreneurial process is not always successful or fun. It is essential that support be genuine and continuous if successes are eventually to emerge.

Actually, most of us can be winners. Practically and realistically, winning is more fun than losing. Winning organizations recognize this, promote the notion of winning and reward winners, regardless of title, level or length of service. Recognize that a winning climate is one which affirms and utilizes human abilities and promotes individual potential. Here, a premium is placed upon those behaviors that actually contribute to organizational effectiveness. In this kind of organization, innovation, creativity, productivity and quality are not just the guideposts of a mission statement, but rather organizational realities. These realities are the hallmark of a first-C.L.A.S.S. organization.

Darryl Hartley-Leonard

Darryl Hartley-Leonard, president of the Hyatt Hotels Corporation, was born in Leeds, England, and educated at the Courtfield School of Hotel Administration at the Lancashire Technical College and School of Art in Blackpool, England. He joined Hyatt in 1964 as a desk clerk and became president in 1986, overseeing all aspects of hotel operations, staffing, sales and marketing, development and strategic planning for the company with more than forty thousand employees and a two-hundred-member corporate staff.

Keys to Innovation

When Jay Pritzker, one of the most innovative and opportunistic guys I know, offered me the position of president of Hyatt Hotels Corporation in February, 1986, he said to me: "Darryl, we're running one of the most successful companies in America. I want that same kind of success to continue, but I don't want more of the same."

When I addressed our hotel general managers at our annual management conference, I passed along a similar message. I was worried that Hyatt — as we grow into a very large company in the next five years — might lose the style, the spirit, the innovation that have kept us successful for nearly three decades. I wanted to remind the managers that today, more than ever in our history, they must be innovators, programmed to make changes, programmed to take risks if they are going to survive in such a crowded, competitive marketplace. Being average simply scares the hell out of me!

Now, you're probably asking yourself, is he crazy? Why would anyone want to mess with a good thing? Why argue with success? After all, when you have a successful meeting, you probably try to duplicate as many elements as possible in the next meeting so you'll get repeats on the accolades. Why would anyone want to take such chances?

I will answer that no one *wants* to take such chances. But everyone *must* take chances to remain on top — because the environment constantly changes, because people and their wants and needs constantly change.

Let's take a quick historical perspective.

The histories of societies, governments and businesses are littered with institutions that were either blind to the need for change — and realizing the need for change is the first step towards innovation — or resisted change. How often have you heard people faced with change say, "But we've always done it that way here" or "If it ain't broke, don't fix it."

Some of you may recall a company so strong that its name became a generic description for its major product — the Stetson Company. In the early 1950s when it was obvious that younger men were not interested in wearing hats, Stetson blindly persisted in offering the same old products. In 1972, Stetson went out of business.

For many years, the name "Underwood" was the major name in typewriters. When IBM successfully introduced a new gadget — the electric typewriter — Underwood continued to stress its manual products, paying no attention to obvious signs that the times had changed and that Underwood had to change with them. Today, Underwood is all but forgotten.

And to make my point even clearer, think back to the recent difficulties of the auto industry. Consider those guys at GM, Ford and Chrysler who said, "Small cars, who needs them? Everyone in America has always wanted to drive a big car — land yachts, I think they call them today — so let's keep giving America what it wants." And so laughed Nissan, Honda and Toyota.

Just take a look at the last fifty years and the environment in which companies have had to operate. Every decade has been very different from the one that came before it — from the American dream in the 1940s to the rebellion and value questioning of the 1960s to the unbelievable competitive pressure of the 1980s.

Look at our everyday lives. Back in the 1950s, when something was made in Japan, we laughed. Now look at the cars, TVs and stereo equipment we have in our houses. Back then our parents thought it was hot stuff to drive to Florida or up to Wisconsin on vacation. Today we're disappointed if our time off doesn't include a trip to Hong Kong or Europe. When our mothers were raising a family, it took them several hours to prepare the evening meal. Today we get frustrated if we can't whip the pot roast into the microwave and sit down at the table half an hour later. In these cases, who would ever argue against innovation?

I don't mean to belabor my point, but I do want to emphasize the *need* for innovation. Actually, it's more than a need. Innovation is a necessity. We have no choice.

A good example can be found right in the hotel industry, and, to a great extent, we have only ourselves to blame. Fifteen years ago, no one had ever heard of turn down, room amenities, concierge service or club levels in hotels. A hotel guest was satisfied with a small bar of soap whether he stayed at the Plaza or at the Holiday Inn. Until we all jumped on the bandwagon, so that today a guest *expects* these things from a hotel. It's no longer a question of extras.

The same can be applied to the meetings business. Fifteen years ago, business people on their way to a meeting or a convention would be happy with a meeting room, some tables and chairs and maybe a sandwich. Today, they're disappointed if they don't get videos, overheads, plush surroundings and a themed coffee break.

We must be innovative simply to keep on top of that monster — customer expectations — that we have all created. Our customers are spoiled, and we have spoiled them. They have become more sophisticated, more knowledgeable. Their expectations are higher. They are better informed. If we don't keep up with them — or, more importantly, ahead of them — we are in danger of becoming the Stetsons and the Underwoods of the 1980s.

So now we all know it's necessary to innovate. I think that before we talk about just how to be innovative, we should define exactly what innovation is. Sounds easy, right? But I've been doing a lot of reading on the subject lately. I think a recent study, which took a hard look at successful, innovative companies, sums up the attributes of innovation best.

What is innovation? Probably, the most important characteristic that distinguishes an innovative company — or an innovative individual, for that matter — is that they don't do business as usual. They recognize the importance of people and are willing to accept mavericks. They're also willing to look the other way when organizational charts and established procedures are disregarded. They are companies and individuals open to new ideas — whenever, wherever and however they emerge. They are continually alert to change — certainly unlike the Stetsons, Underwoods and the auto industry — in the marketplace and in customer attitudes, in the abilities of competitors and in technology. And, after being alerted, they respond to that change.

To understand innovation further, let's look at each of these elements individually. As we go over them and I talk about my company, I don't mean to imply that Hyatt is the only innovative company in existence today. But a very smart young lady in frequent demand as a speaker once told me that you should not try to show how much you know — and obviously don't know — about *other* people's business. All you do is end up making mistakes.

Innovation means not doing business as usual. Now that doesn't mean having polar bears instead of trained staff people passing out information packets. And it doesn't mean designing a new four-color corporate logo when the two-color one serves you well. Innovation is not the introduction of gimmicks. Instead, innovation is a way of thinking about doing business, a unique way of looking at the business you are in. It means you are always willing to step outside the rules, that almost anything goes as long as it has a reasonable chance economically and fits into the ethics of your company's way of doing business. It's a feeling of freedom that permeates a company so that all employees know they can look outside the usual patterns for answers. It means you will never hear these words: "But we've always done it that way here."

Let me give you one example from my own experience. It has to do with the founders of Hyatt who, as the ultimate innovators, the ultimate risk takers, paid nineteen million dollars in 1967 for a hotel in Atlanta that nobody else in the industry would touch.

Back in 1957 — thirty years ago — Jay Pritzker bought a small airport hotel and called it Hyatt. Then he added to that a string of small, motor hotels called Hyatt. Nice little hotels — strung along the west coast — and one in Chicago. They made money, but the world remained unimpressed. Until 1967 — when with luck and good fortune — the Pritzkers bought the John Portman wonder — Hyatt Regency Atlanta — and changed the course of lodging architecture, lodging history and our company.

Now, it took some courage to purchase that hotel. All the other major chains had looked at it and rejected it. They said it didn't look like a hotel, smell like a hotel or feel like a hotel. Basically, what they were saying is that it didn't fit in with what they or what the customer was used to. It didn't fit in with their usual way of doing business.

So not doing business as usual brought the first dramatic atriums into hotels. Those who walked into the first Hyatt atrium were more than a little overwhelmed, and — as our good fortune would have it — they were more than a little impressed. In fact, Hyatt Regency Atlanta became known as the "Jesus Christ" hotel — you walked in, looked up and involuntarily remarked . . .

The innovative architecture helped spark an innovative way of looking at the travel business. In some sense, the early leaders of Hyatt "discovered" the real business travelers — even before they discovered themselves. Before Hyatt Regency Atlanta, the average business traveler wanted only a place to sleep, lounge comfortably, dine efficiently. Correspondingly, the best a hotel could aspire to was to create an environment as nice as home. Travel was going to a place that you would look forward to returning from.

But from early on Hyatt took a unique and unusual worldview of travel. At Hyatt, no one ever tried to recreate someone's home. Our first president believed "If a guest feels our hotels are just like home, we've made a multimillion dollar mistake." Hyatt saw a hotel as one of the major attractions of traveling. A hotel would be a place to be, not merely a place to stay. A hotel would become a place where people could be their best, not simply caught in limbo. Again, we stepped out from the usual way of doing business.

The start of Hyatt Regency Atlanta is really a good capsule example of the three kinds of what I'll call *champions* it takes to bring innovation to reality. First, there was John Portman, the *technical* champion who carried his revolutionary idea into a viable product. Then there was Jay Pritzker, the *business* champion who provided a sound business framework for the idea. Jay and the other leaders of Hyatt were then the *executive* champions who saw an innovative idea and seized the opportunity to exploit it.

So we had an innovative company that had purchased — largely by luck — a unique, unusual product. The next step was to figure out what to do with it. This is where I believe the real innovation of the early Hyatt came into play.

Remember I said that one characteristic of an innovative company is being alert to the marketplace, to the attitudes of the customer — sometimes even before they know themselves they have those attitudes? Although the early leaders of Hyatt didn't formalize the process, they started to think like the customer.

There Hyatt was in 1967 — I was still a boy then, so I'm simply repeating history — suddenly faced with a giant, glamorous world-class hotel in the middle of downtown Atlanta on their hands. Now remember their sum total of hotel experience was the profitable — but small and unassuming — string of motor hotels along the west coast. What did they do? They now had to come up with imaginative, contemporary ways of expressing elegance. Did they run for market research? Certainly not, in 1967. Instead, one day the president of the hotel called a meeting in a hotel room, and they asked each other what *they* like when *they* traveled.

One hated the small bars of soap hotels provided, so the new Hyatt standard would be larger bars. Another noticed what a mess packing shampoo can be, so Hyatt would henceforth provide guests with shampoo. A third liked more pillows in the room; another couldn't stand the small, puny showerheads that spurted a drizzle every morning. As a result, Hyatt has more pillows, all of our hotels have Moen showerheads and so on . . . .

And we've tried our best to carry on that tradition. Just this year, I distributed a new organizational chart. At the top is the customer. At the bottom, the Hyatt corporate office.

Once an organization has agreed upon the need for innovation and has the knowledge necessary to innovate and the desire to act upon that knowledge, it's up to everyone in the organization to foster, create and implement new ideas. The way to make sure that everyone in a company in an innovator — that all employees and colleagues think and act like innovators — is the hardest part of the equation, especially for companies who may have, in the past, been of the "Well, we've always done it that way" variety.

This is where fostering innovation, creating the proper climate to encourage innovation, comes in. And I believe, after looking at many innovative companies and working, fortunately, with many innovative individuals, that you will find six common — what I call emotional — denominators among those who believe in innovation and foster it among others.

First, the innovator has a number-two mentality. Neither he or she nor the company ever believes they are on top. If their industry or peers say they've reached the top — measured by title or by sales or by profits — they believe that they must continually strive to stay there. If you believe you're number one, that no one can do it better, you stop trying. You become complacent, you lose the competitive edge. You stop thinking of and looking for new ideas. In plain language, an individual or a company dies. We've all seen it happen to people and companies we know.

Hyatt was lucky. Our image was created for us when Hyatt Regency Atlanta opened. It said we were glamorous and innovative and had style and flair. It said panache and pizzazz. It said we were leaders in the industry and the community. But a strong image in 1967 wouldn't ensure property in the 1980s. Luckily for me, Hyatt's early leaders were never content with the status quo. They had the number-two mentality.

Second, innovation doesn't mean throwing away the past. It means building upon it. It means taking years of valuable experience and using that as a framework for interpreting the present and, more importantly, the future. Innovation doesn't have to mean a totally different process, procedure or product; it simply means a new way of looking at or thinking about or assessing what's happened to us before.

Third, innovation is fostered by an open flow of communication. Management is an innovative company consciously encourages a top-down/bottom-up approach in which ideas are conceived at all levels of the organization. Ideas can filter down from top management or bubble up from below.

Let me go once again to my favorite example. At Hyatt, innovation is a two-way process. Sure, the corporate staff comes up with some great ideas and spreads them to the hotels in the field. But, more often than not, a great idea gets its beginning at an individual hotel — from a manager or line employee, comes to the top, is refined and then spread back down to the rest of the hotels. Our Regency Clubs started that way. So did our Gold Passport Program, our dessert bars and, way back when, the serving of freshly squeezed orange juice. Our special amenities for female travelers are also the result of an idea that originated in an individual hotel. We make sure this philosophy is spread throughout the company, right down to the maid and the bellperson, so every individual knows he or she has the freedom to communicate, to improve, to innovate.

That leads me to the fourth emotional common denominator of innovation: risk-taking. Innovation means taking risks. It's being unafraid to change or experiment. The secret to successful innovation is to visualize a new and different concept, determine if it may work for you, then put it into action — before the competition and before its been proven successful. That's taking risks. As one of our former Hyatt presidents used to say, if you make one hundred decisions a day and thirty of them are the right ones, then you're in the major leagues. I'm afraid that too many of us today are content to limit our number of decisions because of our concern that every decision be the right one.

To be able to take risks means you must not be afraid of failure — the fifth common denominator. More importantly, a company must let its employees know that it's okay to fail as long as you failed for a good reason. We can fix it and go on. It's unfortunate that there's a common perception about new ideas in many companies today: If they work, they're called innovative; If they don't, they're called dumb. That kind of mentality can only impede efforts to be on top and ahead of the competition.

And, finally, what all this has really been leading to is that to be truly innovative, an individual must be an entrepreneur, and a company must foster that entrepreneurial spirit. Perhaps the most important practice innovators use to bypass the "business-as-usual" syndrome is the deliberate hiring of mavericks who are allowed the leeway necessary to function.

At Hyatt, our emphasis on entrepreneurialism means we cannot be afraid of individual personality. We assume that expression of personality within our organization is more likely to provide original solutions and directions than hinder the pursuit of collective goals.

In short, an innovative company's strategy is to continue to create the company rather than to be "stewards of its success." This results in a constant state of challenge. Creative conflict. This results in a personal assumption of responsibility. Individuals who can make a difference are what counts. They're the innovators.

Ideas are the building blocks of innovation. I'll admit that innovation is easy when a company is new and facing uncharted territory. And I'll admit that even I sometimes fall into the "There's no new idea" syndrome that many people find an easy excuse for sameness. But, while there may be validity to the no-new-idea theory, there are certainly new twists to an old idea. An innovator knows how to take advantage of those twists.

Another example. Hyatt, of course.

Back in the late 1970s, we aggressively started to build resort hotels. As our usual way of doing business, we built those hotels with a good deal of meeting space because of our reputation and success in catering to group business. Now, we could have built a very fine resort hotel with the usual Hyatt services and amenities and the usual swimming pool and golf course of a luxury resort. We would have been successful.

But we started thinking. We wanted to be as different as we were with our hotel in Atlanta. Going into resort development wasn't enough. We wanted to be the innovators in resort development. As a result, today we have Hyatt Regency Maui — a luxury resort with a half-acre free-form pool and waterfalls, not just a swimming pool. Twenty acres of landscaped gardens, not just a beachfront. One million dollars worth of art from around the world, not just a few pictures. And so many birds and other wildlife on staff that we employ a full-time ornithologist.

Still, that hasn't become the standard version of the Hyatt resort. This month we opened the world's longest pool — 1,776 feet — at our hotel in Puerto Rico. Our Scottsdale hotel has a free-form pool with a beach on the end of it for theme parties and the like — right in the middle of the desert. And we've started construction on a new hotel at Waikoloa on the big island of Hawaii where you will be able to swim with porpoises, take a gondola or a tram back to your room at night and see windsurfers on one end of a seven-acre lagoon and snorkelers on the other. We believe resorts are fantasy, so who knows what we will think up next.

So now we have all this raw material to work with. We know what we want to do and how to do it. But we've left out the most important aspect of successful innovation: people. Without them, there are few innovative ideas and no one to implement them creatively.

Here I don't mean managers and supervisors from whom we can demand innovation. I mean the people in the front line, the people carrying out the details, the people primarily responsible for supporting the image we try so hard to project.

Innovative companies recognize that people are their greatest asset. They stay close to their employees. Successful innovation is fueled and shaped by a corporate "vision," which directs and guides the entire company and is clearly communicated throughout the organization.

At Hyatt, from our very beginning, we have been very careful to create and foster a corporate culture that permits employees to be their best. We do it through programs such as training, attitude surveys, promotion from within, decentralized management. But, more importantly, we do it through an attitude that treats the employee as a total person, with a right to a quality life. One of the most important benefits to an innovative employee is the psychic income they derive from working at a company.

What I mean to emphasize here is that as you take a broader, more innovative view of what your customers will appreciate, you should also take an expanded view of the potential your employees represent in terms of individual contribution to your success. They are the center of the innovative process.

Climbing the Corporate Ladder, Part I: Getting There

He was twenty-three, a college graduate and a young person consumed with a desire to earn his place in a society that theoretically promised an aristocracy based on ability, not birth, a hierarchy where status is achieved, not ascribed. A society that rewards on the basis of performance. A structure that remunerates for what you do, not who you are. In effect, all the underlying themes of the great American dream.

She was twenty-one, a college graduate, employed on her first full-time job, and committed to the concept that you always do your very best.

These two young people had a great deal in common. As neophytes in the real world of work, they represented the cream-of-the-crop in terms of schooling and commitment. Further, they were willing to work and give an employer all they had.

After several months on the job in different cities and with different organizations, each came to the independent conclusion that the world of work in practice was radically different from the world of work in theory. Essentially, the gulf between mouth and movement, philosophy and practicality, was poignantly summed up in separate discussions when they lamented they heard "only the bad stuff."

In essence, they felt their supervision was keyed solely to what was wrong rather than also emphasizing what was right. A discouraging state of affairs for the experienced. A chronic source of confusion, anxiety and frustration for the uninitiated. A sobering introduction to a rewritten set of management principles concerned not with function but with form.

A survey of employee attitudes by the U.S. Chamber of Commerce and the Gallup Organization provides some insight into the frustration experienced by today's work force. The survey asked a number of employees, "What do you think it would be possible to change so as to bring about the largest improvement in per- formance and productivity in most companies?" The three most frequently referenced issues were attitudes and abilities of supervisors, management and workers. Other factors like plant, equipment, tools, government regulations and computers were not mentioned collectively as often as the abilities and attitudes of management and employees.

This frustration often devastates the novice employee intent on "proving" himself or herself at work. Managerial attitudes become employee attitudes, and the prevailing attitude in too many organizations reeks of the listlessness that has mired American industry in general and dispirited the new wave of employees in particular. This is the good news. The bad news is that the group of employers most susceptible to the lethargy rampant in organizations is the young, intelligent, aggressive, educated new inductees into the fraternity of organization life.

Every so often, questions are raised about the willingness of young people to work. For the most part, and there are always exceptions, while today's students often lack certain skills, their potential is unlimited, and the desire to perform is present. College and university career planning and placement offices have never been more active than they are today. Many of these offices, inundated with soon-to-be graduates, have resorted to a lottery system that enables only a fraction of those students interested to interview for a position with a visiting firm. At a recent MBA Forum in New York, a barrage of over two thousand students stormed the university representatives seeking information that would enable them to enhance their educational stature in search of a "better" career.

As educators, we find that the lion's share of students are ready to work and become active contributing members of a society that produces. What's lacking in all too many instances is a role model, an organizational mentor to guide, nurture and counsel the newcomer. Ideally, the role-model function should be performed by first-level managers. Sadly, this is often not the case. These young, intelligent, aggressive, educated inductees into the organization fraternity are sometimes subjected to a hazing that systematically diminishes their enthusiasm and steadily depletes their spirit.

In regard to the above, a study conducted by the Public Agenda Foundation of New York dealing with the work ethic concluded that many employees feel there is little relationship between what you do and what you get. Perceptions and prejudices aside, all too many compensation programs are geared not to the ability to produce but, rather, to the ability to survive.

We need to take a careful look at the belief that we can afford the luxury of conducting business as usual, if business as usual implies the conscious or unconscious failure to utilize properly our most valuable resource, human beings.

To all of those committed to reaching that brass ring, take heed. The fact remains that in the long run, excellence shows. The climb is an arduous one. There are, however, three "P"'s for progress: Planning, Preparation and Perseverance.

Planning. The key to planning for success is to identify your own professional mission. Taking into account your background, education and commitment, it is imperative that you assess where you are but, more importantly, where you want to be. *The role of* *planning is to enable you to determine how you want to get to where you want to be.* The quickest route to success is to mirror, mimic and emulate what works. Identify a role model either inside or outside your organization, observe, listen, then do. Examine your plan every six months; some modifications are always necessary. But, if your organization is not moving you to your mission, then move yourself. If you are thwarted within, then move without.

Preparation. Once you have been given one task, assignment or job, you need to *overprepare* yourself for it. There is *no substitute* for preparation. Reading, listening, observing — all contribute to the preparatory process. Amateurs are unprepared, unrehearsed and unimpressive. Professionals devote inordinate amounts of time to preparing for their jobs — indeed, for their careers. There is no "winging it" on the ladder of success. Preparation keeps those corporate demons at bay.

Perseverance. The obstacles and the detractors are everywhere. All too many companies simply do not know how to manage the overproducer, the overachiever, the rate buster. The one catalyst that will continually move you up that ladder of success is perseverance. Don't let up . . . your company needs you, and American industry needs you. You make your own breaks, you create your own luck. Both are achieved by planning, preparation and, most critically, perseverance.

The Right Stuff deals with the early days of this nation's space program. With a collection of individuals who had the right stuff, the United States forged new frontiers in outer space and, in doing so, captivated a world searching for heroes. While these ventures in space required teamwork, individuals with the right stuff were selected, trained and given an opportunity to excel. Not a bad formula for *any* organization committed to the excellence ideal.

A TRW advertisement which appeared in *Fortune* comes to mind. Its caption was, "It Was Just an Idea." In part, the advertisement read, "An idea is a fragile thing. Turning it off is much easier than keeping it lit. . . . Ideas shone because somebody had them and somebody helped them. And nobody turned them off."

This is the approach that creates the right stuff.

Climbing the Corporate Ladder, Part II: Staying There

Now that you've got the job, how do you keep it? More specifically, how do you hang on to the rungs, and what's the most effective way of moving up the ladder?

In theory, a basic element in the great American dream is the notion that status is achieved by performance, not ascribed by birth. This is the stuff that keeps Horatio Alger alive and well and has made the United States, with all its virtues and faults, the promised land for countless millions seeking a better life.

Learn, work hard, produce and move up is an almost sure-fire formula if one is fortunate enough to be employed by an organization that not only embraces the great American dream but also makes it an integral part of the organization's culture. Unfortunately, this is not always the case. That is the bad news. The good news is that many of those frustrated by unrealized and oftentimes unrealistic expectations or the inability to adapt to organizational living don the entrepreneur's mantle and move out on their own. This desire to be one's own boss is vividly reflected in the growing number of those interested in courses and programs dealing with entrepreneurship and small business management.

However, what about the millions who opt for the ranks of management? What can they do to move up, not out? Before the answer, a quick lesson in winning.

The holiday season is a wonderful time for observing a variety of human behaviors. Some of the most incredulous exchanges occur at retail stores between sellers and buyers. An outsider looking in on business transactions can clearly differentiate the responses of winners from those of second-handers. A winner exudes confidence in himself and in his product. A second-hander (as immortalized by Ayn Rand) could care less if a customer buys. A winner thinks career. A second-hander thinks job. A winner puts the customer first, at all times, A second-hander feels that the establishment would be a wonderful place to work if not for the customers. A winner sees the pot-of-gold at the end of the rainbow. A second-hander sees only the rainbow. Winners come early and stay late. Second-handers come late and leave early. During the holiday season both winners as well as second-handers are out in force.

An example. At a department store two weeks before Christmas, an anxious shopper finally spotted the briefcase she had been seeking. She stood at the counter patiently waiting for the salesperson to serve her. Finally, after about thirty minutes, her turn came. She casually remarked to the clerk: "It looks like you could use a little help back there." To that, the clerk responded in second-hand fashion: "Actually, what we could use is fewer customers."

Another example. Our second shopper desperately needed a new pair of running shoes. Lots of stores sell shoes, but very few, he found, sell a *complete product*, which includes knowledge about the right shoes for the right feet. He was not looking for the best price, simply the best shoe for his particular type of long-distance running. At store after store, shoes were handed to him without explanation. One clerk remarked: ". . . some nice colors." Another said: "We have matching warm-ups also." Not a single salesperson could talk product. This was the good news. The bad news was that not a single clerk cared.

Finally, after weeks of searching, he happened upon a winner. A salesperson for an athletic shoe store asked the customer all the right questions. She asked about terrain, distance and frequency of workouts. The shopper anxiously responded. Then, with the preliminaries behind them, she talked product. She discussed the composition of various shoes, their durability and their price. The shoe she finally recommended wasn't the most expensive nor the most attractive. It was, more importantly, the right product for the right customer — the right shoes for the right feet. Following the sale, the pleased customer asked the salesperson: "By the way, do you own this store?" To which she replied: "Not yet." He was watching a winner at work.

A letter in Ann Landers's column in *The Atlanta Constitution* appeared as follows:

> Dear Ann Landers:
>   If it is true, as they say, that there's always room at the top, why is there so much shoving around up there?
> Henry in Morristown
>
> Dear Henry:
> Because getting there is one thing, staying there is another.

We hear it all the time. "It's hard to find good people these days. There just aren't enough qualified people out there." To these detractors we devote a resounding chorus of "baloney!" The fact of the matter is, that for the millions of Americans intent on battling and scraping their way up that ladder, there is a better way. There must, however, be a match, a chemistry, between employer and employee. A winner, in the right organization, will catapult upwards at an amazing speed. A winner (and there are many, many winners around) will move up at a brisk clip. Of course, there are a few things you ought to know.

First of all, recognize that what you don't know *can* hurt you. Knowledge definitely is power, and, as a rule, it is better to know than not to know.

Having said this, you might very well ask: "Know what?" After all, one can't possibly know everything. Therefore, three key areas to know are self, job and organization. Of the three, knowledge of self is probably the most critical and certainly the most demanding.

Just as any organization should understand what kind of business it is in, so should the individual comprehend what kind of business he or she is in, wants to be in and, perhaps, should be in. Actually, responses to the above change from time to time. Recognizing and capitalizing on this is a strength rather than a weakness. Successful second- and third-career people are becoming the norm, not the exception, and being able to change creatively, constructively and realistically is an essential, not an extra. Self-knowledge that includes an accurate assessment of personal strengths and weaknesses seems to be a developed characteristic of those who are there and those aspirants who want to be there.

Job-knowledge, like self-knowledge, should be viewed as a continuous process. Further, knowledge of job for the person who wants to move up involves far more than merely the technical aspects or the routine dimensions of one's work. Comprehending and appreciating the *why* of what a job involves places the true locus of control more directly where it belongs, and that is with you. No amount of gimmickry or magic with mirrors will substitute for this broader job-knowledge.

Now that you understand self and job, how about organization? Do you understand what kind of business the company is in, its philosophy, beliefs and values? Recognize that affiliation with an employing organization — public or private, profit or not-for-profit, large or small — requires adjustments, challenges, rewards, punishments, promotions and setbacks. As a matter of fact, the road to the top (or, for that matter, the road to wherever you want to go) can be not only bumpy but absolutely unpaved.

The more you understand your organization (i.e., what the organization chart depicts and how it actually works), the more effectively you'll understand what it takes to succeed. With this knowledge, you may decide you're willing to pay the price, or you may conclude the price outweighs the rewards. You might even conclude your values and those of the organization simply don't mesh and that it's time to wash up and get out while everyone is on speaking terms.

In essence, geting there and moving up are fairly controllable factors. The means and the end are knowledge-oriented, resting on a foundation of comprehending self, job and organization. Without in-depth understanding of these things, dressing right and performing adequately might keep you in. However, you won't move up with any degree of permanency.

There is no substitute for knowledge, and knowledge is not complete unless it includes knowledge of self, job and organization. For better or for worse, however, knowledge without ability is useless. Ability is not complete unless it includes the ability to do your job and to do the job of others. The learning process never ceases, and those who actively engage in that process will automatically move up faster than those who don't.

Finally, while knowledge and ability are essential for progress up that corporate ladder, there must also be a place for diligence in your quest. In reality, there are few overnight sensations. If you know and if you're able, diligence along with that commitment to self and to organization will put you on top . . . and keep you there.

Frank Perdue

Born on the Delmarva Peninsula east of the Chesapeake Bay, Franklin Parsons (Frank) Perdue found himself in one of the nation's major poultry-producing areas. His father began a table egg business in 1920 in Salisbury, Maryland. At the age of ten, Perdue was given responsibility for fifty chickens. In 1939 he left college to go back into the family business, and today he is in charge of an operation that employs more than thirteen thousand people and has sales in excess of one billion dollars annually.

Quality, Service, Reliability — The Goals of a Flexible Manager

I think my management style is one that needs some change. I started here when there were only my dad, myself and one other fellow. My dad started things in 1920, and I came in 1939. There were three people here. We had enough workload during World War II to employ ten people, and there were only four of us at that time, in 1941. So I've been very much a hands-on manager because I've done almost everything in the company with the exception of actually running a poultry processing plant and the day-to-day selling of the dressed poultry.

I remember when I used to keep the checkbook and decide which growers, excuse me, producers — we never use that word *growers* — I decided which producers got the chickens and I ran the checkbook and I didn't think anybody else could run that checkbook except me. But after awhile, as I got busier and busier and I got more and more balls in the air, I noticed that too many of those balls were hitting the ground. Therefore, I turned the checkbook over to Ms. Mattie Wimbrough, who did a better job with it than I did. That came as a shocking revelation to me, that somebody could do something better than I could do it. That kind of set the pattern for my realizing that I did have to delegate and that didn't come easy for a guy that started with the business, as I almost did.

So in terms of management style, it's been very hard for me to give up the total responsibility, but, obviously, I had to delegate. Another early recognition, equally important, was that you have to have outstanding people. Don Mabe, our president, has been in the company for thirty years, and he's a tremendous asset and force and should be recognized for what he has contributed to the success of this company. Don is the one who started our first hatchery production here on the shore. Don is the one that suggested that we go to North Carolina to produce chickens, which was a salvation for the company. Don has run the Accomack and Salisbury processing plants, so he is an outstanding poultry processing person. He's been in the company since our sales were three million, and they're going to be over a billion dollars in fiscal 1988. Without him and many other people like him, there's no way that I could have built this company. So I think the recognition that you've got to have outstanding people and train them in your way was very important to me and our management style. We're the first company that really conscripted poultry science students and ag engineers and similar graduates right out of school.

Getting the right horses is crucial. Casey Stengel wanted the Yankees because they were the best, but it took them a long time. When somebody asked Andrew Carnegie if he could build his steel empire again, he said someone could take all his plants and everything else, if he could keep his people. Then, he believed, he could build the empire again. But without the people he knew he could never do it.

The first two characteristics you look for in an employee are the personality to handle and to get along with people and boundless energy. I think ours is as hard-working a company, from the top down, as any poultry company in the business. We have not always made all the right decisions. We've made mistakes, as I guess everybody has. Many times people don't want to admit to mistakes, but it doesn't bother me.

In addition to the ability to get along with others and the energy necessary to work hard, leaders must have discipline. I suspect discipline is the quality that explains why heads of companies are usually slimmer than the average person. Discipline is clearly the ingredient that allows leaders to channel their personalities and energies in the direction that's right for the business and for those they lead.

I do, however, believe in Alfred Sloan's philosophy of overlap. I don't think you can run a company the way you run an army with nobody ever going down the line to find out what's happening around him. In business the general cannot talk only to the colonel, the colonel only to his immediate inferior, and so on, down the chain of command. Companies cannot operate with the rigidity of an army. I think Alfred Sloan of General Motors was the first to prescribe that overlap is good as long as it's properly done, with a lot of diplomacy. That is absolutely the case.

You've got to have flexibility. And you have to be alert to change. I saw an incubator once that had the reputation of being the best in the business. In fact, it did give better hatch results by 1 or 2 percent, but the son of the company's founder was afraid to pursue its potential. Meanwhile, competitors were all making their incubators better and better, until they were as good as the best and became better because this leader was afraid to change anything. You cannot be afraid to change. You cannot be afraid of failure.

We want to encourage creativity and creative thinking. Tyson Foods, for instance, started fifteen years ago getting away from just selling a commodity, chicken. We are much later converts, and they've done a very good job with expanding their horizons. So now we're playing catch up in that field. Tyson is located in Arkansas; therefore, they didn't have the big population centers. But they are beautifully located to serve the whole country from the west coast to the east. Thus, they can use network television advertising to advantage. Television advertising wasn't so necessary for us, because we had a tremendous population within overnight truck-haul distance. We can kill chickens today and have them in Boston tomorrow morning, so we didn't have the necessity. However, necessity is the mother of invention, and Tyson had it. We stayed with what worked for us a long time and allowed Tyson a niche that has worked for them.

We recently put in a quality improvement process, using the Quality College of Phil Crosby in Florida. I had gone to Tom Peters's "skunk camp" seminar in California, where I met the President of Milliken Textiles, the only textile company in America that makes money. That alone is impressive. He told me about the quality improvement process, using the Quality College as a base for education and teaching. Now we're in the process of implementing a comprehensive quality improvement program. It is a system synonymous with a people-involvement program. When there were only my dad, myself and two other guys, we didn't have to worry about whether troops down the line felt wanted. There was no room for MBAs at that time in our company. As we have gotten bigger and bigger and bigger, we have had to have some way to motivate people. I've always said if you could get out of the minds of your people all the things that are there about how to create a better company; about how they could do their jobs better; about how to utilize their twenty-five square feet more effectively (because, as Tom Peters says, nobody knows those twenty-five square feet as well as they do); and about how to get them to contribute their ideas for change and efficiency, you would have a terrific company.

Give them the resources, give them a time limit, then see what they achieve in plain dollars and cents. If they don't get the job done, form another corrective action team. Maybe they'll get it done. Today we have corrective action teams, customer action teams and supplier action teams. Take one example, in our case, the boxes that we pack the chickens in. The boxes come from timber and woods. The timber and woods from suppliers vary tremendously. We have, through our own research and laboratory checks of quality of paper, helped our suppliers do a better job for themselves and, therefore, for us and, most importantly, for our customers. If it's a lousy box and it goes into a cooler that's not the best cooler in the world and there's water on the floor, where they set that bottom box down, then stack them eight high, when the guy comes in the cooler the next morning, he finds the whole stack has fallen because the bottom box collapsed. Well, the quality of that bottom box has got to get better! Simple, isn't it?

I think my legacy will be my tremendous obsession with quality, service and reliability. I used to think just quality, but now I put service and reliability almost equal to quality. And I think that zeal for those things is what has helped build our business. We have always endeavored to make a product better. Someone once asked me: "Who makes a better chicken than we make?" I did not choose to answer that question. I chose instead to ask: "Can we make our product any better?" And the answer to my question is patently clear. The wider the edge that we place between us and the next fellow, the better premium that we will get. The consumer is not an idiot, and while I believe in advertising, a valuable product is mightier than a gifted advertiser's intent.

The Quest for Quality

When was the last time you walked away from a business exchange truly satisfied? When was the last time you completed a business or personal transaction truly pleased? When was the last time you exited a place of business absolutely certain that you would be honored to conduct proceedings with that establishment in the future?

If you respond: I don't know, I don't remember, or Never, you shouldn't assume that a personal vendetta is being waged against you by the commercial establishments of the world. All too often most of us walk away from transactions battered and beaten, humiliated and humbled, but rarely, if ever, really pleased.

In fact, the general consensus of the consuming public is that we're lucky if we're not hurt too badly. We settle for mediocrity when we should be demanding excellence. We accept rudeness and curtness only because it's better than being beaten. We all too often allow ourselves to be coaxed into situations and transactions knowing that in the game of winners and losers, we lose, once again. In general, we've encouraged and sustained a mind set that is ruled by the dictum of the "minimum shaft expectation." In short, we walk away from transactions grateful that we are not hurt or abused too badly. We leave establishments thankful that we're not followed. We accept the average. We promote the mundane. We demand mediocrity . . . and guess what? . . . we get it.

Our quest for quality today is not hampered by the invasion of foreign operations onto American soil. Our quest for quality is not impeded by hypercompetitive markets pitting East against West, North against South. Our quest for quality and success is not thwarted by a lack of technological competence or expertise. Quite simply, the greatest adversaries battling our quest for quality are the millions of consumers who settle for second-best. The enemy is us . . . . and we represent a formidable foe. We have systematically lowered our expectations, and our lowered expectations have been fulfilled. We are inundated with products that occasionally work, people who fail to show up and service-oriented organizations that have made service a four-letter word.

Before you throw in the towel and admit defeat, we need to reassess and evaluate what works. After all, what better way to improve performance, quality, service and profitability than to emulate, to copy what has already proven successful? The shortest, most direct route to excellence in both quality and service is to identify the outstanding corporate role model and follow the leader. There is nothing wrong with the Pied Piper approach to management as long as the Pied Piper is a winner, in every sense of the word. There is a great deal to be learned from others, particularly successful others. The key is to extract the ingredients of the formula and use them to the best advantage for you and your organization. A quick look at some of the Pied Pipers of quality illustrates our point.

I remember an ad in *The Wall Street Journal* which read: "A picture worth $111,000,000." The ad was presented by COMPAQ Computer Corporation, and touted that firm's record-breaking sales performance in its first year of operation. Indeed, COMPAQ's revenues for its first full year in business, $111 million, were greater than those of any company in the history of American business. The success of COMPAQ is attributable to a number of factors. Sure, the software options are immense, the work-processing capabilities and graphics are superb, and it's a durable piece of equipment. More importantly, the firm's quality control is exceptionally impressive, service (a key factor in the computer industry) is superlative and COMPAQ is truly IBM-compatible.

This is, in fact, a major ingredient of COMPAQ's success. Viewing IBM as the Pied Piper of the computer industry, COMPAQ's founders sought to develop a machine that was portable, rugged and IBM-compatible. What better formula for success than to follow the leader? What better way to vault your organization to preeminence than to identify critical ingredients for success, modify them for your organization and "Go?" COMPAQ's quest for quality has created a winner. After all, there is much to admire about IBM's formula for success and its "striving for perfection every time" by staff members who truly believe quality means never having to say "It's not my job."

Since 1930, when George Jenkins founded the Publix grocery store chain in Winter Haven, Florida, the company has been driven by Jenkins's simple philosophy: "Be fair, be honest, work hard and put the customer above everything else." Today, with more than twenty-four thousand employees, and sales in excess of three billion dollars, Jenkins serves as a Pied Piper for many in the grocery industry.

The very first reflection of quality readily evident to a Publix shopper is the pristine cleanliness of the unit. Cleanliness sets a tone for this organization that rings quality, loud and clear. This is the kind of cleanliness that encourages you to pick up merchandise that has fallen on the floor and put it back on the shelves. Cleanliness, along with a belief in employees who share the "Publix Dream" of desire, loyalty and allegiance to shared goals, creates an incredibly productive and profound work environment. Jenkins has established a standard of quality that many others in this industry have sought to emulate. There, quality is a top-to-bottom effort that sets a tiptop example for both employees and consumers.

Some say if you've never seen a Mary Kay convention, you haven't lived. While many summarily discount the enthusiasm and *esprit de corps* cultivated at the annual meeting of Mary Kay beauty consultants, it is difficult to argue with a winning formula.

What has catapulted this organization from a nondescript cottage business to a multimillion-dollar, multinational success story in just two decades is a belief in people and product — two very simple ingredients in the Mary Kay success formula. The Mary Kay cosmetic line is marketed through a unique person-to-person party plan that focuses on individual products contoured for individual consumers. Emphasis is placed on only two components, the beauty consultant and the beauty product consumer. Educated salespeople convey a knowledge and an integrity that breeds confidence in consumers. This confidence breeds sales. It's a simple, straightforward process, and Mary Kay has perfected it as few others have.

The United States is confronting one of the greatest competitive corporate challenges in the history of business. Major industries that dominated the industrial scene in this country for years have found themselves at a competitive disadvantage that seems formidable at best, insurmountable at worst.

The fact remains, however, that we have the expertise, the resources and the ability to combat the global challenge. Our quest for quality, which is really a quest for success, starts with the individual players in the game. We must put to rest the notion that paying one's dues is a one-time affair. In fact, in today's business environment, paying one's dues simply entitles you to get back in line and pay again and again. Quality is a top-to-bottom proposition in organizations of all kinds, public and private, profit and nonprofit. Some classic examples of quality have been highlighted in this essay. Fortunately, there are thousands more where those came from.

At an IBM conference, particular emphasis was placed on the following approaches to quality, quality, quality:

Defect-free output. Everyone's work output should be defect-free.

Do it right. Everyone's job should be done right the first time.

Do the right thing. Everyone should be doing the right job.

Remembering who your customers are and committing yourself and your organization to quality are simple steps that are all too often ignored. Simply put, handle every transaction as if you will have to live with that customer in a very small room for the rest of your life. The quest for quality is not a one-time challenge. It is a never-ending process that must be continuously refueled and refined. We must, however, learn from our mistakes and emulate our successes. The competition won't wait . . . will you?

Karl D. Bays

Karl D. Bays is chairman of the board and chief executive officer of IC Industries, Inc., a firm headquartered in Chicago. He formerly served as chairman of the board and chief executive officer of Baxter Travenol Laboratories, Inc. A former Marine officer, he holds degrees from Eastern Kentucky University and Indiana University.

The Force of Entrepreneurship

Back in 1916, Henry Ford the original was heard to say: "The only history that's worth a tinker's dam is the history we make today."

It was in 1942 that Thurman Wesley Arnold, the lawyer and judge, said: "The only type of economic system in which government is free and in which the human spirit is free is one in which commerce is free."

And it was sometime more recently that J. Fred Bucy from Texas Instruments said: "Nothing is ever accomplished by a reasonable man."

In quoting those various thinkers from the past, I don't mean to say that I agree with all of them. I have more regard for history than Ford and more respect for reason than Bucy. But I'm quoting all of them as one way to let you know that I've done some thinking — about what distinguished entrepreneurship means.

When we think of entrepreneurs, most of us tend to think about the guy in the garage with a wrench and an idea or the one upstairs with a new computer program or the one out looking for a shoestring worth of backing to launch a new company. But I hardly know a microchip from a carburetor. I knew and loved the founder of American Hospital Supply Corporation, where I started my career, but I certainly wasn't the founder myself.

So I've never really thought of myself as an entrepreneur.

But then Webster's New Collegiate Dictionary broke the ice on that issue. It defines an entrepreneur as "one who organizes, manages and assumes the risks of a business or enterprise."

Well, there you go. I've organized. I've managed. In fact, all I ever wanted to be was the manager of something. I've also assumed some risk from time to time. So I'm an entrepreneur. Webster's Dictionary says so.

Having arrived at that grateful conclusion, I've also done some thinking about what the organizational, managerial and risk-taking elements of entrepreneurship might mean for U.S. business today and tomorrow. I've thought about it in connection with my own business.

It was in August 1958 that I went to work for American Hospital Supply Corporation, as a salesman in Kentucky. I received my MBA from Indiana University one day and started work the next.

My compensation package was a one-hundred-dollars-a-week draw. If my commissions fell short of one hundred dollars a week, I was in an overdraft, and there were red overdraft brackets all over my commission statement for many, many months. It made me wonder sometimes why a former Marine Corps officer with a couple of college degrees had ever gotten into such an arrangement.

In fact, during my last year at Indiana, I'd talked to a lot of companies — IBM, Procter & Gamble and many others. I was offered jobs with them. But there was something that really turned me on about American. It was a feeling of progress and service. As I look back on it, I realize that it was basically a feeling of entrepreneurship. In any case, it looked to me like an opportunity to be involved in something that was really moving ahead. More important, I felt — if I stuck my head above the crowd — it was an opportunity to be a manager.

Remember that managing something was all I wanted to do. During my time in the Marines, for example, I did a lot of thinking about the possibilities there. The honest truth is that I was sure enough of myself to think I might be able to run the Corps but impatient enough to think it'd take too long to get to the top. So I went to business school instead.

Indiana University is where I really got into the ideas and principles of management. By that, I mean all the classic teachings about planning, organization, motivation and control. I truly believed what I learned there, and I've never forgotten it.

So there I was — travelling the two-lanes of Kentucky, selling syringes and intravenous solutions and thinking about managing something. Over the next twelve years, I ended up in Columbus (Ohio), Kansas City, Cincinnati, Chicago and a few other places. But American and its founder, Foster McGaw, held true to my initial impression. Starting in 1970, after twelve years with American and at age thirty-five, I got my chance to run the company.

American moved from about $500 million in sales in 1970 to $3.5 billion in 1984. We laid out a strategy of breadth, automation and utmost efficiency in marketing, here and overseas, and it worked well for us over those years.

We got quite a bit of press for reshaping the marketing of health-care products, systems and services. The industry-watchers generally called our strategies innovative, but with some inherent risk because we were departing from the traditional way of marketing in health care.

But then came 1985, a year when we took the ultimate risk. We bet the company on a new direction in health care. The industry was in a period of terrific change at that point. The change had started a few years prior, and it continues today.

Our nation was coming off a time of tremendous investment and growth in health care. In the forty years after World War II, we expanded our hospital system, created new surgical and medical capabilities and insured people with what amounted to a blank check for their health-care costs.

But it was Medicare and Medicaid, beginning in the mid-1960s, that really sent us into hyperspace. I'm not even sure we realized what a massive commitment we were making when we began to apply tax dollars to the health care of the poor, the aged and the disabled.

We made the commitment nevertheless. Health care continued to get better. More people were covered, and — as you well know — the costs went through the roof.

I never viewed the changes in the mid-1980s as a reduction in our national commitment to meeting the health needs of the American people. But I did see them as a clear and rather loud statement that the system had to get more cost-effective than ever before.

You're familiar with what started happening. The Feds changed the funding mechanism and, thus, the economic incentive under Medicare. Business corporations started changing their benefits programs to encourage people to use health care as wisely as possible.

I know that some of the reports on the changing scene in health care have been fairly murky. When you read the paper one morning, it's the diagnostic-related groups that were created under the Social Security Amendments to Medicare in 1983 — the DRGs, as they're called, who are supposed to be the driving force.

Then you pick up the paper the next day to learn that, no, the really important thing is the emergence of capitated coverage through the proliferation of HMOs, IPAs, PPOs and XYZs. The next day, it's the methods of utilization-review and managed-care that corporations are getting into — they're the wave of change in the delivery of health care.

Well, it's really not all that convoluted.

The fact is, there used to be an awfully low level of risk in the delivery of health care. The money was flowing like the Delaware River. About the only way a hospital could goof it up was to get crosswise with the doctors.

That's what's changing. There's risk now. There's the potential to succeed (and many hospitals have done better than ever in the past several years). But there's the opportunity to fail as well. In short, there's been an increase in the entrepreneurial atmosphere that surrounds health care, and it's a very healthy development, in my view. I'm not saying that the past was totally easy. But I'm saying that the present is different, and it holds the promise of better health care for the future.

What's happening here is not unlike what's happened elsewhere in the U.S. economy. I'm a director of an airline, so I've had the chance to watch and take part in a whole new way of thinking in that industry. Believe me, it's not over yet. Banking is another example. The U.S. Supreme Court has given its blessing to the interstate spread of the so-called "nonbank bank" — the limited-service or specialized type of institution. And guess who expects to be the nation's largest issuer of bank credit cards by the end of the year. It's Sears, Roebuck. They'll give you a Discover card, then sell you some overalls to put it in.

It just seems to me that there's some heavy entrepreneuring going on throughout the economy, including the $500-billion health-care segment. It's a new mindset — a new view of the horizon — whether you run a hospital, an insurance company, a bank, a university, an airline or a chain of hotels. And I say it's to the good. That surely doesn't mean it's easy. Along with the potential, there always comes the risk. You have to react quickly to changing circumstances, and that's what we were doing at American in the mid-eighties.

Beginning in 1983, our market changed faster than anyone ever dreamed it could change. Hospital admissions and lengths of stay dropped like a rock. Supply usage went down. Hospitals formed some heavy-duty buying groups, and they started squeezing their supply nickels tight enough to make President Jefferson turn blue. American Hospital was out in front on a lot of that change. We'd been working for quite a few years to build on our efficiency and be ready to serve the needs of the national hospital chains. But I thought we needed to do more.

In fact, we had a meeting in March 1985 of our top two hundred managers, and I said to them at that time:

"We're a dynamic company in a changing industry. We've made some changes in response. But I won't say we're done changing. We're not — and I hope we never are."

I went on to point out that:

"Business history tells us, when industries change as dramatically as ours, a few companies emerge more powerful and with greater long-term growth potential than others. They're the ones that move boldly, seize opportunities and are willing to adapt and change."

In making those points, I was trying to send a signal to our managers because it was only a couple of weeks later that our directors and those of the Hospital Corporation of America voted to merge our two companies.

I'll tell you something else, too: If controversy is any sort of measurement of the boldness of a plan, then that plan was bold. We really were betting the company. I needn't go through the play-by-play. Our attempts to put together a fully integrated health-care company (everything from supplies to inpatient care to financing) were debated on Wall Street and around the health system.

The debate itself was part of what encouraged Baxter Travenol to think about taking over American instead of watching us merge with Hospital Corporation of America. Indeed, just about eight days before the HCA deal was to go through, in July 1985, Baxter proposed buying us — and, of course, that's what ultimately happened. The reason for going through those events is not just to bring you war stories from out on the merger front. Instead, it's because I think there are some lessons to be learned about management, organization, risk and entrepreneurship.

For one thing, risks are risks.

I can't think of a single example of progress in medicine, technology, industry or anywhere else that came about without some measure of risk — financial, physical or political. But I can think of a lot of gambles that failed and, if we spend too much time wringing our hands over those that didn't make it, we'll never get anywhere. I was deeply committed to putting American together with HCA. I'm no less committed to making the Baxter-American combination a lasting success. To act in any other way would be pouting, and that's hardly an entrepreneurial virtue.

A second lesson is that organization itself does no work, produces no product, serves no customer and adds no value for shareholders. It's only when organization is animated by human effort and the direction of management that beneficial results begin to happen.

Baxter today has the potential for preeminence in international health care. But it's not because we've wired two companies together. Our leadership will emerge only inasmuch as we succeed in finding new ways to bring better health care with greater cost-effectiveness to more people. If we do that, we'll win. If we don't, we're headed for history. (A year and a half after our merger, by the way, I'm more convinced than ever that we will win.)

By the same token, I've been disturbed by some of what I've seen happening in the restructuring of U.S. industry over the past several years. That restructuring is permanent and necessary, in my view. If we're at all realistic about the size and the interdependence of the world today, then we have to recognize the need to think and work globally, to get more productive and to compete fiercely. What I'm against are those changes in ownership and organization that create an illusion of greater wealth but lead to no increase in competitiveness, efficiency or innovation. In that light, I see some of the takeover moves that have been made as parasitical at worst and hypocritical at best.

To me, the idea of entrepreneurship mixes an unapologetic desire for personal gain with the knowledge that you'll gain only if you're serving other people in a way that they deem worthwhile. If there's no service, there's no gain. Nor should there be.

A third and very important lesson, I believe, is that entrepreneurship is possible not just in a back-room business but in a large corporation as well. I'm referring in particular to the managerial aspect that's included in Webster's definition. The discipline of management is what makes today's large, international corporations possible. Without management, such organizations cannot exist or function. But one of the things we're learning about large companies today is that they're far from omnipotent. No organization can do all things or serve every market. In fact, large firms are not even the best generators of jobs or new technology.

Well, I have no problem with that. We still need the small, pioneering organizations. They're an integral part of a free society where the human spirit is free. But what we are learning is that large organizations — in their management, organization and risk-taking — can constantly revitalize themselves, their markets, products and strategic direction. They do it in health care or telecommunications or automotive or education or anywhere else. To me, that's a real and fruitful form of entrepreneurship.

In fact, one final lesson is that revitalization is a necessary type of entrepreneurship.

In a large corporation, just as anywhere else, the force of entrepreneurship is what makes progress possible. It's a voice that says the status quo is not enough. It's a recognition that risks are real. But it's also the knowledge that the rewards — the benefits to humanity — of real entrepreneurship are lasting and highly worthwhile.